GUIDE TO MOBILE PHONE REPAIR

SMARTPHONE

TROUBLESHOOTING & REPAIR

Guide To Mobile Phone Repair

FIRST EDITION

AMERICAN TRAINED EXPERT

All Rights Reserved

Introduction

Before You Start

As a technician, you must understand a basic rule of business, time is money. Whether you are boss or work for someone else, the ability to identify and isolate a fault quickly and decisively is very important to the success of your business. It requires some common sense, and a little bit of focus. It also requires an understanding of the troubleshooting process, and reliable plan of action. Even though the number of configuration and setups are virtually unlimited, the methodology used to approach each repair is always about the same. This introduction is intended to isolate the concepts of basic troubleshooting and show you how to apply basic repair steps that will help you narrow the problem down before you even take a screwdriver to the mobile phone. By applying a constant technique. You can safe precious time from every repair.

The General Troubleshooting Steps

Regardless of how your particular smartphone might be, a dependable Troubleshooting steps can be broken down into four basic steps.
#1:Define your symptoms,
#2: identify and isolate the location of your problem
#3: replace the suspected component, and
#4:re-test the component thoroughly to be sure that you have solve the problem.
If you have not solved the problem, start again from step #1:This is a "universal" procedure that you can apply to any sort of troubleshooting __not just for phones.

DEFINE YOUR SYMPTOMS

When a phones breaks down, the cause might be a simple as a loose wire or a connector, or as complicated as an IC or component failure. Before you start, you must have a good understanding of all the symptoms. Think about the symptoms carefully. By recognizing and understanding your symptoms, it can be much easier to trace a problem to the appropriate component. Take the time to write down as many symptoms as you can. As a technician, you must often write problems and solutions for reference purposes.

IDENTIFY AND ISOLATE

Before you try to isolate a problem within a piece of hardware, you must first be sure that the equipment itself is causing the problem. In many cases, this will be fairly obvious, but some situation might not be. A faulty or improperly configured piece of software can cause confusing system errors. When you are sure that it is a system's hardware failure, you can begin to identify which component fails.

REPLACE

Because phones are designed as a sub-unit, it is almost always easier to replace a sub-unit outright, rather than attempt to repair the sub-unit to its component level. Even if you had the time, to isolate defective component, many parts are not inter-changeable, so it is better to replace the defective part than try to repair it

RE-TEST

When a repair is finally complete, the system must be reassembly carefully before testing it. All guards, housings, cables and shields must replaced before final testing. If symptoms persist, you will have to reevaluate the symptoms and narrow the problem to another parts of the equipment. If normal operation is restored (or greatly improved), test the phones's various function. When you can verify that the symptoms have stop during actual operation, the equipment can be returned to service. As a general rule, it is wise to let the system run for at least 24 hours to ensure that the replacement sub-assembly will not fail prematurely.

Do not be discouraged if the equipment still malfunctions. Maybe software settings and device drivers may need to be updated to. If you are tired simply walk away, clear your hand, and start again by defining the current symptoms. Never continue with a repair if you are tired or frustrated tomorrow is another day. Even the most experienced troubleshooters get overwhelmed from time to time.

Course Contents

Part 1 : Introduction to Cell Phone Repair

How Cellphone Works
Learning with Block Diagrams
Hardware Repair Techniques
Software Handling
Flashing
Unlocking
software, unlocking, flashing
What is Unlocking, user lock, SPC, MSL, FSC, OTKSL, Flashing
When to use these Terms
GSM unlocking: using codes
GSM Flashing
using software to remove user lock, SPC
what is prl
what is ESN/MEID
Introduction to CDMA software

Part 2: Basic Electronics Declassified:

Ohm's Law
Series Circuit
Parallel Circuit
Identifying Electronics Components and Circuit Symbols
Resistors
Capacitors
Transistors
Diodes
Fuse
Coils & Inductors
Crystal Oscillators
RF & IF Amplifiers and Filters
EMI and ESD Filters

Part 3: Tools and Test Equipment

Safety Procedures and Proper Handling of Tools and Test Equipment
How To Use and Read a Multimeter Tester
Test and Check up Procedures on Electronics Components
Preparing the Proper Tools For Repairing
Opening Tools and Tweezers

Soldering and Desoldering Tools
Muti Tester
SMD Rework Stations
DC Power Supply
Cleaning Kits
Reballing Kits
Working Table Equipments

Part 4: Schematic Diagrams

How to Read Cellphone's Schematic Diagrams
Identifying Component Symbols and Layout in Schematic Diagram
How to Identify The Follwing:

Resistor's Symbols and Layout
Capacitor's Symbols and Layout
Transistor's Symbols and Layout
Diodes Symbols and Layout
Coil Symbols and Layout
Integrated Circuit Symbols and Layout
DC to DC Voltage Drivers, Regulators
Convertes Symbols and Layout
EMI-ESD Symbols and Layout
RF Filter Symbols and Layout
Battery Cell Symbols and Layout
Power Switch , Mouthpiece, Earpiece and Ringtones Speakers
User Interface Symbols and Layout
Clock Crystal Oscillator Symbols and Layout
Fuse Symbol and Layout
Lines and Symbols on Schematic Diagram

Part 5: SOLDERING, SOLDERING, SOLDERING

How to Find and Locate Components on PC Board
How to Solder SMD Components Manually by Hand
Master soldering on any electric board
BASICS OF SOLDERING
Advantages of Soldering
What is Soldering & de-soldering? Lead free or not?
Hand soldering vs. machine soldering
Electric tools used in soldering: Soldering machines, Hot-Air machines, Pre-heaters, Infrared machines,
Rework stations...etc
Soldering tips & soldering irons

Hand tools & accessories used in soldering: magnifier, tweezers, Fume Extractor , sponges.etc
Chemicals used in soldering: flux, lead, solder wire, flux remover, tin

Part 6: APPLICATION OF SOLDERING IN CELL PHONE REPAIR

Types of circuit boards: PCB solder types and cell phone generations
Which electronic components are found in a cell phone PCB
diode, transceiver, transistor, integrated circuit, 2 point solder joints or 3 joints multi points?
Underfill & under film
Practical basic soldering trainings
Basic and intermediate applications for training
Soldering charging ports
Soldering power buttons
Soldering flex cables
Soldering SIM card trays
Memory modules
Camera modules
Battery sockets
LCD Connector modules
How to Reball BGA Chips Manually by Hand
Identifying and Familiarization of Common Mobile Phones Components and Spare Parts
LCD's Touch Screen Panels Microphones Micro Speakers Switches Charging Pins Antenna's
Battery
USB connectors

Part 7:Integrated Circuits

Understanding Major Integrated Circuits (IC) on Mobile Phones
Power Management IC
Application Processor
Flash IC
RAM IC
Hardware Handling Procedures
Proper Disassembling and Assembling Methods
How to Test Mobile phone Speaker,Buzzer or Ringer
How to Test Mobile phone Microphone or Mouthpiece
How to test Mobile Phone Charger Voltage
How to Test Mobile Phone Vibra Motor
How to check Mobile Phone Battery Voltage
How to test Power ON OFF Switch

Part 8: LIQUID DAMAGE

Types of liquid damage: Toilet, fresh, salt, food
Tools used in treatment
Chemicals used in treatment

Part 9 : Troubleshooting

Hardware Troubleshooting Basics
How to Troubleshoot Not Charging Issues
How charging circuit works
No Charging Response
Charger Not Supported
Not Charging
How SIM Circuits works
Insert Sim Card Problem
Invalid Sim Card
How Keypad Circuits Works
How to Map and Trace keypads Lines
Understanding The LED light Circuits
Explanation on How Audio Circuits work
Mouthpiece
Earpiece
Buzzer
Ringer
Headset
Vibra motor
How LCD Display Circuit Works
Understanding How RF circuit works

PART 1

Introduction:

How Cellphone Works

As a basic Part of a Technician, It is fully advice that he/she must have a basic knowledge of what technology he or she come up to..

Before we proceed further, please take a simple brief to enhanced your knowledge about the Field of What we are going to discuss hereafter.... Now first come first we all ever wonder how does the cellphone works?

have you ever wondered how a cell phone works? What makes it different from a regular phone? what's inside of it and how do they created it? What do all those terms like **PCS, GSM, CDMA** and **TDMA** mean? To start with, one of the most interesting things about a cell phone is that it is actually a radio -- an extremely sophisticated radio, but a radio nonetheless. The telephone was invented by Alexander Graham Bell in 1876, and wireless communication can trace its roots to the invention of the radio by Nikolai Tesla in the 1880s (formally presented in 1894 by a young Italian named Guglielmo Marconi). It was only natural that these two great technologies would eventually be combined.

If you prepare to take a deep knowledge, i recommended you to visit this site and have a brief Fundamentals of <u>Wireless Communication</u>
A basic technician all need is just to have a simple understanding about cellphones, we do not need extreme and intimate deeper meaning about it,
that's because what we are going to take around here is to fix what those various mobile phones company created and build....to make it as simple as that...

Cell Phone Network Technologies:

2G Technology

There are three common technologies used by 2G cell-phone networks for transmitting information:

  * Frequency division multiple access (FDMA)

  * Time division multiple access (TDMA)

  * Code division multiple access (CDMA)

Although these technologies sound very intimidating, you can get a good sense of how they work just by breaking down the title of each one.

The first word tells you what the access method is. The second word, division, lets you know that it splits calls based on that access method.

  * FDMA puts each call on a separate frequency.
  * TDMA assigns each call a certain portion of time on a designated frequency.
  * CDMA gives a unique code to each call and spreads it over the available frequencies.

The last part of each name is multiple access. This simply means that more than one user can utilize each cell.

FDMA

FDMA separates the spectrum into distinct voice channels by splitting it into uniform chunks of bandwidth. To better understand FDMA, think of radio stations: Each station sends its signal at a different frequency within the available band. FDMA is used mainly for analog transmission. While it is certainly capable of carrying digital information, FDMA is not considered to be an efficient method for digital transmission.

In FDMA, each phone uses a different frequency.

TDMA

TDMA is the access method used by the Electronics Industry Alliance and the Telecommunications Industry Association for Interim Standard 54 (IS-54) and Interim Standard 136 (IS-136). Using TDMA, a narrow band that is 30 kHz wide and 6.7 milliseconds long is split time-wise into three time slots.

Narrow band means "channels" in the traditional sense. Each conversation gets the radio for one-third of the time. This is possible because voice data that has been converted to digital information is compressed so that it takes up significantly less transmission space. Therefore, TDMA has three times the capacity of an analog system using the same number of channels. TDMA systems operate in either the 800-MHz (IS-54) or 1900-MHz (IS-136) frequency bands.

TDMA splits a frequency into time slots.

Unlocking Your GSM Phone
Any GSM phone can work with any SIM card, but some service providers "lock" the phone so that it will only work with their service. If your phone is locked, you can't use it with any other service provider, whether locally or overseas. You can unlock the phone using a special code -- but it's unlikely your service provider will give it to you. There are Web sites that will give you the unlock code, some for a small fee, some for free.

GSM

TDMA is also used as the access technology for Global System for Mobile communications (GSM). However, GSM implements TDMA in a somewhat different and incompatible way from IS-136. Think of GSM and IS-136 as two different operating systems that work on the same processor, like Windows and Linux both working on an Intel Pentium III. GSM systems use encryption to make phone calls more secure. GSM operates in the 900-MHz and 1800-MHz bands in Europe and Asia and in the 850-MHz and 1900-MHz (sometimes referred to as 1.9-GHz) band in the United States. It is used in digital cellular and PCS-based systems. GSM is also the basis for Integrated Digital Enhanced Network (IDEN), a popular system introduced by Motorola and used by Nextel.

GSM is the international standard in Europe, Australia and much of Asia and Africa. In covered areas, cell-phone users can buy one phone that will work anywhere where the standard is supported. To connect to the specific service providers in these different countries, GSM users simply switch subscriber identification module (SIM) cards. SIM cards are small removable disks that slip in and out of GSM cell phones. They store all the connection data and identification numbers you need to access a particular wireless service provider.

Unfortunately, the 850MHz/1900-MHz GSM phones used in the United States are not compatible with the international system. If you live in the United States and need to have cell-phone access when you're overseas, you can either buy a tri-band or quad-band GSM phone and use it both at home and when traveling or just buy a GSM 900MHz/1800MHz cell phone for traveling. You can get 900MHz/1800MHz GSM phones from Planet Omni, an online electronics firm based in California. They offer a wide selection of Nokia, Motorola and Ericsson GSM phones. They don't sell international SIM cards, however. You can pick up prepaid SIM cards for a wide range of countries at Telestial.com.

CDMA

CDMA takes an entirely different approach from TDMA. CDMA, after digitizing data, spreads it out over the entire available bandwidth. Multiple calls are overlaid on each other on the channel, with each assigned a unique sequence code. CDMA is a form of spread spectrum, which simply means that data is sent in small pieces over a number of the discrete frequencies available for use at any time in the specified range.

In CDMA, each phone's data has a unique code.

All of the users transmit in the same wide-band chunk of spectrum. Each user's signal is spread over the entire bandwidth by a unique spreading code. At the receiver, that same unique code is used to recover the signal. Because CDMA systems need to put an accurate time-stamp on each piece of a signal, it references the GPS system for this information. Between eight and 10 separate calls can be carried in the same channel space as one analog AMPS call. CDMA technology is the basis for Interim Standard 95 (IS-95) and operates in both the 800-MHz and 1900-MHz frequency bands.

Ideally, TDMA and CDMA are transparent to each other. In practice, high-power CDMA signals raise the noise floor for TDMA receivers, and high-power TDMA signals can cause overloading and jamming of CDMA receivers.

2G is a cell phone network protocol. Click here to learn about network protocols for Smartphones.

Now let's look at the distinction between multiple-band and multiple-mode technologies.

Multi-band vs. Multi-mode Cell Phones

Dual Band vs. Dual Mode
If you travel a lot, you will probably want to look for phones that offer multiple bands, multiple modes or both. Let's take a look at each of these options:

  * Multiple band - A phone that has multiple-band capability can switch frequencies. For example, a dual-band TDMA phone could use TDMA services in either an 800-MHz or a 1900-MHz system. A quad-band GSM phone could use GSM service in the 850-MHz, 900-MHz, 1800-MHz or 1900-MHz band.

* **Multiple mode** - In cell phones, "mode" refers to the type of transmission technology used. So, a phone that supported AMPS and TDMA could switch back and forth as needed. It's important that one of the modes is AMPS -- this gives you analog service if you are in an area that doesn't have digital support.

* **Multiple band/Multiple mode** - The best of both worlds allows you to switch between frequency bands and transmission modes as needed.

Cellular vs. PCS

Personal Communications Services (PCS) is a wireless phone service very similar to cellular phone service, but with an emphasis on personal service and extended mobility. The term "PCS" is often used in place of "digital cellular," but true PCS means that other services like paging, caller ID and e-mail are bundled into the service.

While cellular was originally created for use in cars, PCS was designed from the ground up for greater user mobility. PCS has smaller cells and therefore requires a larger number of antennas to cover a geographic area. PCS phones use frequencies between 1.85 and 1.99 GHz (1850 MHz to 1990 MHz).

Technically, cellular systems in the United States operate in the 824-MHz to 894-MHz frequency bands; PCS operates in the 1850-MHz to 1990-MHz bands. And while it is based on TDMA, PCS has 200-kHz channel spacing and eight time slots instead of the typical 30-kHz channel spacing and three time slots found in digital cellular.

Changing bands or modes is done automatically by phones that support these options. Usually the phone will have a default option set, such as 1900-MHz TDMA, and will try to connect at that frequency with that technology first. If it supports dual bands, it will switch to 800 MHz if it cannot connect at 1900 MHz. And if the phone supports more than one mode, it will try the digital mode(s) first, then switch to analog.

You can find both dual-mode and tri-mode phones. The term "tri-mode" can be deceptive. It may mean that the phone supports two digital technologies, such as CDMA and TDMA, as well as analog. In that case, it is a true tri-mode phone. But it can also mean that it supports one digital technology in two bands and also offers analog support. A popular version of the tri-mode type of phone for people who do a lot of international traveling has GSM service in the 900-MHz band for Europe and Asia and the 1900-MHz band for the United States, in addition to the analog service. Technically, this is a dual-mode phone, and one of those modes (GSM) supports two bands.

3G and 3GS Technology

In the next section, we'll take a look at 3G mobile-phone technology.

3G technology is the latest in mobile communications. 3G stands for "third generation" -- this makes analog cellular technology generation one and digital/PCS generation two. 3G technology is intended for the true multimedia cell phone -- typically called smartphones -- and features increased bandwidth and transfer rates to accommodate Web-based applications and phone-based audio and video files.

3G comprises several cellular access technologies. The three most common ones as of 2005 are:

  * CDMA2000 - based on 2G Code Division Multiple Access (see Cellular Access Technologies)
  * WCDMA (UMTS) - Wideband Code Division Multiple Access
  * TD-SCDMA - Time-division Synchronous Code-division Multiple Access

3G networks have potential transfer speeds of up to 3 Mbps (about 15 seconds to download a 3-minute MP3 song). For comparison, the fastest 2G phones can achieve up to 144Kbps (about 8 minutes to download a 3-minute song). 3G's high data rates are ideal for downloading information from the Internet and sending and receiving large, multimedia files. 3G phones are like mini-laptops and can accommodate broadband applications like video conferencing, receiving streaming video from the Web, sending and receiving faxes and instantly downloading e-mail messages with attachments.

3GS feels wonderfully familiar – it's design is almost identical to the 3G, and it's not until you switch the device on that you start to appreciate the differences. The "S" stands for speed – Apple has used a faster processor in the 3GS, and the impact is immediate, with applications loading more briskly, programs running noticeably faster, and the already slick user-interface getting an extra layer of go-faster stripes. It's also HSDPA compatible, a step up from 3G, meaning it can surf the web at faster speeds. Battery life is longer too; I was able to squeeze a full day out of my iPhone without needing to give it a lunchtime charging boost.

Block diagram on how cell-phone works

How Cell-phone works

In this lesson we are going to take a brief familiarization of a typical block diagram of a cellphone.
Block Diagram can help us understand the flow of a certain part of a cellphone's circuit.
A Cell-phone handset is basically composed of two sections,
which is RF and Baseband Sections.

RF

RF refers to radio frequency, the mode of communication for wireless technologies of all kinds, including cordless phones, radar, ham radio, GPS, and radio and television broadcasts. RF technology is so much a part of our lives we scarcely notice it for its ubiquity. From baby monitors to cell phones, Bluetooth® to remote control toys, RF waves are all around us. RF waves are electromagnetic waves which propagate at the speed of light, or 186,000 miles per second (300,000 km/s). The frequencies of RF waves, however, are slower than those of visible light, making RF waves invisible to the human eye.

Baseband

In signal processing, baseband describes signals and systems whose range of frequencies is measured from zero to a maximum bandwidth or highest signal frequency. It is sometimes used as a noun for a band of frequencies starting at zero.
In telecommunications, it is the frequency range occupied by a message signal prior to modulation.
It can be considered as a synonym to low-pass.
Baseband is also sometimes used as a general term for part of the physical components of a wireless communications product. Typically, it includes the control circuitry (microprocessor), the power supply, and amplifiers.
A baseband processor is an IC that is mainly used in a mobile phone to process communication functions.

Basically Baseband also composed of to sections which is the Analog and Digital Processing Sections. So, we are going to separate each other for better and easier to understand.
Cell-phone have three different sections which is the following.
I prepare this to be simple and easy instead of using or explaining it with deep technical terms .

In this manner, it is easy for us to understand the concepts and methods of how basically the cellphone works.

Cell-phone have three sections since baseband is differentiated by into two which is the Analog and Digital function while the RF section remains as a whole circuit section..

which consists of following

1. Radio Frequency (RF Section)
2. The Analog Baseband Processor
3. And the Digital Baseband Processor.

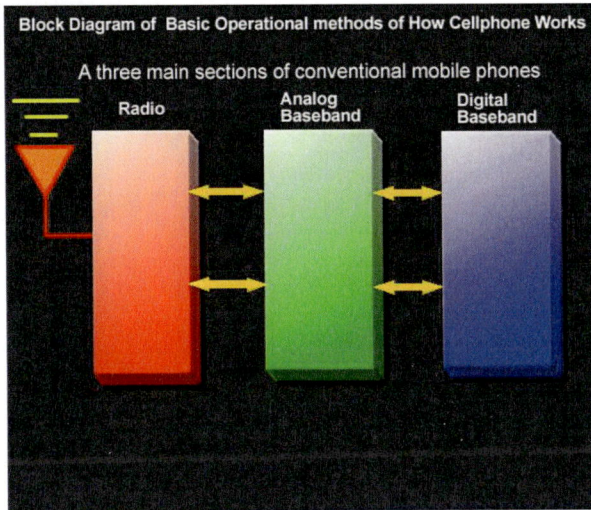

Block Diagram of Basic Operational methods of How Cellphone Works

A three main sections of conventional mobile phones

Radio   Analog Baseband   Digital Baseband

Radio Frequency Processing Section
The RF section is the part of the cell-phone circuit is also known as RF Transceiver.
It is the section that transmit and receive certain frequency to a network and synchronize to other phone.

The RF - A radio section is based on two main Circuits.
1 Transmitter
2 Reciever
A simple mobile phone uses these two circuits to correspond to an other mobile phone. A Transmitter is a circuit or device which is used to transmit radio signals in the air.and a reciever is simply like radios which are used to recieve transmissions(Radiation) which is spread in the air by any transmitter on a specific frequency.
The two way communication is made possible by setting two transmitters and two recievers sycronized in this form that a trasmitter in a cell phone is syncronised with the frequency of other

15

cell phone's recieving frequency same like the transmitter of second cell phone is syncronised with the recieving frequency of first cell phone. So first cell phone transmits its radiation in the air while the other phone listens it and same process is present in the opposit side. so these hand held two cell phones correspond to one another.

the technology used in these days is a little bit different but it is based on the basic theory prescribed before. the today's technology will be discussed in later on.

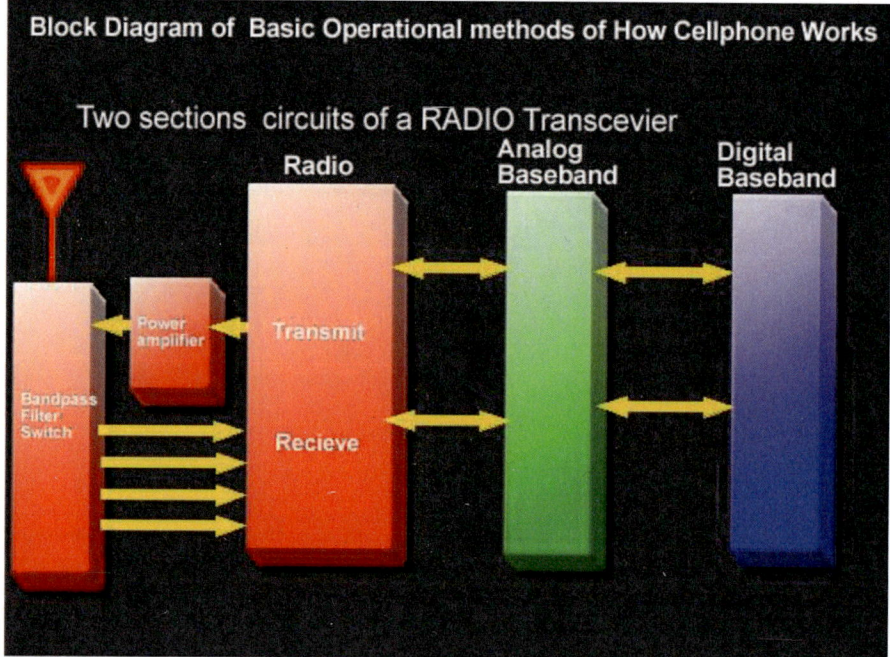

Block Diagram of Basic Operational methods of How Cellphone Works

Analog Baseband Processor

A/D and D/A section

The analog baseband processing section is composed of different types of circuits.
This section converts and process the analog to digital (A/D) signals and digital to analog signals (D/A).

Control section

This is the section acts as the controller of the the input and output of any analog and digital signal.

Power Management

A power management section in mobile phones is designed to handle energy matters that is

consumed in mobile phones. There are two main sub sections in a single power section.
• Power Distribution and switching section
• **Charging Section**
A power distribution section is designed to distribute desired Voltages and current to the other sections of a phone. this section takes power from a battery (which is figured commonly 3.6 Volts)and in some places it converts or step down to various volts like 2.8 V 1.8V 1.6V etc. while on other place it also
steps up the voltage like 4.8 V. this section is commonly designed around a power IC(and integrated circuit) which is used to distribute and regulate the voltage used in other components. The Charging section is based on a charging IC which takes power from an external source and gives it to battery to make it again power up when it is exhausted. this section uses convertibly 6.4 V from an external battery charger and regulates it to 5.8V wile giving it to battery. The battery is made charged by this process and it is ready to use for the next session (a battery session is a time which is provided by the manufacturer of a cell phone for standby by condition of a mobile phone or talk condition.)

Audio Codecs Section
This section where analog and digital audio properties being process like the microphone, earpiece speaker headset and ring-tones and also the vibrator circuits.

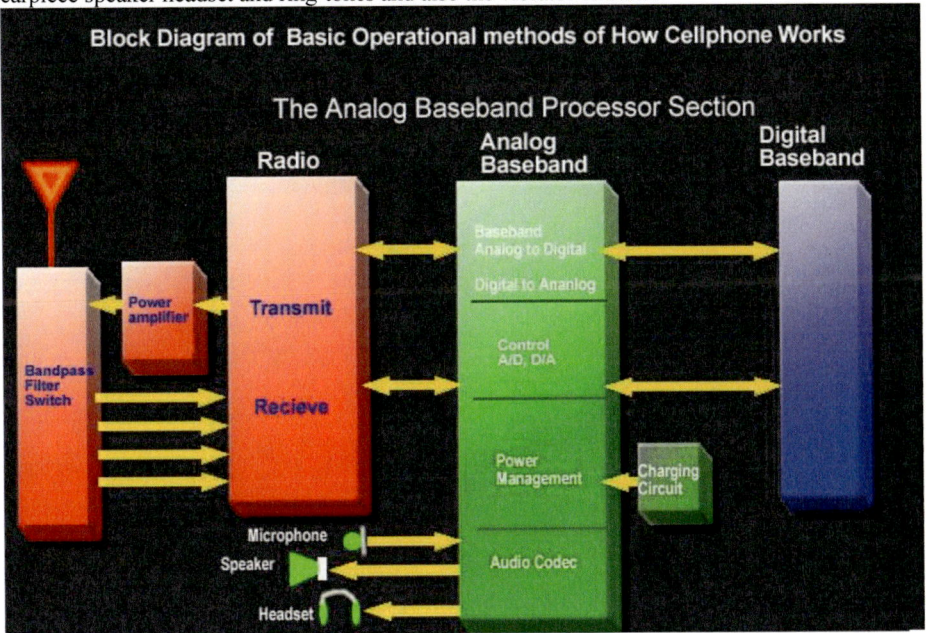

Block Diagram of Basic Operational methods of How Cellphone Works

The Analog Baseband Processor Section

Digital Baseband Processor
This is the part where All Application being process. Digital Baseband Processor section is used

in mobile phones to handle data input and output signal like switching, driving applications commands and memory accessing and executing.

These are the parts and sections o a Digital Baseband Circuit were installed.

CPU

CPU(Central Processing Unit) The Central Processing Unit (CPU) is responsible for interpreting and executing most of the commands from the users interface. It is often called the "brains" of the microprocessor, central processor, "the brains of the computer"

Flash and Memory Storage Circuits

*RAM(Random Access Memory)

*ROM,Flash(Read Only Memory

Interfaces such as the following were also part on this section:

*Blutooth

*Wi-fi

*Camera

*Screen Display

*Keypads

*USB

*SIM-Card

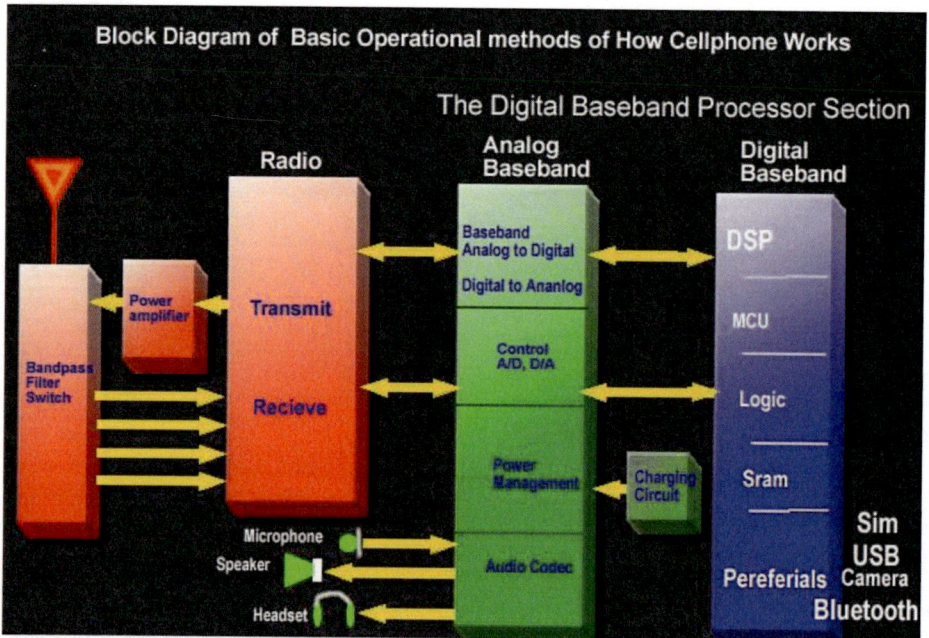

Block Diagram of Basic Operational methods of How Cellphone Works

Here a typical overview of a block diagram on latest mobile phone designs.

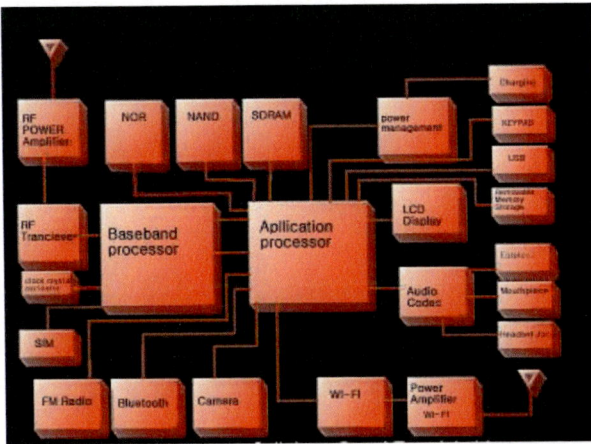

Various mobile phones have different concepts and design on every aspects, but the methods and operational flow are all exactly the same. It differs on how and what certain IC chips and parts they are being used and installed to a certain mobile phone circuitry.

PART 2

Basic Electronics

Definition of Electronics:

Electronics is the branch of science that deals with the study of flow and control of electrons (electricity) and the study of their behavior and effects in vacuums, gases, and semiconductors, and with devices using such electrons. This control of electrons is accomplished by devices that resist, carry, select, steer, switch, store, manipulate, and exploit the electron.

Electronics isn't always easy, but you can learn. And you can do it without memorizing theories and formulas belong in a Physics text. the focus of this program is learning how things work. Electronics may defined as an art of knowledge to make such impossible things work. Things such as Televisions, AM/FM Radios, Computers and of course the mobile phones and etc. We are surrounded by electronics....

Learning how things work can be fun.
With this skill you can Build things.
make better use of things
and repair things..
have better job opportunities

An important part of learning electronics
is the need to visualize the action inside a piece of equipment. In electronics things happen at a sub-atomic level. to understand what is happening, you need a mental picture, a visualization of events you can see directly. You need a in your mind of how events are turned on and off. you need to visualize signals being amplified and attenuated. (These are long words for being made bigger and smaller)

take an overview of electronic equipment. Inside anything what's happening can be describe as some kind of source delivering power to some kind of a load. The terms source and load become clearer as you can discover a few basics. A source is where the energy comes from. A load is what does the work. When power is delivered to a load, the load produces sound, heat, pictures or anything else that can be produced electronically..

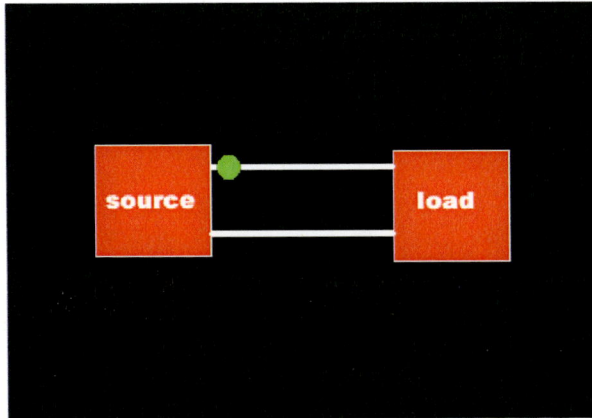

On successful completion of this lesson you will be able to:

describe the structure of a simple atom
recognize a series resistor circuit
calculate the expected current in a series circuit
calculate the power dissipated in a resistor from color code
measure the voltage across a resistor or circuit
measure the current through a resistor circuit
recognize several types of switches
determine circuit paths in switched circuits

Basic Electronics

The Enteractive Lesson

A Practice Exercise

Introduction to Troubleshooting

Ohm's Law

What is Ohm's Law?

Ohm's Law is made from 3 mathematical equations that shows the relationship between electric voltage, current and resistance.

What is voltage? An **analogy** would be a huge water tank filled with thousands of gallons of water high on a hill.
The difference between the pressure of water in the tank and the water that comes out of a pipe connected at the bottom leading to a faucet is determined by the size of the pipe and the size of the outlet of the faucet. This difference of pressure between the two can be thought of as potential Voltage.

What is current? An analogy would be the amount of flow determined by the pressure (voltage) of the water thru the pipes leading to a faucet. The term current refers to the quantity, volume or intensity of electrical flow, as opposed to voltage, which refers to the force or "pressure" causing the current flow.

What is resistance? An analogy would be the size of the water pipes and the size of the faucet. The larger the pipe and the faucet (less resistance), the more water that comes out! The smaller the pipe and faucet, (more resistance), the less water that comes out! This can be thought of as resistance to the flow of the water current.
All three of these: voltage, current and resistance directly interact in Ohm's law.
Change any two of them and you effect the third.

Info: Ohm's Law was named after Bavarian mathematician and physicist Georg Ohm.

Ohm's Law can be stated as mathematical equations, all derived from the same principle.
In the following equations,
V is voltage measured in volts (the size of the water tank),

I is current measured in amperes (related to the pressure (Voltage) of water thru the pipes and faucet) and

R is resistance measured in ohms as related to the size of the pipes and faucet:

V = I x R (Voltage = Current multiplied by Resistance)

R = V / I (Resistance = Voltage divided by Current)

I = V / R (Current = Voltage Divided by Resistance)

Knowing any two of the values of a circuit, one can determine (calculate) the third, using Ohm's Law.

For example, to find the Voltage in a circuit:

If the circuit has a current of 2 amperes, and a resistance of 1 ohm, (< these are the two "known"), then according to Ohms Law and the formulas above, voltage equals current multiplied by resistance:

(V = 2 amperes x 1 ohm = 2 volts).

To find the current in the same circuit above assuming we did not know it but we know the voltage and resistance:
I = 2 volts divided by the resistance 1 ohm = 2 amperes.

In this third example we know the current (2 amperes) and the voltage (2 volts)....what is the resistance?
Substituting the formula:
R = Volts divided by the current (2 volts divided by 2 amperes = 1 ohm

Sometimes it's very helpful to associate these formulas Visually. The Ohms Law "wheels" and graphics below can be a very useful tool to jog your memory and help you to understand their relationship.

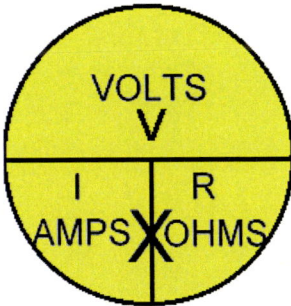

The wheel above is divided into three sections:

Volts V (on top of the dividing line)
Amps (amperes) I (lower left below the dividing line)
Resistance R (lower right below the dividing line)
X represents the (multiply by sign)
Memorize this wheel

To use, just cover the unknown quantity you need with your minds eye and what is left is the formula to find the unknown.

Example:

To find the current of a circuit (I), just cover the I or Amps section in your mines eye and what remains is the V volts above the dividing line and the R ohms (resistance) below it. Now substitute the known values. Just divided the known volts by the known resistance.
Your answer will be the current in the circuit.
The same procedure is used to find the volts or resistance of a circuit!

Here is another example:

You know the current and the resistance in a circuit but you want to find out the voltage.

Just cover the voltage section with your minds eye...what's left is the I X R sections. Just multiply the I value times the R value to get your answer! Practice with the wheel and you'll be surprised at how well it works to help you remember the formulas without trying!

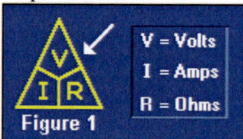

Figure 1

V = Volts
I = Amps
R = Ohms

This Ohm's Law Triangle graphic is also helpful to learn the formulas. Just cover the unknown value and follow the graphic as in the yellow wheel examples above.

You'll have to insert the X between the I and R in the graphic and imagine the horizontal divide line but the principal is just the same.

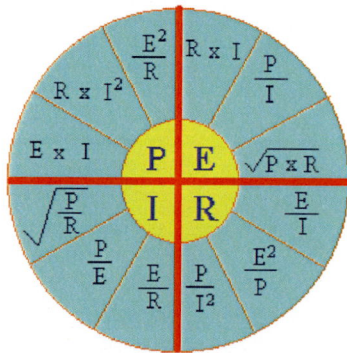

In the above Ohm's law wheel you'll notice that is has an added section (P) for Power and the letter E* has been used instead of the letter V for voltage.

This wheel is used in the exact same fashion as the other wheels and graphics above.

You will also notice in the blue/green areas there are only two known values with the unknown value in the yellow sections. The red bars separate the four units of interest.

An example of the use of this wheel is:

Let's say that you know the power and the current in a circuit and want to know the voltage. Find your unknown value in the yellow areas (V or E* in this wheel) and just look outward and pick the values that you do know. These would be the P and the I. Substitute your values in the formula, (P divided by I) do the math and you have your answer!

Info: Typically, Ohm's Law is only applied to DC circuits and not AC circuits.
* The letter "E" is sometimes used in representations of Ohm's Law for voltage instead of the "V" as in the wheel above.

OHM's LAW Calculator

Series Circuit

A circuit composed solely of components connected in series is known as a **series circuit**

A Simple Series Circuit
Let's start with a series circuit consisting of three resistors and a single battery:

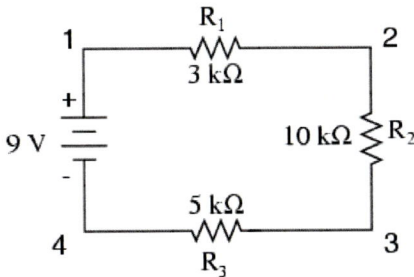

The first principle to understand about series circuits is that the amount of current is the same through any component in the circuit. This is because there is only one path for electrons to flow in a series circuit, and because free electrons flow through conductors like marbles in a tube, the rate of flow (marble speed) at any point in the circuit (tube) at any specific point in time must be equal.

From the way that the 9 volt battery is arranged, we can tell that the electrons in this circuit will flow in a counter-clockwise direction, from point 4 to 3 to 2 to 1 and back to 4. However, we have one source of voltage and three resistances. How do we use Ohm's Law here?

An important caveat to Ohm's Law is that all quantities (voltage, current, resistance, and power) must relate to each other in terms of the same two points in a circuit. For instance, with a single-battery, single-resistor circuit, we could easily calculate any quantity because they all applied to the same two points in the circuit:

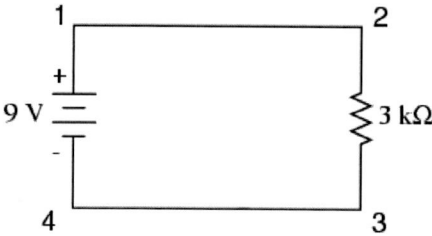

$$I = \frac{E}{R}$$

$$I = \frac{9 \text{ volts}}{3 \text{ k}\Omega} = 3 \text{ mA}$$

Since points 1 and 2 are connected together with wire of negligible resistance, as are points 3 and 4, we can say that point 1 is electrically common to point 2, and that point 3 is electrically common to point 4. Since we know we have 9 volts of electromotive force between points 1 and 4 (directly across the battery), and since point 2 is common to point 1 and point 3 common to point 4, we must also have 9 volts between points 2 and 3 (directly across the resistor). Therefore, we can apply Ohm's Law (I = E/R) to the current through the resistor, because we know the voltage (E) across the resistor and the resistance (R) of that resistor. All terms (E, I, R) apply to the same two points in the circuit, to that same resistor, so we can use the Ohm's Law formula with no reservation.

However, in circuits containing more than one resistor, we must be careful in how we apply Ohm's Law. In the three-resistor example circuit below, we know that we have 9 volts between points 1 and 4, which is the amount of electromotive force trying to push electrons through the series combination of R_1, R_2, and R_3. However, we cannot take the value of 9 volts and divide it by 3k, 10k or 5k Ω to try to find a current value, because we don't know how much voltage is across any one of those resistors, individually.

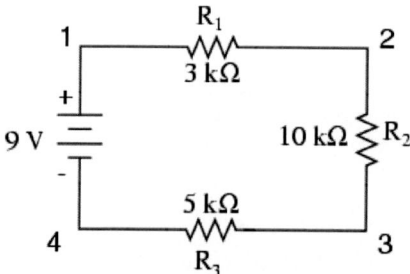

The figure of 9 volts is a *total* quantity for the whole circuit, whereas the figures of 3k, 10k, and

5k Ω are *individual* quantities for individual resistors. If we were to plug a figure for total voltage into an Ohm's Law equation with a figure for individual resistance, the result would not relate accurately to any quantity in the real circuit.

For R_1, Ohm's Law will relate the amount of voltage across R_1 with the current through R_1, given R_1's resistance, 3kΩ:

$$I_{R1} = \frac{E_{R1}}{3\ k\Omega} \qquad\qquad E_{R1} = I_{R1}(3\ k\Omega)$$

But, since we don't know the voltage across R_1 (only the total voltage supplied by the battery across the three-resistor series combination) and we don't know the current through R_1, we can't do any calculations with either formula. The same goes for R_2 and R_3: we can apply the Ohm's Law equations if and only if all terms are representative of their respective quantities between the same two points in the circuit.

So what can we do? We know the voltage of the source (9 volts) applied across the series combination of R_1, R_2, and R_3, and we know the resistances of each resistor, but since those quantities aren't in the same context, we can't use Ohm's Law to determine the circuit current. If only we knew what the *total* resistance was for the circuit: then we could calculate *total* current with our figure for *total* voltage (I=E/R).

This brings us to the second principle of series circuits: the total resistance of any series circuit is equal to the sum of the individual resistances. This should make intuitive sense: the more resistors in series that the electrons must flow through, the more difficult it will be for those electrons to flow. In the example problem, we had a 3 kΩ, 10 kΩ, and 5 kΩ resistor in series, giving us a total resistance of 18 kΩ:

$$R_{total} = R_1 + R_2 + R_3$$

$$R_{total} = 3\ k\Omega + 10\ k\Omega + 5\ k\Omega$$

$$R_{total} = 18\ k\Omega$$

In essence, we've calculated the equivalent resistance of R_1, R_2, and R_3 combined. Knowing this, we could re-draw the circuit with a single equivalent resistor representing the series combination of R_1, R_2, and R_3:

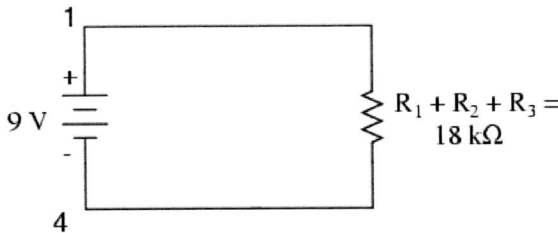

Now we have all the necessary information to calculate circuit current, because we have the voltage between points 1 and 4 (9 volts) and the resistance between points 1 and 4 (18 kΩ):

$$I_{total} = \frac{E_{total}}{R_{total}}$$

$$I_{total} = \frac{9 \text{ volts}}{18 \text{ k}\Omega} = 500 \text{ }\mu A$$

Knowing that current is equal through all components of a series circuit (and we just determined the current through the battery), we can go back to our original circuit schematic and note the current through each component:

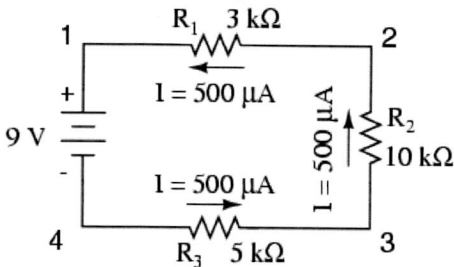

Now that we know the amount of current through each resistor, we can use Ohm's Law to determine the voltage drop across each one (applying Ohm's Law in its proper context):

$$E_{R1} = I_{R1} R_1 \qquad E_{R2} = I_{R2} R_2 \qquad E_{R3} = I_{R3} R_3$$

$$E_{R1} = (500 \text{ }\mu A)(3 \text{ k}\Omega) = 1.5 \text{ V}$$

$$E_{R2} = (500 \text{ }\mu A)(10 \text{ k}\Omega) = 5 \text{ V}$$

$$E_{R3} = (500 \text{ }\mu A)(5 \text{ k}\Omega) = 2.5 \text{ V}$$

Notice the voltage drops across each resistor, and how the sum of the voltage drops (1.5 + 5 + 2.5) is equal to the battery (supply) voltage: 9 volts. This is the third principle of series circuits: that the supply voltage is equal to the sum of the individual voltage drops.

However, the method we just used to analyze this simple series circuit can be streamlined for better understanding. By using a table to list all voltages, currents, and resistances in the circuit, it becomes very easy to see which of those quantities can be properly related in any Ohm's Law equation:

	R_1	R_2	R_3	Total	
E					Volts
I					Amps
R					Ohms

↑ Ohm's Law   ↑ Ohm's Law   ↑ Ohm's Law   ↑ Ohm's Law

The rule with such a table is to apply Ohm's Law only to the values within each vertical column. For instance, E_{R1} only with I_{R1} and R_1; E_{R2} only with I_{R2} and R_2; etc. You begin your analysis by filling in those elements of the table that are given to you from the beginning:

	R_1	R_2	R_3	Total	
E				9	Volts
I					Amps
R	3k	10k	5k		Ohms

As you can see from the arrangement of the data, we can't apply the 9 volts of E_T (total voltage) to any of the resistances (R_1, R_2, or R_3) in any Ohm's Law formula because they're in different columns. The 9 volts of battery voltage is *not* applied directly across R_1, R_2, or R_3. However, we can use our "rules" of series circuits to fill in blank spots on a horizontal row. In this case, we can use the series rule of resistances to determine a total resistance from the *sum* of individual resistances:

	R_1	R_2	R_3	Total	
E				9	Volts
I					Amps
R	3k	10k	5k	18k	Ohms ←

Rule of series circuits
$$R_T = R_1 + R_2 + R_3$$

Now, with a value for total resistance inserted into the rightmost ("Total") column, we can apply Ohm's Law of I=E/R to total voltage and total resistance to arrive at a total current of 500 µA:

	R_1	R_2	R_3	Total	
E				9	Volts
I				500µ	Amps
R	3k	10k	5k	18k	Ohms

↑
Ohm's Law

Then, knowing that the current is shared equally by all components of a series circuit (another "rule" of series circuits), we can fill in the currents for each resistor from the current figure just calculated:

	R_1	R_2	R_3	Total	
E				9	Volts
I	500µ	500µ	500µ	500µ	Amps ←
R	3k	10k	5k	18k	Ohms

Rule of series circuits

$$I_T = I_1 = I_2 = I_3$$

Finally, we can use Ohm's Law to determine the voltage drop across each resistor, one column at a time:

	R_1	R_2	R_3	Total	
E	1.5	5	2.5	9	Volts
I	500µ	500µ	500µ	500µ	Amps
R	3k	10k	5k	18k	Ohms

↑   ↑   ↑
Ohm's   *Ohm's*   *Ohm's*
Law   *Law*   *Law*

Just for fun, we can use a computer to analyze this very same circuit automatically. It will be a good way to verify our calculations and also become more familiar with computer analysis. First, we have to describe the circuit to the computer in a format recognizable by the software. The SPICE program we'll be using requires that all electrically unique points in a circuit be numbered, and component placement is understood by which of those numbered points, or "nodes," they share. For clarity, I numbered the four corners of our example circuit 1 through 4. SPICE, however, demands that there be a node zero somewhere in the circuit, so I'll re-draw the circuit, changing the numbering scheme slightly:

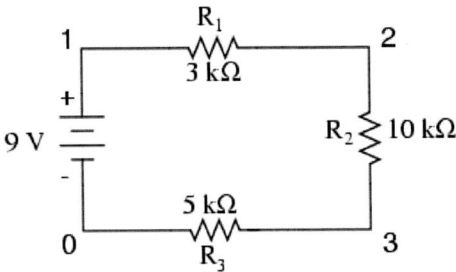

All I've done here is re-numbered the lower-left corner of the circuit 0 instead of 4. Now, I can enter several lines of text into a computer file describing the circuit in terms SPICE will understand, complete with a couple of extra lines of code directing the program to display voltage and current data for our viewing pleasure. This computer file is known as the *netlist* in SPICE terminology:

```
series circuit
v1 1 0
r1 1 2 3k
r2 2 3 10k
r3 3 0 5k
.dc v1 9 9 1
.print dc v(1,2) v(2,3) v(3,0)
.end
```

Now, all I have to do is run the SPICE program to process the netlist and output the results:

```
v1              v(1,2)      v(2,3)      v(3)        i(v1)
9.000E+00       1.500E+00   5.000E+00   2.500E+00   -5.000E-04
```

This printout is telling us the battery voltage is 9 volts, and the voltage drops across R_1, R_2, and R_3 are 1.5 volts, 5 volts, and 2.5 volts, respectively. Voltage drops across any component in SPICE are referenced by the node numbers the component lies between, so v(1,2) is referencing the voltage between nodes 1 and 2 in the circuit, which are the points between which R_1 is located. The order of node numbers is important: when SPICE outputs a figure for v(1,2), it regards the polarity the same way as if we were holding a voltmeter with the red test lead on node 1 and the black test lead on node 2.

We also have a display showing current (albeit with a negative value) at 0.5 milliamps, or 500 microamps. So our mathematical analysis has been vindicated by the computer. This figure appears as a negative number in the SPICE analysis, due to a quirk in the way SPICE handles current calculations.

In summary, a series circuit is defined as having only one path for electrons to flow. From this definition, three rules of series circuits follow: all components share the same current; resistances add to equal a larger, total resistance; and voltage drops add to equal a larger, total voltage. All of these rules find root in the definition of a series circuit. If you understand that definition fully, then the rules are nothing more than footnotes to the definition.

- **REVIEW:**

- Components in a series circuit share the same current: $I_{Total} = I_1 = I_2 = \ldots I_n$
- Total resistance in a series circuit is equal to the sum of the individual resistances: $R_{Total} = R_1 + R_2 + \ldots R_n$
- Total voltage in a series circuit is equal to the sum of the individual voltage drops: $E_{Total} = E_1 + E_2 + \ldots E_n$

Parallel Circuit

One connected completely in parallel is known as a **parallel circuit**.

Simple Parallel Circuit
Let's start with a parallel circuit consisting of three resistors and a single battery:

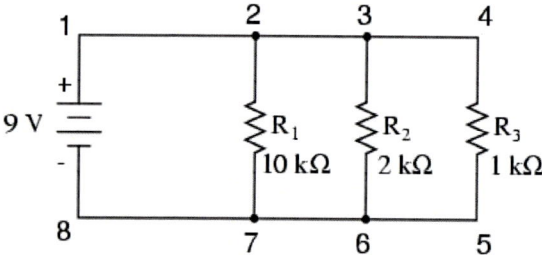

The first principle to understand about parallel circuits is that the voltage is equal across all components in the circuit. This is because there are only two sets of electrically common points in a parallel circuit, and voltage measured between sets of common points must always be the same at any given time. Therefore, in the above circuit, the voltage across R_1 is equal to the voltage across R_2 which is equal to the voltage across R_3 which is equal to the voltage across the battery. This equality of voltages can be represented in another table for our starting values:

	R_1	R_2	R_3	Total	
E	9	9	9	9	Volts
I					Amps
R	10k	2k	1k		Ohms

Just as in the case of series circuits, the same caveat for Ohm's Law applies: values for voltage, current, and resistance must be in the same context in order for the calculations to work correctly. However, in the above example circuit, we can immediately apply Ohm's Law to each resistor to find its current because we know the voltage across each resistor (9 volts) and the resistance of each resistor:

$$I_{R1} = \frac{E_{R1}}{R_1} \qquad I_{R2} = \frac{E_{R2}}{R_2} \qquad I_{R3} = \frac{E_{R3}}{R_3}$$

$$I_{R1} = \frac{9 \text{ V}}{10 \text{ k}\Omega} = 0.9 \text{ mA}$$

$$I_{R2} = \frac{9 \text{ V}}{2 \text{ k}\Omega} = 4.5 \text{ mA}$$

$$I_{R3} = \frac{9 \text{ V}}{1 \text{ k}\Omega} = 9 \text{ mA}$$

	R_1	R_2	R_3	Total	
E	9	9	9	9	Volts
I	0.9m	4.5m	9m		Amps
R	10k	2k	1k		Ohms

Ohm's Ohm's Ohm's
Law Law Law

At this point we still don't know what the total current or total resistance for this parallel circuit is, so we can't apply Ohm's Law to the rightmost ("Total") column. However, if we think carefully about what is happening it should become apparent that the total current must equal the sum of all individual resistor ("branch") currents:

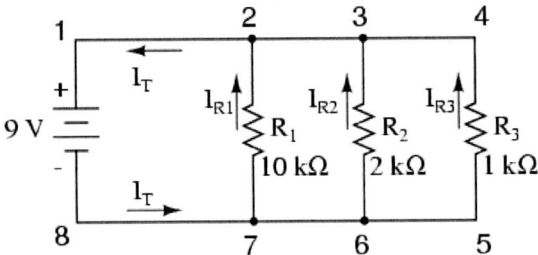

As the total current exits the negative (-) battery terminal at point 8 and travels through the circuit, some of the flow splits off at point 7 to go up through R_1, some more splits off at point 6 to go up through R_2, and the remainder goes up through R_3. Like a river branching into several smaller streams, the combined flow rates of all streams must equal the flow rate of the whole river. The same thing is encountered where the currents through R_1, R_2, and R_3 join to flow back to the positive terminal of the battery (+) toward point 1: the flow of electrons from point 2 to point 1 must equal the sum of the (branch) currents through R_1, R_2, and R_3.

This is the second principle of parallel circuits: the total circuit current is equal to the sum of the individual branch currents. Using this principle, we can fill in the I_T spot on our table with the sum of I_{R1}, I_{R2}, and I_{R3}:

	R_1	R_2	R_3	Total	
E	9	9	9	9	Volts
I	0.9m	4.5m	9m	14.4m	Amps ←
R	10k	2k	1k		Ohms

Rule of parallel
circuits
$$I_{total} = I_1 + I_2 + I_3$$

Finally, applying Ohm's Law to the rightmost ("Total") column, we can calculate the total circuit resistance:

	R_1	R_2	R_3	Total	
E	9	9	9	9	Volts
I	0.9m	4.5m	9m	14.4m	Amps
R	10k	2k	1k	625	Ohms

$$R_{total} = \frac{E_{total}}{I_{total}} = \frac{9\ V}{14.4\ mA} = 625\ \Omega \qquad \text{Ohm's Law}$$

Please note something very important here. The total circuit resistance is only 625 Ω: *less* than any one of the individual resistors. In the series circuit, where the total resistance was the sum of the individual resistances, the total was bound to be *greater* than any one of the resistors individually. Here in the parallel circuit, however, the opposite is true: we say that the individual resistances *diminish* rather than *add* to make the total. This principle completes our triad of "rules" for parallel circuits, just as series circuits were found to have three rules for voltage, current, and resistance. Mathematically, the relationship between total resistance and individual resistances in a parallel circuit looks like this:

$$R_{total} = \frac{1}{\dfrac{1}{R_1} + \dfrac{1}{R_2} + \dfrac{1}{R_3}}$$

The same basic form of equation works for *any* number of resistors connected together in parallel, just add as many 1/R terms on the denominator of the fraction as needed to accommodate all parallel resistors in the circuit.

Just as with the series circuit, we can use computer analysis to double-check our calculations.

First, of course, we have to describe our example circuit to the computer in terms it can understand. I'll start by re-drawing the circuit:

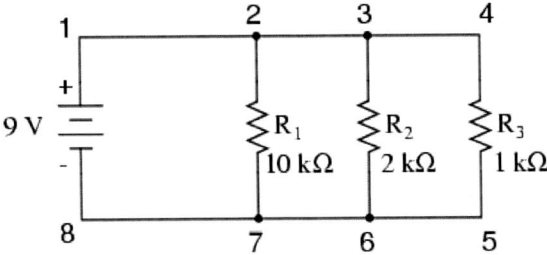

Once again we find that the original numbering scheme used to identify points in the circuit will have to be altered for the benefit of SPICE. In SPICE, all electrically common points must share identical node numbers. This is how SPICE knows what's connected to what, and how. In a simple parallel circuit, all points are electrically common in one of two sets of points. For our example circuit, the wire connecting the tops of all the components will have one node number and the wire connecting the bottoms of the components will have the other. Staying true to the convention of including zero as a node number, I choose the numbers 0 and 1:

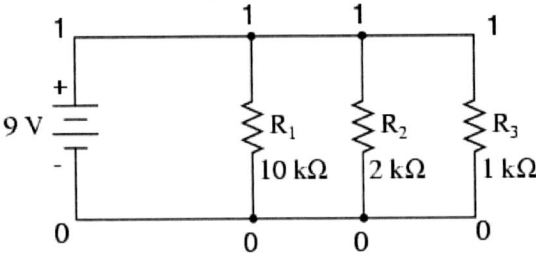

An example like this makes the rationale of node numbers in SPICE fairly clear to understand. By having all components share common sets of numbers, the computer "knows" they're all connected in parallel with each other.

In order to display branch currents in SPICE, we need to insert zero-voltage sources in line (in series) with each resistor, and then reference our current measurements to those sources. For whatever reason, the creators of the SPICE program made it so that current could only be calculated *through* a voltage source. This is a somewhat annoying demand of the SPICE simulation program. With each of these "dummy" voltage sources added, some new node numbers must be created to connect them to their respective branch resistors:

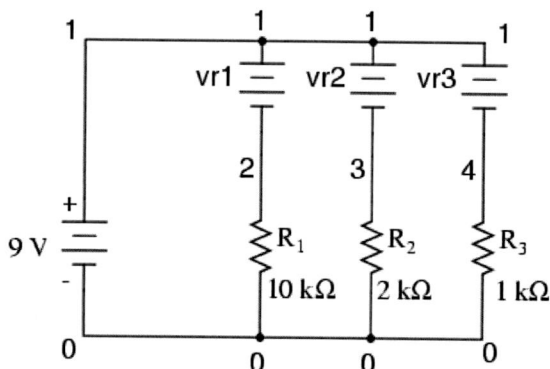

NOTE: vr1, vr2, and vr3 are all
"dummy" voltage sources with
values of 0 volts each!!

The dummy voltage sources are all set at 0 volts so as to have no impact on the operation of the circuit. The circuit description file, or *netlist*, looks like this:

```
Parallel circuit
v1 1 0
r1 2 0 10k
r2 3 0 2k
r3 4 0 1k
vr1 1 2 dc 0
vr2 1 3 dc 0
vr3 1 4 dc 0
.dc v1 9 9 1
.print dc v(2,0) v(3,0) v(4,0)
.print dc i(vr1) i(vr2) i(vr3)
.end
```

Running the computer analysis, we get these results (I've annotated the printout with descriptive labels):

```
v1              v(2)            v(3)            v(4)
9.000E+00       9.000E+00       9.000E+00       9.000E+00
battery         R1 voltage      R2 voltage      R3 voltage
voltage


v1              i(vr1)          i(vr2)          i(vr3)
9.000E+00       9.000E-04       4.500E-03       9.000E-03
battery         R1 current      R2 current      R3 current
voltage
```

These values do indeed match those calculated through Ohm's Law earlier: 0.9 mA for I_{R1}, 4.5 mA for I_{R2}, and 9 mA for I_{R3}. Being connected in parallel, of course, all resistors have the same voltage dropped across them (9 volts, same as the battery).

In summary, a parallel circuit is defined as one where all components are connected between the same set of electrically common points. Another way of saying this is that all components are connected across each other's terminals. From this definition, three rules of parallel circuits follow: all components share the same voltage; resistances diminish to equal a smaller, total resistance; and branch currents add to equal a larger, total current. Just as in the case of series circuits, all of these rules find root in the definition of a parallel circuit. If you understand that definition fully, then the rules are nothing more than footnotes to the definition.

- **REVIEW:**
- Components in a parallel circuit share the same voltage: $E_{Total} = E_1 = E_2 = \ldots E_n$
- Total resistance in a parallel circuit is *less* than any of the individual resistances: $R_{Total} = 1 / (1/R_1 + 1/R_2 + \ldots 1/R_n)$
- Total current in a parallel circuit is equal to the sum of the individual branch currents: $I_{Total} = I_1 + I_2 + \ldots I_n$.

Identifying Electronics Component's Circuit Symbols and Functions

Identifying **Electronic Component and Symbol** is very important rule when fixing mobile phones problems..
Be familiar of its circuit symbols below for easy troubleshooting guide.
Every Electronics Component has its own symbols visualizing its function in every circuit diagram...
This is a very big help especially when working on hardware problems. This **Components Symbol** is a standard guides when reading or writing **service schematic diagram** with various mobile phone products..
Electronic Components: Symbols & Functions

Circuit Symbols
Circuit symbols are used in circuit diagrams which show how a circuit is connected together. The actual layout of the components is usually quite different from the circuit diagram. To build a circuit you need a different diagram showing the layout of the parts on strip board or printed circuit board. Circuit symbols are used in circuit diagrams, which show how a circuit is connected together. The actual layout of the components is usually quite different from the circuit diagram. To build a circuit you need a different diagram showing the layout of the parts on the printed circuit board. However understanding electronics circuit give you a better understanding of how to find faults in an electronic circuit
Wires and connections Component Circuit Symbol Function of Component

Wire

To conduct or pass current from one part of a circuit to another. Wires joined

A 'blob' should be drawn where wires are connected (joined), but it is sometimes omitted. Wires connected to another wire should be staggered slightly to form two T-junctions, as shown. Such help to transmitted current to other paths Wires not joined

In diagrams it is often necessary to draw wires crossing even though they are not connected. It is preferred to have the 'hump' symbol as shown because the simple crossing of the wire may be misread as a join where you have forgotten to add a 'blob'!
Power Supplies Component Circuit Symbol Function of Component
Cell

Supplies electrical energy. The larger terminal indicates the positive (+).A single cell is often interpreted and called a battery, but a battery is two or more cell joined together. Battery

Supplies electrical energy. A battery is more than one cell. The larger terminal is the positive (+). And the small terminal is called the negative (
-
)DC supply
+ -
Supplies electrical energy. DC = Direct Current, always flowing in one direction.AC supply

Supplies electrical energy.AC = Alternating Current, continually changing direction of it currents it is negative and then Positive which alternates again. Fuse

A safety device, which will 'blow' or melt if the current flowing through it exceeds a specified value. Used as a protection for electrical circuits. Transformer Two coils of wire linked by an iron core. Transformers are used to step up(increase) and step down (decrease) AC voltages. Energy is transferred between the coils by the magnetic field in the core. There is no electrical connection between the coils. Earth(Ground) A connection to earth. For many electronic circuits this is the 0V (zero volts)of the power supply, but for mains electricity and some radio circuits it really means the earth. It is also known as ground.
Output Devices: Lamps, Heater, Motor, etc. Component Circuit Symbol Function of Component

Circuit Symbols

Circuit symbols are used in circuit diagrams which show how a circuit is connected together. The actual layout of the components is usually quite different from the circuit diagram. To build a circuit you need a different diagram showing the layout of the parts on strip board or printed circuit board.

Circuit symbols are used in circuit diagrams, which show how a circuit is connected together. The actual layout of the components is usually quite different from the circuit diagram. To build a circuit you need a different diagram showing the layout of the parts on the printed circuit board. However understanding electronics circuit give you a better understanding of how to find faults in an electronic circuit

Wires and connections

Component	Circuit Symbol	Function of Component
Wire		To conduct or pass current from one part of a circuit to another.
Wires joined		A 'blob' should be drawn where wires are connected (joined), but it is sometimes omitted. Wires connected to another wire should be staggered slightly to form two T-junctions, as shown. Such help to transmitted current to other paths
Wires not joined		In diagrams it is often necessary to draw wires crossing even though they are not connected. It is preferred to have the 'hump' symbol as shown because the simple crossing of the wire may be misread as a join where you have forgotten to add a 'blob'!

Power Supplies

Component	Circuit Symbol	Function of Component
Cell		Supplies electrical energy. The larger terminal indicates the positive (+). A single cell is often interpreted and called a battery, but a battery is two or more cell joined together.
Battery		Supplies electrical energy. A battery is more than one cell. The larger terminal is the positive (+). And the small terminal is called the negative (-)
DC supply		Supplies electrical energy. DC = Direct Current, always flowing in one direction.
AC supply		Supplies electrical energy. AC = Alternating Current, continually changing direction of it currents it is negative and then Positive which alternates again.
Fuse		A safety device, which will 'blow' or melt if the current flowing through it exceeds a specified value. Used as a protection for electrical circuits.
Transformer		Two coils of wire linked by an iron core. Transformers are used to step up (increase) and step down (decrease) AC voltages. Energy is transferred between the coils by the magnetic field in the core. There is no electrical connection between the coils.
Earth (Ground)		A connection to earth. For many electronic circuits this is the 0V (zero volts) of the power supply, but for mains electricity and some radio circuits it really means the earth. It is also known as ground.

Output Devices: Lamps, Heater, Motor, etc.

Output Devices: Lamps, Heater, Motor, etc.

Component	Circuit Symbol	Function of Component
Lamp (lighting)		A transducer, which converts electrical energy to light. This symbol is used for a lamp providing illumination, for example a car headlamp.
Lamp (indicator)		A transducer which converts electrical energy to light. This symbol is used for a lamp which is an indicator, for example a warning light on a car dashboard.
Heater		A transducer which converts electrical energy to heat.
Motor		A transducer, which converts electrical energy to kinetic energy (motion).
Bell		A transducer, which converts electrical energy to sound.

Component	Circuit Symbol	Function of Component
Buzzer		A transducer, which converts electrical energy to sound.
Inductor (Coil, Solenoid)		A coil of wire, which creates a magnetic field when current, passes through it. It may have an iron core inside the coil. It can be used as a transducer converting electrical energy to mechanical energy by pulling on something.

Switches

Component	Circuit Symbol	Function of Component
Push Switch (push-to-make)		A push switch allows current to flow only when the button is pressed. This is the switch used to operate a doorbell. It is a abbreviated NO for normally open .
Push-to-Break Switch		This type of push switch is normally closed abbreviated NC for normally closed. (on), it is open (off) only when the button is pressed.
On-Off Switch (SPST)		SPST = Single Pole, Single Throw. An on-off switch allows current to flow only when it is in the closed (on) position.
2-way Switch (SPDT)		SPDT = Single Pole, Double Throw. A 2-way changeover switch directs the flow of current to one of two routes according to its position. Some SPDT switches have a central off position and are described as 'on-off-on'.
Dual On-Off Switch (DPST)		DPST = Double Pole, Single Throw. A dual on-off switch, which is often used to switch mains electricity because it can isolate both the live and neutral connections.

Scribd - Mozilla Firefox

File Edit View History Bookmarks Tools Help

Free Cellphone Repair Tutorial Sitema... | Scribd | phonewreck.com | How to Reball BGA Chips of a Mobile... | Inbox (1,344) - verneka@gmail.com -... | +

www.scribd.com/fullscreen/105191337access_key=key-v7jbrczzk396p2ulg4&allow_share=true&view_mode=scroll | Google

Most Visited | Getting Started

2-way Switch (SPDT)		A 2-way changeover switch directs the flow of current to one of two routes according to its position. Some SPDT switches have a central off position and are described as 'on-off-on'.
Dual On-Off Switch (DPST)		DPST = Double Pole, Single Throw. A dual on-off switch, which is often used to switch mains electricity because it can isolate both the live and neutral connections.
Reversing Switch (DPDT)		DPDT = Double Pole, Double Throw. This switch can be wired up as a reversing switch for a motor. Some DPDT switches have a central off position.
Relay	NO COM NC	An electrically operated switch, for example a 9V battery circuit connected to the coil can switch a 230V AC mains circuit. NO = Normally Open, COM = Common, NC = Normally Closed.

Scribd - Mozilla Firefox

File Edit View History Bookmarks Tools Help

Free Cellphone Repair Tutorial Sitema... | Scribd | phonewreck.com | How to Reball BGA Chips of a Mobile... | Inbox (1,344) - verneka@gmail.com -... | +

www.scribd.com/fullscreen/105191337access_key=key-v7jbrczzk396p2ulg4&allow_share=true&view_mode=scroll | Google

Most Visited | Getting Started

Resistors

Component	Circuit Symbol	Function of Component
Resistor		A resistor restricts the flow of current, for example to limit the current passing through an LED. A resistor is used with a capacitor in a timing circuit.
Variable Resistor (Rheostat)		This type of variable resistor with 2 contacts (a rheostat) is usually used to control current. Examples include: adjusting lamp brightness, adjusting motor speed, and adjusting the rate of flow of charge into a capacitor in a timing circuit.
Variable Resistor (Potentiometer)		This type of variable resistor with 3 contacts (a potentiometer) is usually used to control voltage. It can be used like this as a transducer converting position (angle of the control spindle) to an electrical signal.
Variable Resistor (Preset)		This type of variable resistor (a preset) is operated with a small screwdriver or similar tool. It is designed to be set when the circuit is made and then left without further adjustment. Presets are cheaper than normal variable resistors so they are often used in projects to reduce the cost.

Capacitors

Component	Circuit Symbol	Function of Component
Capacitor		A capacitor stores electric charge. A capacitor is used with a resistor in a timing circuit. It can also be used as a filter, to block DC signals but pass AC signals.
Capacitor, polarized	+	A capacitor stores electric charge. This type must be connected the correct way round. A capacitor is used with a resistor in a timing circuit. It can also be used as a filter, to block DC signals but pass AC

Capacitor, polarized		A capacitor stores electric charge. This type must be connected the correct way round. A capacitor is used with a resistor in a timing circuit. It can also be used as a filter, to block DC signals but pass AC signals.
Variable Capacitor		A variable capacitor is used in a radio tuner.
Trimmer Capacitor		This type of variable capacitor (a trimmer) is operated with a small screwdriver or similar tool. It is designed to be set when the circuit is made and then left without further adjustment.

Diodes

Component	Circuit Symbol	Function of Component
Diode		A device, which only allows current to flow in one direction.
LED Light Emitting Diode		A transducer, which converts electrical energy to light.

Transistors

Component	Circuit Symbol	Function of Component
Transistor NPN		A transistor amplifies current. It can be used with other components to make an amplifier or switching circuit.
Transistor PNP		A transistor amplifies current. It can be used with other components to make an amplifier or switching circuit.
Phototransistor		A light-sensitive transistor.

Audio and Radio Devices

Component	Circuit Symbol	Function of Component
Microphone		A transducer, which converts sound to electrical energy.

Audio and Radio Devices

Component	Circuit Symbol	Function of Component
Microphone		A transducer, which converts sound to electrical energy.
Earphone		A transducer, which converts electrical energy to sound.
Loudspeaker		A transducer, which converts electrical energy to sound.
Piezo Transducer		A transducer, which converts electrical energy to sound.
Amplifier (general symbol)		An amplifier circuit with one input. Really it is a block diagram symbol because it represents a circuit rather than just one component.

Aerial (Antenna)		A device, which is designed to receive or transmit radio signals. It is also known as an antenna.

Meters and Oscilloscope

Component	Circuit Symbol	Function of Component
Voltmeter	(V)	A voltmeter is used to measure voltage. The proper name for voltage is 'potential difference', but most people prefer to say voltage!
Amp-meter	(A)	An amp-meter is used to measure current. As known as amps
Galvanometer	(↑)	A galvanometer is a very sensitive meter which is used to measure tiny currents, usually 1mA or less.
Ohmmeter	(Ω)	An ohmmeter is used to measure resistance. Most Multimeter have an ohmmeter setting.
Oscilloscope		An oscilloscope is used to display the shape of electrical signals and it can be used to measure their voltage and time period.

Sensors (input devices)

Component	Circuit Symbol	Function of Component
LDR		A transducer which converts brightness (light) to resistance (an electrical property). LDR = Light Dependent Resistor
Thermistor		A transducer which converts temperature (heat) to resistance (an electrical property).

Logic Gates

Logic gates process signals, which represent **true** (1, high, +Vs, on) or **false** (0, low, 0V, off). There are two sets of symbols: traditional and IEC (International Electrotechnical Commission).

Gate Type	Traditional Symbol	IEC Symbol	Function of Gate
NOT		=1	A NOT gate can only have one input. The 'o' on the output means 'not'. The output of a NOT gate is the inverse (opposite) of its input, so the output is true when the input is false. A NOT gate is also called an inverter.

Gate Type	Traditional Symbol	IEC Symbol	Function of Gate
AND		&	An AND gate can have two or more inputs. The output of an AND gate is true when all its inputs are true.
NAND		&	A NAND gate can have two or more inputs. The 'o' on the output means 'not' showing that it is a Not AND gate. The output of a NAND gate is true unless all its inputs are true.
OR		≥1	An OR gate can have two or more inputs. The output of an OR gate is true when at least one of its inputs is true.
NOR		≥1	A NOR gate can have two or more inputs. The 'o' on the output means 'not' showing that it is a Not OR gate. The output of a NOR gate is true when none of its inputs are true.
EX-OR		=1	An EX-OR gate can only have two inputs. The output of an EX-OR gate is true when its inputs are different (one true, one false).
EX-NOR		=1	An EX-NOR gate can only have two inputs. The 'o' on the output means 'not' showing that it is a Not EX-OR gate. The output of an EX-NOR gate is true when its inputs are the same (both true or both false).

SMT Resistor

SMT Resistor (Unprinted)

In Mobile Phones **Surface Mount Molded (SMD) Resistor** where not printed with numerical value and it is left blank, the problem is that it is too tiny or small to print at..

You can refer only its value by an aide of Schematic Diagram Available for that certain products. Or you can Identify and check its value by using Resistance Tester...

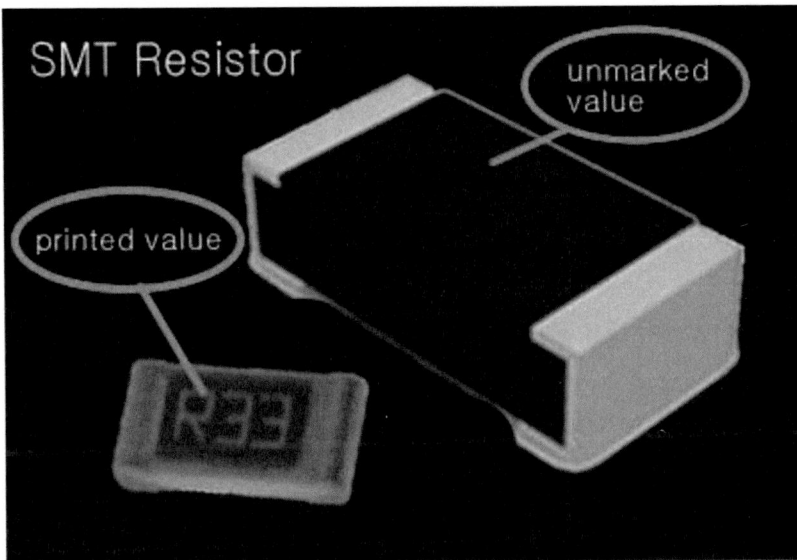

In Schematic Diagram Its Original value where indicated: For Example:

Resistances less than 1000 ohms or 1K with "R" indicated in the middle indicates a decimal point like:

4R7 = 4.7Ω
2R2 = 2.2Ω

and the rest just like how it does indicated like:

100Ω = 100 ohms
220Ω = 200 ohms

and up
4.7K = 4.7 kiloohms

The Printed SMD Resistor

Zero ohm resistors Surface mounted resistors are printed with numerical values in a code related to that used on axial resistors.

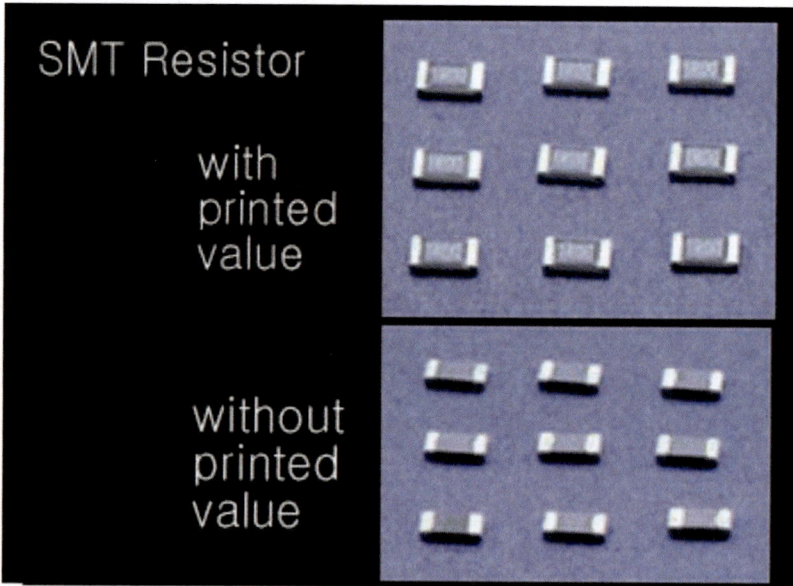

Standard-tolerance Surface Mount Technology (SMT) resistors are marked with a three-digit code, in which the first two digits are the first two significant digits of the value and the third digit is the power of ten (the number of zeroes). For example:

334   = 33 × 10,000 Ω = 330 kΩ

222   = 22 × 100 Ω = 2.2 kΩ
473   = 47 × 1,000 Ω = 47 kΩ
105   = 10 × 100,000 Ω = 1 MΩ

Resistances less than 100 ohms are written: 100, 220, 470. The final zero represents ten to the power zero, which is 1. For example:

100   = 10 × 1 Ω = 10 Ω
220   = 22 × 1 Ω = 22 Ω

Resistances less than 10 ohms have 'R' to indicate the position of the decimal point (radix point). For example:

4R7   = 4.7 Ω
0R22   = 0.22 Ω
0R01   = 0.01 Ω

Precision resistors are marked with a four-digit code, in which the first three digits are the significant figures and the fourth is the power of ten. For example:

1001   = 100 × 10 ohms = 1 kΩ
4992   = 499 × 100 ohms = 49.9 kΩ
1000   = 100 × 1 ohm = 100 Ω

"000" and "0000" sometimes appear as values on surface-mount zero-ohm links, since these have (approximately) zero resistance.

SMD Capacitor

The types of capacitor which is commonly used in small space circuit like the cellphone uses the **Tantalum** type of capacitor,
Tantalum capacitors are used in smaller electronic devices including portable telephones, pagers, personal computers, and automotive electronics.
It also offer smaller size and lower leakage than standard. .
There are two types of Capacitors used in Mobile Phones Circuits,

The **Polarized** and **Non-Polarized** Capacitors.

This are the Capacitors may look like that are being used in mobile phones circuit.

SMT Capacitor

Surface Mounted Technology Designed

The Polarized Capacitor

Tantalum Capacitors which is polarized, and may be used in DC circuits. Typical values range form 0.1uF to 470uF.

Standard Tantalum values change in multiples of 10, 22, 33, and 47. Normal Temperature Coefficient [TC] for Tantalum Capacitors is ±5%.

Polarized capacitors are typically used in large voltage situations, such as DC line filtering to reduce noise related to uneven voltage levels after rectification from an AC source. Mainly measured in microfarads. Polarity is critical to these devices. They are marked with the voltage rating (usually double the circuit voltage used) as well as the farad marking.

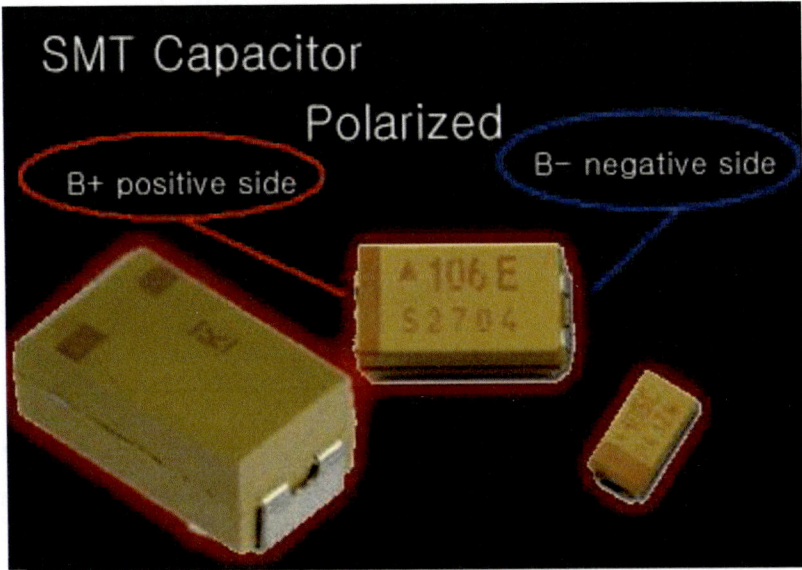

SMT Capacitor

Polarized

B+ positive side

B– negative side

▲ 106 E
S2704

Non-Polarized Capacitor

Non-polarized are similar to polarized except the plates are similar metal.

Polarized caps are typically used in large voltage situations, such as DC line filtering to reduce noise related to uneven voltage levels after rectification from an AC source. Mainly measured in microfarads. Polarity is critical to these devices. They are marked with the voltage rating (usually double the circuit voltage used) as well as the farad marking.

SMT Capacitor
Bi-polar or
Non polarized

non-polarized caps are typically used in low voltage situations, both AC and DC. Polarity is not critical. Measured in pico farads typically.

Decimal multiplier prefixes are in common use to simplify and shorten the notations of quantities such as component values.

Capacitance, for example, is measured in Farads, but the Farad is far too large a unit to be of practical use in most cases. For convenience, we use sub-multiples to save a lot of figures. For example, instead of writing 0.000000000001 Farads, we write 1pF (1 picofarad).

The more common prefixes and the relationships to one another are as follows.

Abbrev.	Prefix	Multiply by	or
p	pico	0.000000000001	10^{-12}
n	nano	0.000000001	10^{-9}
μ	micro	0.000001	10^{-6}
m	milli	0.001	10^{-3}
-	UNIT	1	10^{0}

k	kilo	1000	10^3
M	mega	1000000	10^6

1000 pico units	=	1 nano unit
1000 nano units	=	1 micro unit
1000 micro units	=	1 milli unit
1000 milli units	=	1 unit
1000 units	=	1 kilo unit
1000 kilo units	=	1 mega unit

Tolerance

All components differ from their marked value by some amount. Tolerance specifies the maximum allowed deviation from the specified value. Tolerances are normally expressed as a percentage of the nominal value.

For example, a component with a marked value of 100 and a tolerance of 5% could actually be any value between 5% below the marked value (95) and 5% above the marked value (105).

SMT Transistor

transistor is a semiconductor device used to amplify and switch electronic signals. It is made of a solid piece of semiconductor material, with at least three terminals for connection to an external circuit.

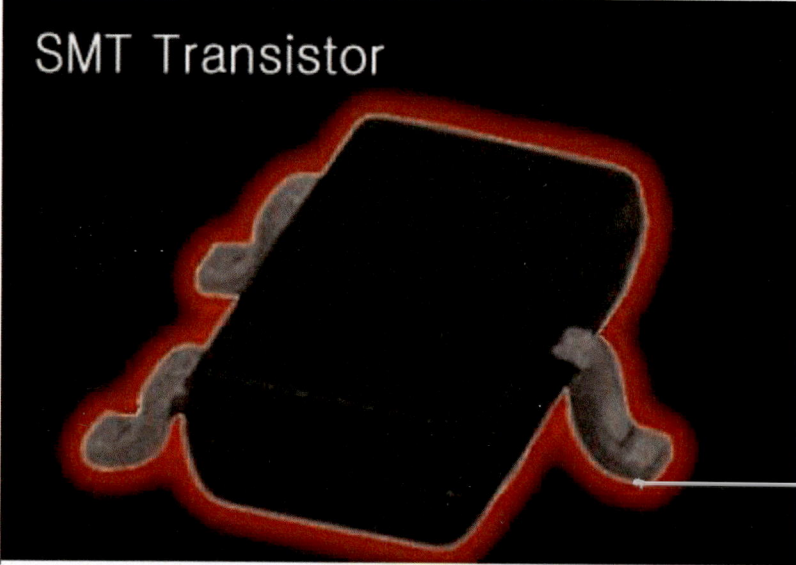

A voltage or current applied to one pair of the transistor's terminals changes the current flowing through another pair of terminals. Because the controlled (output) power can be much more than the controlling (input) power, the transistor provides amplification of a signal. Some transistors are packaged individually but many more are found embedded in integrated circuits.

The transistor is the fundamental building block of modern electronic devices, and its presence is ubiquitous in modern electronic systems.

Types of transistor

Transistor circuit symbols

There are two types of standard transistors, **NPN** and **PNP**, with different circuit symbols. The letters refer to the layers of semiconductor material used to make the transistor. Most transistors used today are **NPN** because this is the easiest type to make from silicon. This page is mostly about **NPN** transistors and if you are new to electronics it is best to start by learning how to use these first. The leads are labeled **base (B)**, **collector (C)** and **emitter (E)**.

The leads are labeled base (B), collector (C) and emitter (E).
These terms refer to the internal operation of a transistor but they are not much help in understanding how a transistor is used, so just treat them as labels!

Diodes - Surface Mounted

In electronics, a **diode** is a two-terminal electronic component that conducts electric current in only one direction. The term usually refers to a **semiconductor diode**, the most common type today, which is a crystal of semiconductor connected to two electrical terminals, a P-N junction. A **vacuum tube diode**, now little used, is a vacuum tube with two electrodes; a plate and a cathode.
The most common function of a diode is to allow an electric current in one direction (called the diode's *forward* direction) while blocking current in the opposite direction (the *reverse* direction). Thus, the diode can be thought of as an electronic version of a check valve. This unidirectional behavior is called rectification, and is used to convert alternating current to direct current, and extract modulation from radio signals in radio receivers.
However, diodes can have more complicated behavior than this simple on-off action, due to their complex non-linear electrical characteristics, which can be tailored by varying the construction of their P-N junction. These are exploited in special purpose diodes that perform many different functions. Diodes are used to regulate voltage (Zener diodes), electronically tune radio and TV receivers (varactor diodes), generate radio frequency oscillations (tunnel diodes), and produce light (light emitting diodes). Diodes were the first semiconductor electronic devices. The discovery of crystals' rectifying abilities was made by German physicist Ferdinand Braun in 1874. The first semiconductor diodes, called cat's whisker

diodes were made of crystals of minerals such as galena. Today most diodes are made of silicon, but other semiconductors such as germanium are sometimes used.

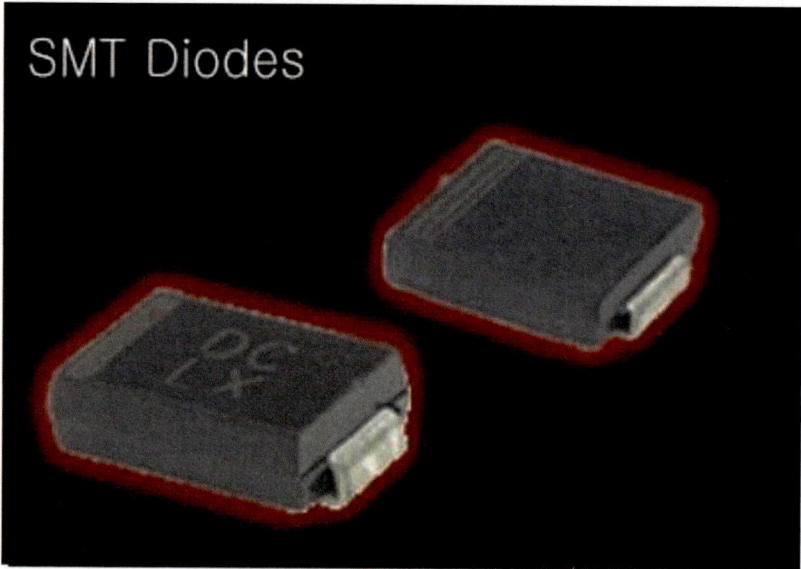

SMT Diodes

Types of semiconductor diode in Mobile Phones Circuit

Zener diodes

Diodes that can be made to conduct backwards. This effect, called Zener breakdown, occurs at a precisely defined voltage, allowing the diode to be used as a precision voltage reference. In practical voltage reference circuits Zener and switching diodes are connected in series and opposite directions to balance the temperature coefficient to near zero. Some devices labeled as high-voltage Zener diodes are actually avalanche diodes (see above). Two (equivalent) Zeners in series and in reverse order, in the same package, constitute a transient absorber (or Transorb, a registered trademark). The Zener diode is named for Dr. Clarence Melvin Zener of Southern Illinois University, inventor of the device.

SMD Type Zener Diodes

Light-emitting diodes (LEDs)

In a diode formed from a direct band-gap semiconductor, such as gallium arsenide, carriers that cross the junction emit photons when they recombine with the majority carrier on the other side. Depending on the material, wavelengths (or colors) from the infrared to the near ultraviolet may be produced. The forward potential of these diodes depends on the wavelength of the emitted photons: 1.2 V corresponds to red, 2.4 V to violet. The first LEDs were red and yellow, and higher-frequency diodes have been developed over time. All LEDs produce incoherent, narrow-spectrum light; "white" LEDs are actually combinations of three LEDs of a different color, or a blue LED with a yellow scintillator coating. LEDs can also be used as low-efficiency photodiodes in signal applications. An LED may be paired with a photodiode or phototransistor in the same package, to form an opto-isolator.

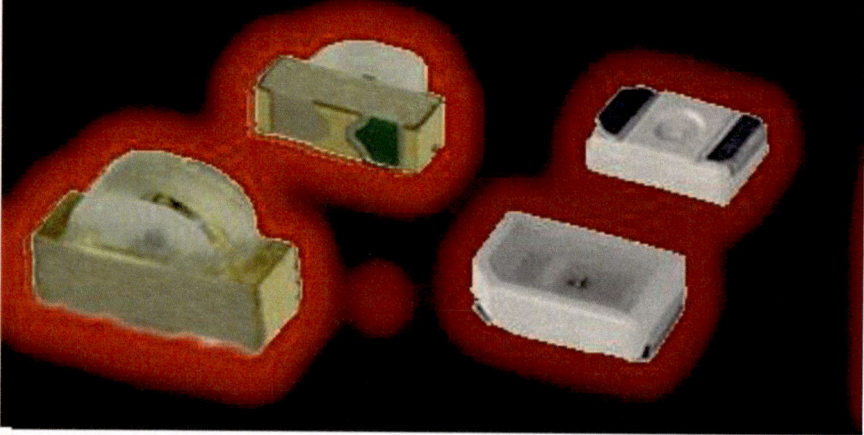

SMT LED

Light Emitting Diode

Photodiodes

All semiconductors are subject to optical charge carrier generation. This is typically an undesired effect, so most semiconductors are packaged in light blocking material. Photodiodes are intended to sense light(photodetector), so they are packaged in materials that allow light to pass, and are usually PIN (the kind of diode most sensitive to light). A photodiode can be used in solar cells, in photometry, or in optical communications. Multiple photodiodes may be packaged in a single device, either as a linear array or as a two-dimensional array. These arrays should not be confused with charge-coupled devices.

SMD Type Photo Diodes

Fuse - Surface Mounted

In electronics and electrical engineering a fuse (from the Latin "fusus" meaning to melt) is a type of sacrificial overcurrent protection device. It's essential component is a metal wire or strip that melts when too much current flows, which interrupts the circuit in which it is connected. Short circuit, overload or device failure is often the reason for excessive current.

A fuse interrupts excessive current (blows) so that further damage by overheating or fire is prevented. Wiring regulations often define a maximum fuse current rating for particular circuits. Overcurrent protection devices are essential in electrical systems to limit threats to human life and property damage. Fuses are selected to allow passage of normal current and of excessive current only for short periods.

A fuse was patented by Thomas Edison in 1890 [1] as part of his successful electric distribution system.

SMT Inductors

An **inductor** or a reactor is a passive electrical component that can store energy in a magnetic field created by the electric current passing through it. An inductor's ability to store magnetic energy is measured by its inductance, in units of **henries**. Typically an inductor is a conducting wire shaped as a coil, the loops helping to create a strong magnetic field inside the coil due to **Faraday's Law of Induction**. Inductors are one of the basic electronic components used in electronics where current and voltage change with time, due to the ability of inductors to delay and reshape alternating currents.

SMT Coils or Inductors

Inductance (L) (measured in henries) is an effect resulting from the magnetic field that forms around a current-carrying conductor which tends to resist changes in the current. Electric current through the conductor creates a magnetic flux proportional to the current, and a change in this current creates a corresponding change in magnetic flux which, in turn, by Faraday's Law generates an electromotive force (EMF) that opposes this change in current. Inductance is a measure of the amount of EMF generated per unit change in current. For example, an inductor with an inductance of 1 henry produces an EMF of 1 volt when the current through the inductor changes at the rate of 1 ampere per second. The number of loops, the size of each loop, and the material it is wrapped around all affect the inductance. For example, the magnetic flux linking these turns can be increased by coiling the conductor around a material with a high permeability such as iron. This can increase the inductance by 2000 times, although less so at high frequencies.

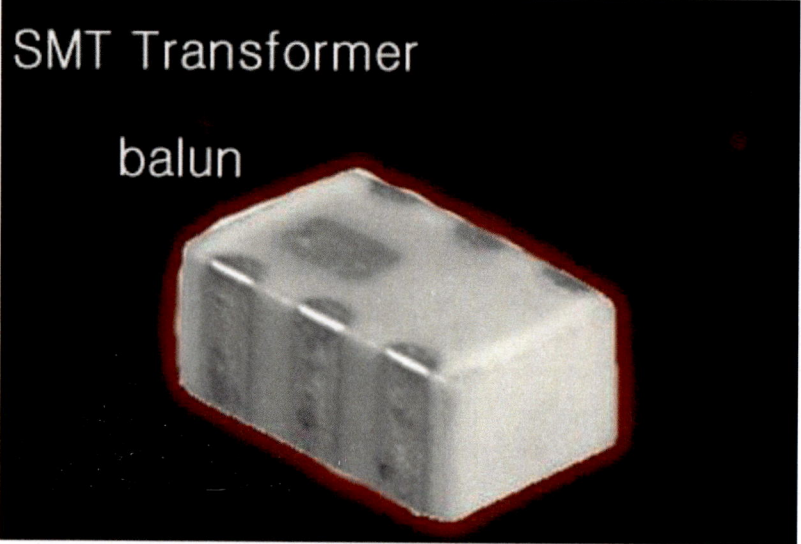

SMT Transformer

balun

Inductors are used extensively in analog circuits and signal processing. Inductors in conjunction with capacitors and other components form tuned circuits which can emphasize or filter out specific signal frequencies. Applications range from the use of large inductors in power supplies, which in conjunction with filter capacitors remove residual hums known as the Mains hum or other fluctuations from the direct current output, to the small inductance of the ferrite bead or torus installed around a cable to prevent radio frequency interference from being transmitted down the wire. Smaller inductor/capacitor combinations provide tuned circuits used in radio reception and broadcasting, for instance.

Oscillators

An electronic oscillator is an electronic circuit that produces a repetitive electronic signal, often a sine wave or a square wave.

A low-frequency oscillator (LFO) is an electronic oscillator that generates an AC waveform at a frequency below ≈20 Hz. This term is typically used in the field of audio synthesizers, to distinguish it from an audio frequency oscillator.

Oscillators designed to produce a high-power AC output from a DC supply are usually called inverters. The waveform generators which are used to generate pure sinusoidal waveforms of fixed amplitude and frequency are called oscillators.

Crystal oscillator

A crystal oscillator is an electronic circuit that uses the mechanical resonance of a vibrating crystal of piezoelectric material to create an electrical signal with a very precise frequency. This frequency is commonly used to keep track of time (as in quartz wristwatches), to provide a stable clock signal for digital integrated circuits, and to stabilize frequencies for radio transmitters and receivers. The most common type of piezoelectric resonator used is the quartz crystal, so oscillator circuits designed around them were called "crystal oscillators".

Quartz crystals are manufactured for frequencies from a few tens of kilohertz to tens of megahertz. More than two billion (2×109) crystals are manufactured annually. Most are small devices for consumer devices such as wristwatches, clocks, radios, computers, and cellphones. Quartz crystals are also found inside test and measurement equipment, such as counters, signal generators, and oscilloscopes.

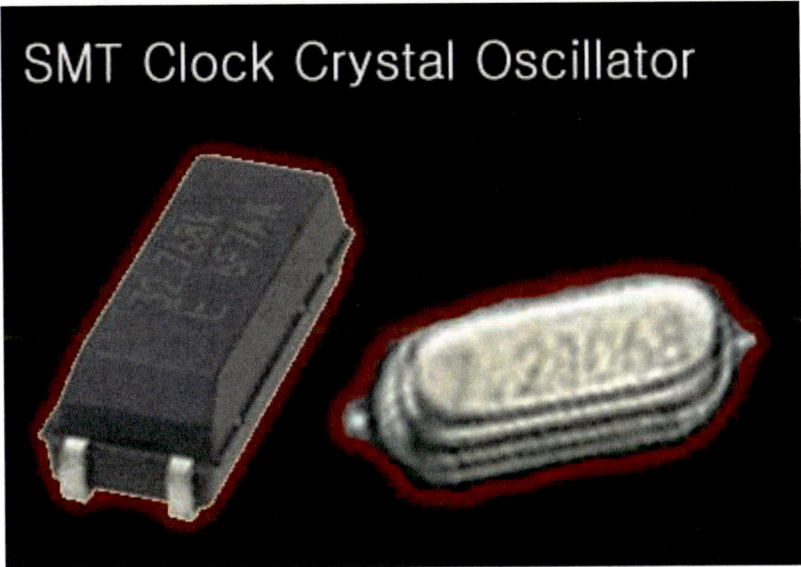

SMT Clock Crystal Oscillator

Voltage-controlled oscillator

A voltage-controlled oscillator or VCO is an electronic oscillator designed to be controlled in oscillation frequency by a voltage input.

SMT Voltage Controlled Oscillator

The frequency of oscillation is varied by the applied DC voltage, while modulating signals may also be fed into the VCO to cause frequency modulation (FM) or phase modulation (PM); a VCO with digital pulse output may similarly have its repetition rate (FSK, PSK) or pulse width modulated (PWM).

RF and IF Amplifiers and Filters

Electronic filters are electronic circuits which perform signal processing functions, specifically to remove unwanted frequency components from the signal, to enhance wanted ones, or both. Electronic filters can be:

Radio frequency (RF) and microwave filters represent a class of electronic filter, designed to operate on signals in the megahertz to gigahertz frequency ranges (medium frequency to extremely high frequency). This frequency range is the range used by most broadcast radio, television, wireless communication (cellphones, Wi-Fi, etc...), and thus most rf and microwave devices will include some kind of filtering on the signals transmitted or received.

Such filters are commonly used as building blocks for duplexers and diplexers to combine or separate multiple frequency bands.

EMI - ESD Filters

Electrostatic discharge (**ESD**) is the sudden and momentary electric current that flows between two objects at different electrical potentials caused by direct contact or induced by an electrostatic field. The term is usually used in the electronics and other industries to describe momentary unwanted currents that may cause damage to electronic equipment.

ESD is a serious issue in solid state electronics, such as integrated circuits. Integrated circuits are made from semiconductor materials such as silicon and insulating materials such as silicon dioxide. Either of these materials can suffer permanent damage when subjected to high voltages; as a result there are now a number of antistatic devices that help prevent static build up.

Below are common types of EMI-ESD protection chips used among various mobile phone's circuit.

SMT EMI/ESD Filters

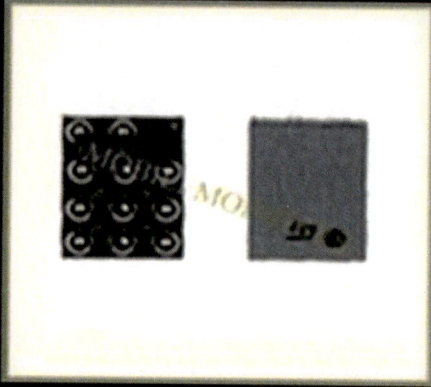

Electromagnetic interference (or **EMI**, also called **radio frequency interference** or **RFI**) is a disturbance that affects an electrical circuit due to either electromagnetic conduction or electromagnetic radiation emitted from an external source. The disturbance may interrupt, obstruct, or otherwise degrade or limit the effective performance of the circuit. The source may be any object, artificial or natural, that carries rapidly changing electrical currents, such as an electrical circuit, the Sun or the Northern Lights.

EMI can be intentionally used for radio jamming, as in some forms of electronic warfare, or can occur unintentionally, as a result of spurious emissions for example through intermodulation products, and the like. It frequently affects the reception of AM radio in urban areas. It can also affect cell phone, FM radio and television reception, although to a lesser extent.

PART 03

Repair Tools and Test Equipment

Preparing the Proper Tools For Repairing..

There are many different variety and Cellphone Repair Tools. A lot companies offers online purchasing for such certain tools for beginning into business... You can choose which is which for such certain product.

In my opinion, when you are into a planning to purchased any tools, Ask some experts first for that certain products you are going to buy...

Basically these are the primary tools when you are going to repair cellphones.

1. **Multi-Tester** (Analog/Digital)- Used to measure Voltages, Currents and Resistance in electronic

components.

2. **Screwdrivers** - Used to loosen the phones screws.

3. **Tweezers** - used to hold and pick small cellphone component parts.

4. **Soldering iron** - used to solder / resolder electronic parts.

5. **Soldering lead** - used to bonds Electronic components.

6. **Soldering Flux and Paste** - Used to tightened soldering quality.

7. **BGA Rework station** - Applied Heat to remove and replaced parts and IC chips.

8. **Re balling Kits** - Tools for re balling IC bumps, this composed of Stencil plates, Ball Leads and Spatula

9. **DC Regulated Power Supply**- Used to substitute battery voltage when working on hardware troubleshooting.

10. Flashing and Unlocking Device- it is Software Tools that used to unlock and flash mobile phones programmable circuits.

11. Cables and Wires - Used as an Interface from PC to cellphones when working on like flashing, unlocking and jailbreaking.

Test Equipment

Electronic test equipment is specialized equipment which is used in the testing of electronics. It can be utilized in the construction of prototypes and new products, and in maintenance and troubleshooting. A huge family of components are included under the umbrella of electronic test equipment, ranging from simple equipment which is used for routine home repair to sophisticated systems which are used exclusively by engineers. Many companies sell used electronic test equipment, which is often far less costly than brand new products and just as useful.

All of the devices in the family of electronic test equipment are capable of providing some sort of information about an electronic device or circuit. This information can vary from something simple, like whether or not current is flowing through a circuit, to something complex, like whether or not the components of a motherboard are working properly. Electronic test equipment may be passive, or it may emit an active signal and register a response, and it can provide specific measurements, or more generic data.

Typically, electronic test equipment includes a way to interface with an item being tested, such as a probe or clip, and a readout which provides information, ranging from a light which becomes illuminated when something is working properly to a readout with measurements. Sophisticated equipment may hook up to a computer for the purpose of performing diagnostics, with the equipment running several different tests at once and compiling the information in a computer program. This type of electronic test equipment is often used in the development of new products, to confirm that they are safe and to test their limits.

One of the simplest examples of electronic test equipment is a continuity tester, a device which many people may be familiar with. A continuity tester is used to determine whether a circuit is open or closed. If the circuit is open, it indicates a fault or ground, while if it is closed, it is working correctly. Continuity testers are often used to diagnose home electrical problems, such as a suspected fault in an outlet.

More sophisticated equipment can measure current, resistance, voltage, capacitance, charge, and digital circuits. Testgear, as electronic test equipment is sometimes known, may also combine multiple functions for convenience. Electricians, phone repair men, and cable installers typically carry testgear for use in their work, and electronic test equipment is also used by engineers, physicists, and numerous other researchers and inventors.

Opening Tools and Tweezers

Opening Tools

Proper opening tools is used to avoid damaged and insure safety in handling mobile phones, which prior to avoid risk of scratches and breakage.

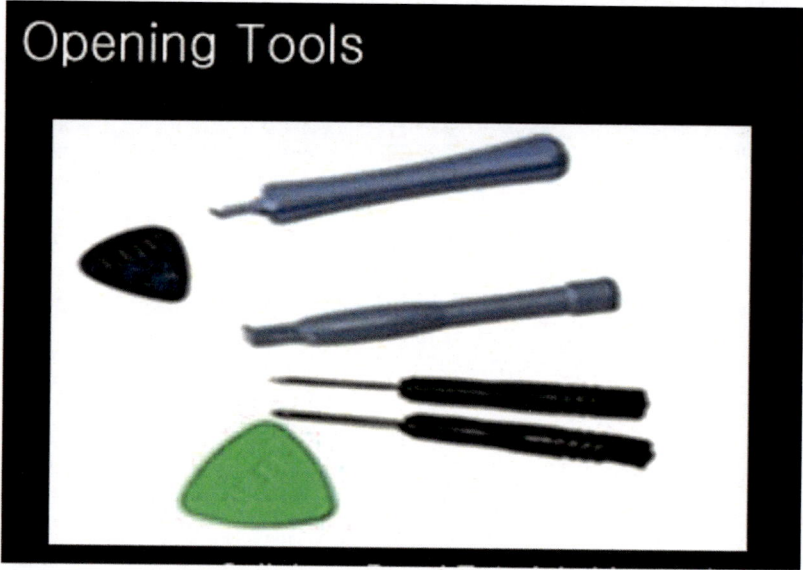

Tweezers

Tweezers are tools used for picking up small objects that are not easily handled with the human hands and very useful in surface mounted electronics components.

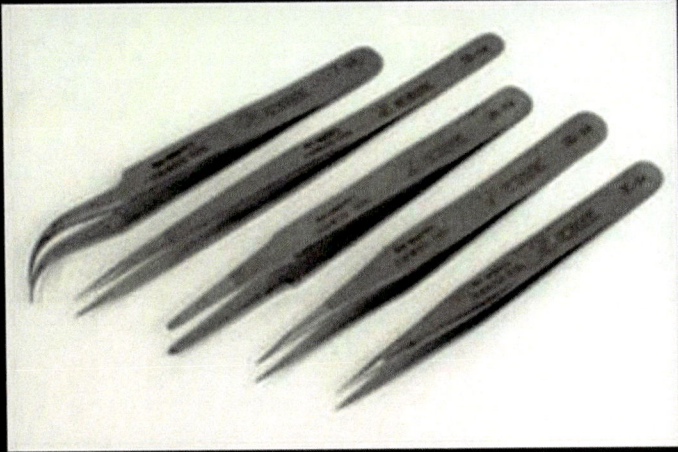

Tweezers

Torx and Precision Screwdrivers

Various Mobile phone uses variety of screws mounted to every products.

Do not try to attempt opening any screws that did not match with the screwdriver you have or you might end up a loosen tread screw, and find it hard enough to open it up...

Selecting and collecting of Torx and precision screwdrivers is highly recommended.

Torx and Precision comes with different code and number..

T6 is the most commonly used in mobile phones.

Soldering and Desoldering Tools

Soldering Iron

A soldering iron is a tool normally used for applying heat to two or more adjoining metal parts such that solder may melt and flow between those parts, binding them securely, conductively and hermetically.

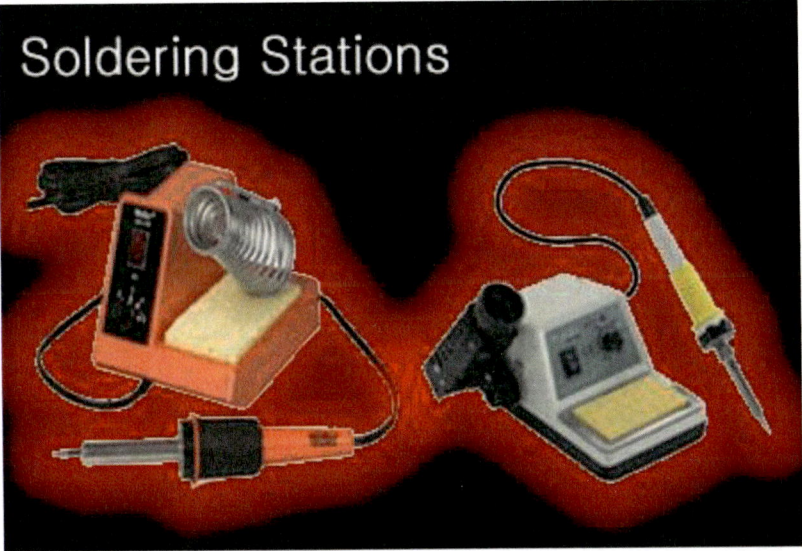

Soldering Stations

A soldering iron is composed of a heated metal tip and an insulated handle. Heating is often achieved electrically, by passing an electrical current (supplied through an electrical cord or battery cables) through the resistive material of a heating element. Another heating method includes combustion of a suitable gas, which can either be delivered through a tank mounted on the iron (flameless), or through an external flame.

Soldrering SMD Components

Some soldering irons heat up and cool down in a few seconds, while others may take several minutes.

Soldering LEAD
 Soldering lead is used to bond or connect electronic components.
Solder is a fusible metal alloy with a melting point or melting range of 90 to 450 degree Celsius (190 to 840 °F), used in a process called soldering where it is melted to join metallic surfaces. It is especially useful in electronics . Alloys that melt between 180 and 190 °C (360 and 370 °F) are the most commonly used. By definition, using alloys with melting point above 450 °C (840 °F) is called brazing. Solder can contain lead and/or flux but in many applications solder is now lead free.

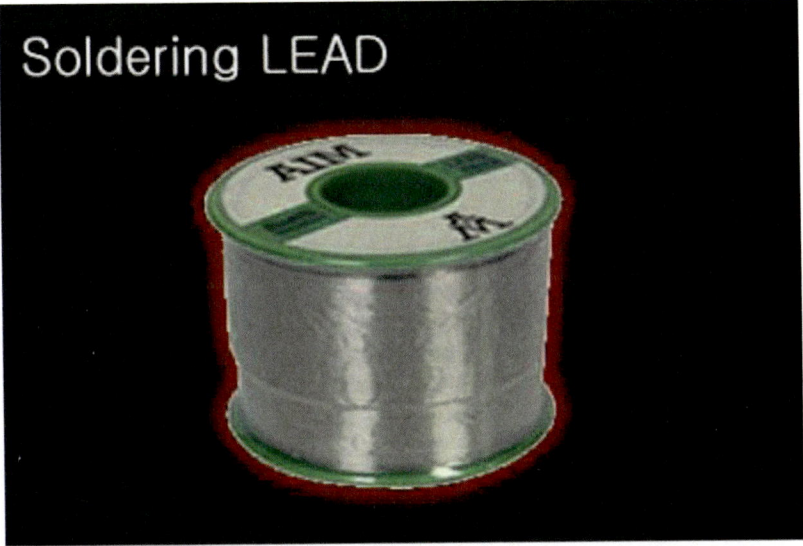
Soldering LEAD

While it is possible to do some wiring without soldering connections, soldering is the preferred approach. Proper soldering is easy with the right tools and techniques. One item that is critical is the right solder. DO NOT use the environmentally friendly lead free solders, they don't work worth a damn. Even in carefully controlled industrial conditions, lead free solders produce inferior connections. As much as the politicians backed by environmentalists would like to, they can't legislate metallurgy.

Soldering Paste
Solder paste (or solder cream) is used for connecting the terminations of integrated chip packages with land patterns on the printed circuit board. The paste is applied to the lands by printing the solder using a stencil, while other methods like screening and dispensing are also used. A majority of defects in mount assemblies are caused due to the issues in printing process or due to defects in the solder paste. An electronics manufacturer needs to have a good idea about the printing process, specifically the paste characteristics, to avoid reworking costs on the assemblies.

Soldering Paste

Characteristics of the paste, like viscosity and flux levels, need to be monitored periodically by performing in-house tests.

Soldering flux Soldering flux is just a safe, convenient acid for dissolving the oxide skin off the metal you want your solder to wet well. Also dissolves oxide off the liquid solder, making it less crusty and therefore more shiny.

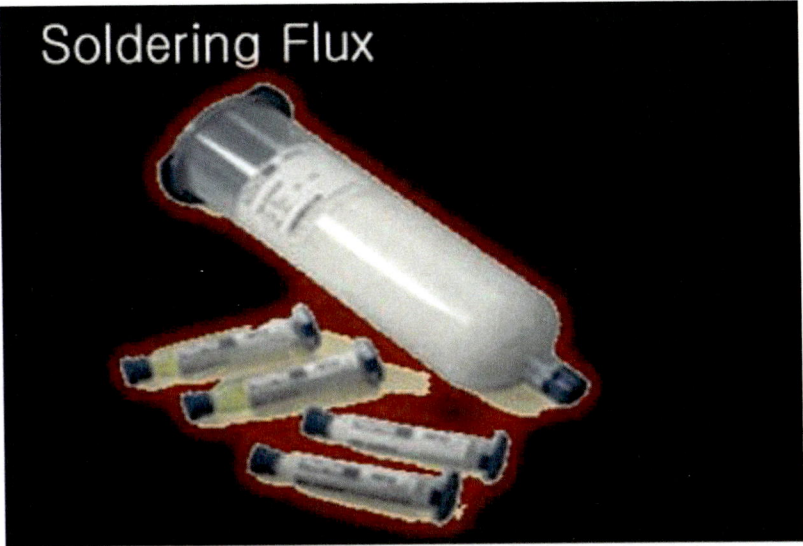

Soldering Flux

"Acid" flux is the stronger class of flux; it has something like hydrochloric acid in it. (The paste form has zinc chloride.)
This is good for making difficult oxides dissolve so difficult metals like stainless steel can be solder-wetted.
But the acid can hang around later trying to corrode the metal it just cleaned for you.
So for electronic stuff we mostly do not use it.
If we do, we scrub it off with things like toothbrush, water, soap, alcohol, baking soda, to minimize acid residues.

The flux built into most solder wire is called rosin flux.
I think it is an organic acid (so is vinegar, and tart-tasting "citric acid"),
stuck onto larger molecules that melt only at soldering temperatures.
That is the clear yellow-brownish plaque that sits on the solder's surface when you are done.
It does the same stuff as acid flux, but it is milder two ways.
It is only strong enough to reduce weakly oxidizable metals like copper, tin, lead, silver.
So it is just strong enough for electronics use, but not for soldering to stainless steel or iron or anything with chrome or aluminum.
And rosin-flux goes back to its plastic-like solid form after use, so it does not act

very corrosive to the metals later on.

So we do not need to clean it away carefully.

It can be cleaned away if you want to work at it, with brush-scrubbing and the right "polar solvents".

"Flux remover" is sold in spray-cans for this. Rubbing alcohol with a dash of dish-soap sort of works for me.

Try it and see what it looks like.

Soldering Wick

A solder wick (also desoldering wick or desoldering braid) is a tool for removing solder from any solder joint. Usually, it is a roll of fine, braided 18 to 42 AWG wire, typically oxygen free copper, which has been treated with a rosin solder flux.

Close up to a piece of solder wick

Close up to the netting of a solder wick

To remove solder with it, one presses the wick onto the solder joint to be removed and then heats the wick portion that is on the connection with the tip of a soldering iron. As the rosin melts onto the wick and the connection and the solder reaches its melting point the solder rushes via capillary action onto the clean copper braid. Once everything has melted and the solder fuses with the braided copper, the wick is lifted along with the solder and is then cut off and disposed of.

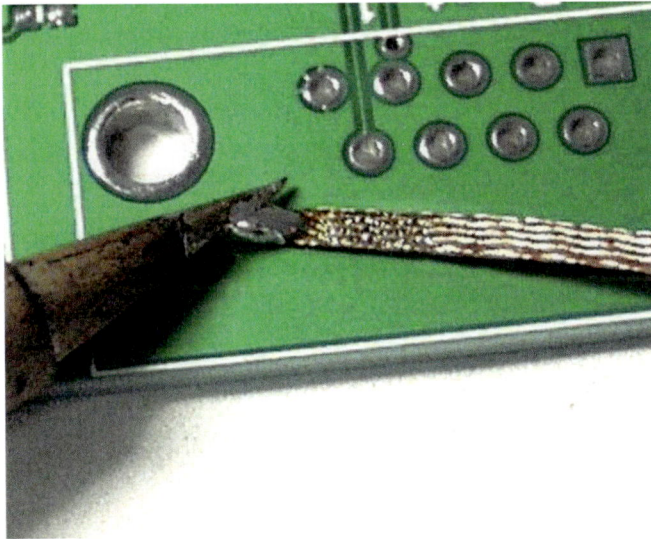

Multimeter Tester

What is a multimeter tester?

A multitester or multimeter is a device which can be used to gather data about electronics circuits. A basic multitester can measure resistance, voltage, current and continuity, while more advanced versions may be able to provide additional data.

Multitesters can be used with the current off or on in most cases, although using the device with the current on can sometimes result in damage to the device. This device is hand held, and powered by batteries. It consists of two probes attached to a central pack which can be digital or analog. The device has a series of buttons or switches which can be used to set the type of measurement being performed.

Analog Multitester
Analog types are been able to read manually to its Reading the needle pointing to a gauge, it requires a some computation when checking some components or where the selector is being set.
Basic Multitester has features like as follows:
Resistance Set Value: x1,
                    x10, = multiply by 10
                      x1K= it means multiply it by 1000
                        x10K = it means multiply it by 10,000

DC Set Value: from 0.1 to 1000 DC Voltage (Direct Current)
AC Set Value: from 10 to 1000 AC Voltage (Alternating Current)
DC Current Set Value: from 0.5micro ampere to 50 micro ampere

Continuity, the most basic measurement provided by a multitester, determines whether or not a circuit is complete. For a continuity test, the device is set to "ohms" and AC or DC, depending on the current being measured, before the probes on the device are inserted into the circuit. If the circuit is complete, the readout will measure between 0 and .05 ohms. A measurement of infinity indicates that the circuit is open, which means there is a problem. In addition to being used as a basic continuity tester,

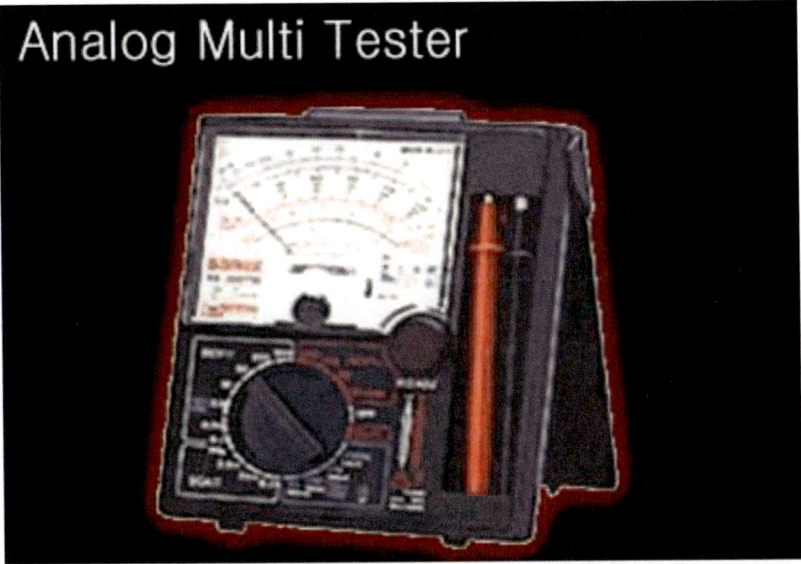

Analog Multi Tester

Digital Multitester

A digital multimeter is a tool that can measure amps, volts, and ohms. It is different from an analog meter, which has a needle and a gauge, in that it has a digital light-emitting diode (LED) display. Digital multimeters are typically more accurate than their old analog counterparts. A digital multimeter can also have other functions; obviously, the more expensive meters will have more features, but all of them measure the three basic currents.

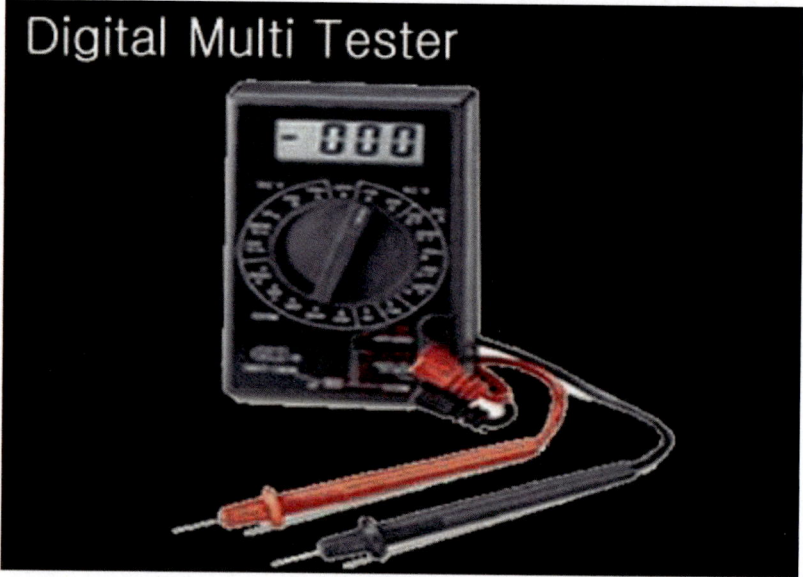

Digital Multi Tester

Another specification to consider when purchasing a DMM is its range. Regardless of what current is being tested, the proper range for that measurement is critical to the accuracy of the measurement. If the operator were testing a 12-volt battery, for instance, then a range setting of 0 to 25 volts would result in a more accurate measurement then a range setting of 0 to 500 volts. Thankfully, many DMM's have an automatic range feature, which will set the proper range for the circuit being tested automatically; all the operator has to do is set the DMM to the proper current being tested, and the meter does the rest.

When using a DMM for the first time, it is essential that a person read the instruction manual that comes with it. Many DMM's require different steps for taking measurements; this will entail pressing certain buttons before hooking up the leads, and so on. Most digital multimeters require a battery for operation. The instruction manual will most likely specify which type of battery to use. If the battery type is not specified, alkaline batteries are typically used.

A DMM's maximum reading capacity is extremely important as well. This is the maximum amount of current that the meter can measure. Usually, the current limit is printed on the face of the DMM. A common limit is 10 amps. This means that if the meter is hooked up to a current of 12 amps, the internal fuse will pop to prevent damaging the meter. Installing a bigger fuse will not increase the limit of the DMM; it will only burn it out permanently.

SMD Rework Stations

SMD(Surface Mounted) Rework station is used to remove, replace, do re-balling **BGA**(Ball Grid Alley) chips and **SMD components.**

Make sure that the re-balling station are controllable and match to standard temperature for PCB's and SMD Electronic Components..

It is made of high quality heating material. desoldering and soldering of BGA's are precisely controlled. Air flow and and Temperature are adjustable in wide range to produce high temperature breeze. Movable and Replaceable heating heads and very easy to operate...

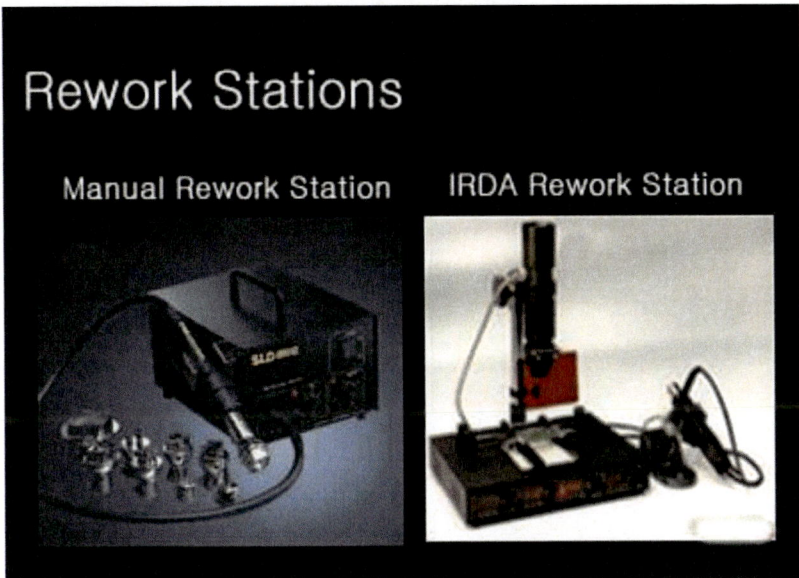

In the market today there are two types of rework station to choose that match your needs and budget. The Oldest type is the **Standard Filament Type Rework Station** and the latest is called **Infrared or IRDA Rework Station.**

The Standard Type is Consist of a heating filament which is by then blown by an air to produce a very hot air temperature.

A technical view of an SMD Rework Station with filament and an air blowing to produce hot temperature air flow...

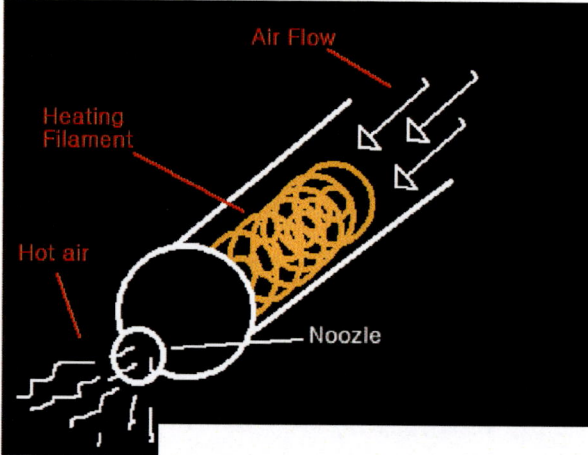

Thermostat adjustment is applied by controlling the heat temperature and the amount of air to flow.

Some types of Filament SMD Rework Station are digital in which the amount of heat and air were displayed on a seven segment LED and a push button adjustment were placed.

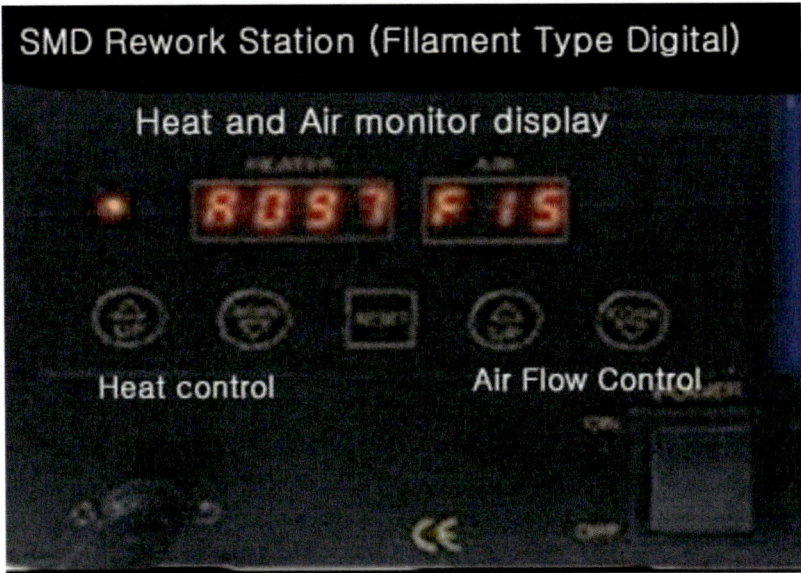

Infrared or IR SMD Rework Station

This one was designed by an Infrared (IR) Technology. Uses infrared heat wave technology instead of the conventional hot air, effectively solves the major problem being encountered when using the hot air gun, which is the movement of surrounding components while reworking.

The small amount of Infrared light is amplified to produce a very high temperature Lazer Beam. It is digitally designed and can be set automatically.

A simple overview of an IR SMD Rework Station.

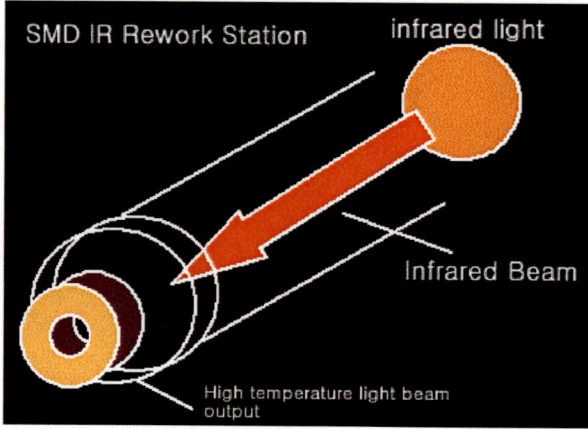

A set example of an IR SMD rework Station. Note: the Author is not endorsing any product.

SMD IR Rework Station

Adjustable DC Power Supply

The Dc power Supply can be used to substitute for the Battery Voltage when do live voltage checking on the PCB circuits... This is being used to trace the power supply line in electronic circuit.

Linear DC Power Supply

Linear Adjustable DC Power Supply is a equipment with high stability, high reliability, low noise, its output voltage or current can be continuously adjusted, and its constant voltage and current can auto-conversion. This universal power supply can be used in many different areas, from test of R&D equipment to test of production lines.

Here's a sample of substituting DC voltage in working cellphone repair tracing B+ line.

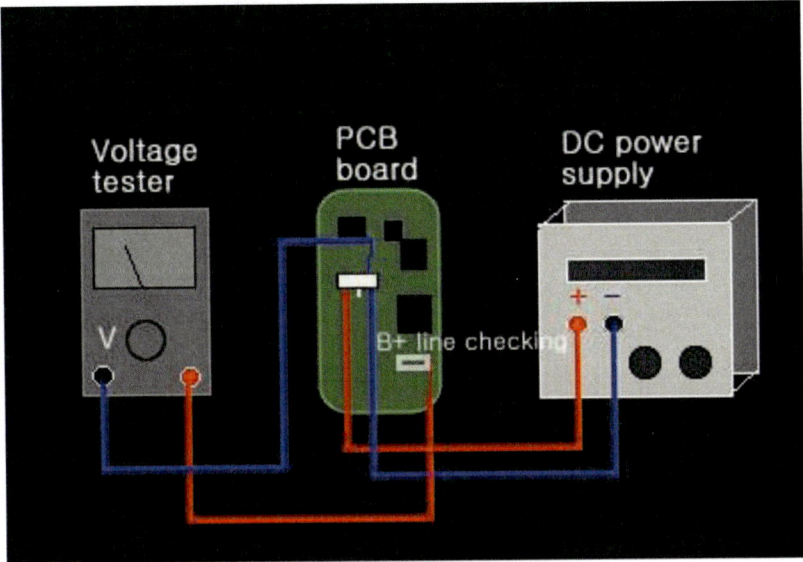

Voltage tester   PCB board   DC power supply

B+ line checking

Cleaning Tools

Cleaning kits and tools is also necessary when repairing specially when working wet units, corroded or rusted PCP boards. Some cleaning tools may found at household or home products and not so hard to find and prepare it. here's; some cleaning tools that may you find at home.

Brushes can help eliminate and wipe dust on PCB Components. Make sure that the brushes you may use have low electrostatic ability.

Small Paint Brush

Old toothbrush

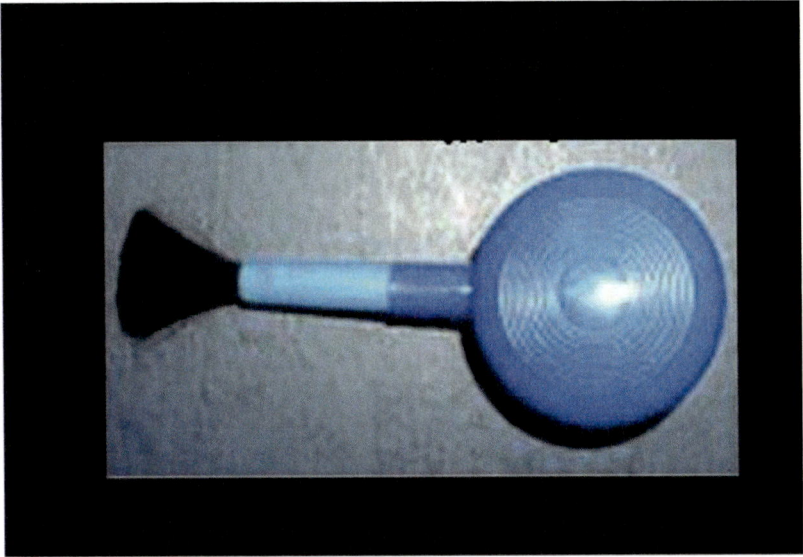

A **cotton cloth** or **sponge** and **cotton buds** which help to wipe extra solvents, dust,rust and dirt.

Cotton Cloth

Sponge

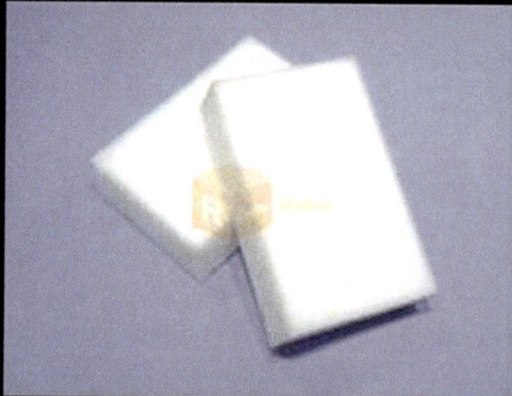

Anti Static Spray or liquids used to eliminate water residues and corrosive element in PCB component.

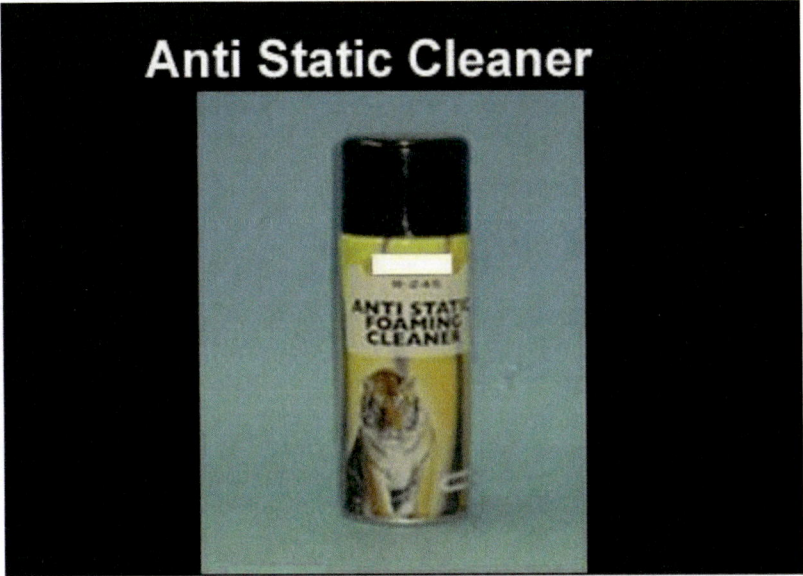

A **lacquer thinner** is a substitute to anti static cleaner and commonly and widely used by many technician's.

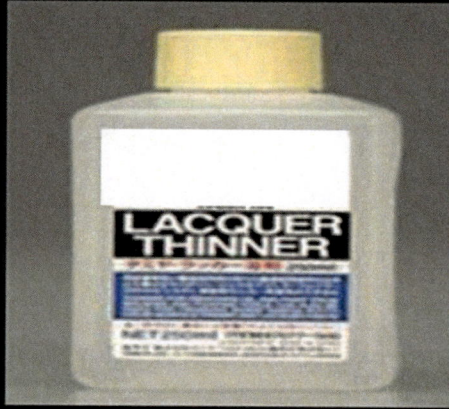

Lacquer Thinner

An **Ultrasonic Cleaner**- A machine that cleans by using a fluid that is vibrated at 20,000 cycles per second. When the vibration speed rises above the ultrasonic frequency level, bubbles explode and generate strong power, cleaning the surfaces and cavities of hard-to-clean objects.

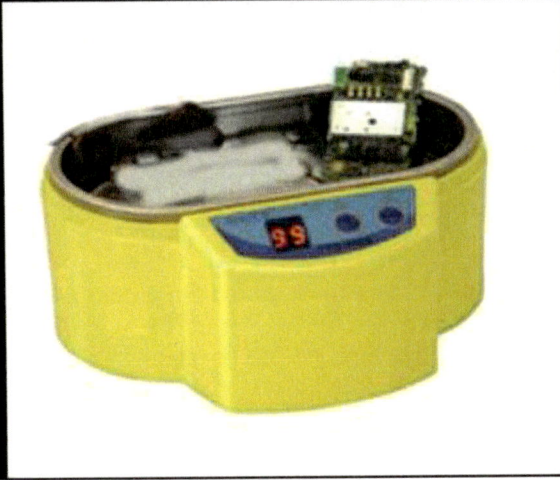

Reballing Kits

Re-balling kits are used to repair broken or weak soldered BGA (Ball Grid Array) Chips.

This is very important tools when it comes to hardware problem troubleshooting in various mobile phones.

This is only being used when an IC or chips was being suspected having fault or causes the problem.

That is because Mobile phones used BGA (ball grid array) solder balls that holds as connection terminal of every chips.

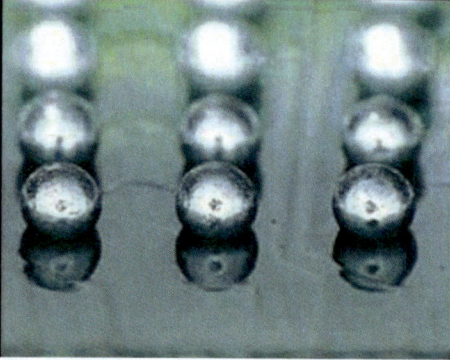

BGA Solder balls

There are many kits you can buy via online this days unlike before that most of mobile phone technician was unable to used this kits for it was not too easy to find and purchase. The process is that they just remove the entire solder balls and flattened out the entire bump terminal then replace the chips again. It may work but not totally effective as like for my years experience for the soldering process is too weak and easy to break , because the amount of soldered balls that holds the chips is not strong enough to hold it.

Although reballing IC's is not that easy for beginners to tackle to. it needs training and proper procedures to follow, further we will discuss the easiest way on how to reball IC chips.

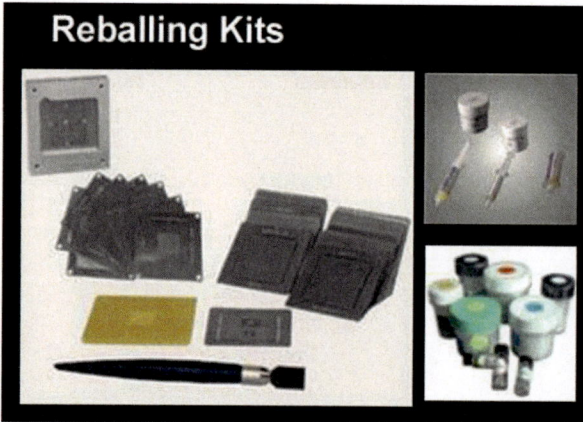

Reballing Kits

These are the kits you must prepare to be able to proceed in reballing BGA chips.

A Solder Balls

Solder balls have different sizes and measured by diameter, that match on every chips bumps sizes also. These are the common Soldering Ball diameter ranges for mobile phones chips.

0.05, 0.10, 0.15, 0.20, 0.25mm, 0.30mm, 0.35mm, 0.40mm,0.45mm,0.50mm ,0.55mm ,0.60mm, 0.65mm, 0.76mm

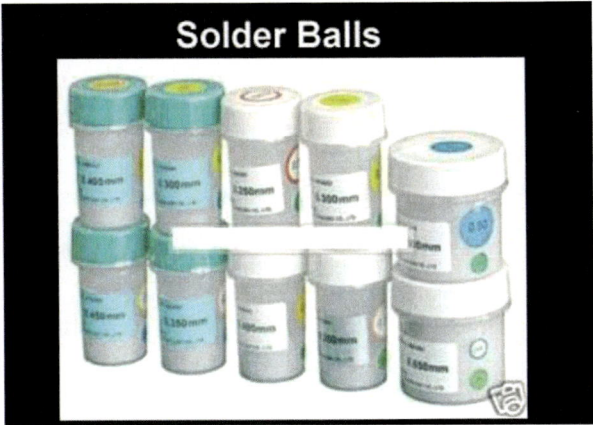

A BGA Stencil Pattern Plates

This is being used to properly align the solder ball on every bumps of the chips.

every chips have different bumps pattern and alignment designs.

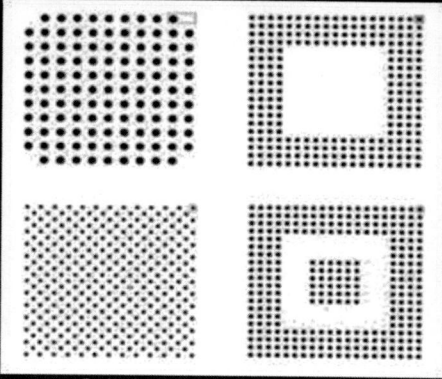
Stencil Patterns

Spatula

this is used to gathered the solder ball on each holes of the Stencil plates.

Spatula

A liquid Flux

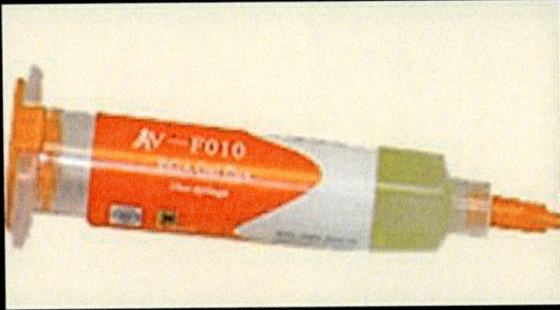

Liquid Soldering Flux

A PCB Board Holder

a PCB holder is being used to maintain the accuracy while working soldering and to avoid gripping and misalignment of solder balls.

PCB Board Holder

(a)

A Cleaning liquid

Too many cleaning product offered today that is non flammable.

A lacquer thinner will work, and still widely used for many mobile phone technician.

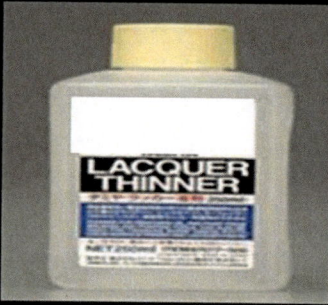

Lacquer Thinner

A cotton buds

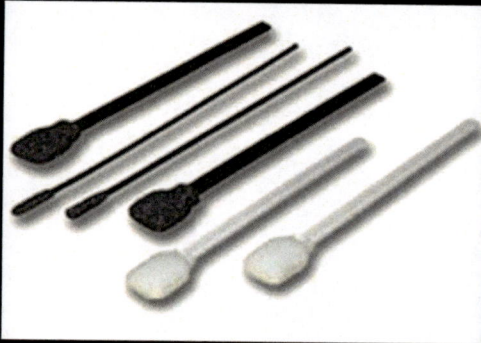

Cotton Buds

A Brush

Old toothbrush

Working Table Equipment

Additional working table equipment such **PC** or **laptop**, **table lamp** or a **magnifying lamp,** are very useful and important for cellphone repair...

A Personal Computer may help for storing support guides and manuals, A PC is also the key tool when it comes working on software like flashing and unlocking mobile phones. It is also being used to apply any applications such as Themes, Games, Mp3 music and ring-tones and any other application and add-ons to the cellphones by using a USB cable wire or blue-tooth device attach to it. A large Memory storage or Hard disk is also required for storing many software and programs just only for mobile phones.

Desktop Computer or Laptop

a table lamp is also require on a working table, it adds visibility when fixing things on a table like cellphone because cellphone parts are too small enough to handle.

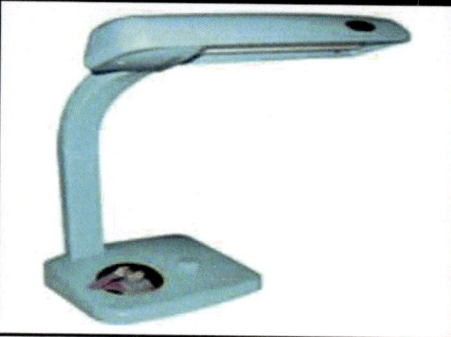

table Lamp

A magnifying lamp is much better for repairing tiny parts on a cellphone specially when it comes working on soldering a component and to avoid risk of damaging to other parts.

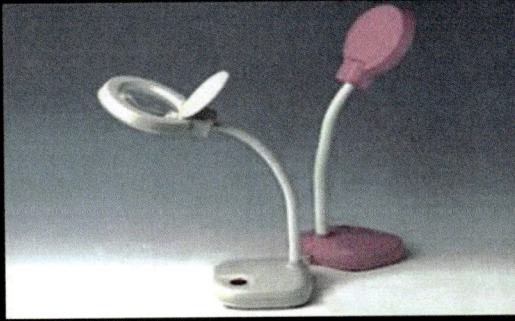

Desktop Magnifying Lamp

A microscope is used by many experts in finding problems such as cracks, breakage and damaged PCB's (printed circuit board) which is invisible to human eyesight.

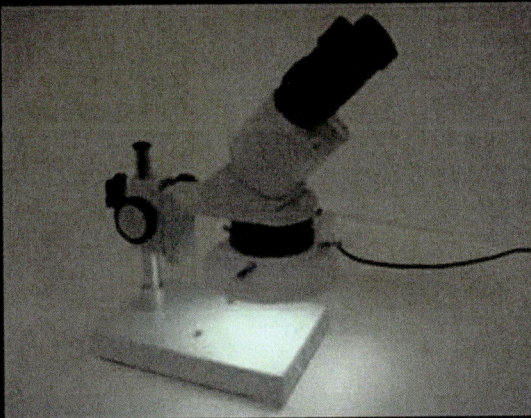

Microscope

If you feel too heavy and have not enough money yet to buy this devices don't worry you can still fix cellphones without this equipment. You can still do repair such as, LCD replacements and other problems that this devices is not necessarily to apply. Feel free to start from scratch and buy all you can when you start to have enough money to purchase it.

PART 04

Safety Procedures and Proper Handling of Tools and Test Equipment on Cellphone Repair

Safety procedure and proper handling of tool is highly observed when working any electronic components to avoid risk of unnecessary further damages whatever you are working at. These are the following thing that always to remind when working any electronic components such as cellphones.

Antistatic Wrist Strap

Wear a Ground Strap.
 Anti static wrist strap is used to avoid risk of electrostatic discharge from a human body to an electronic component circuit.
An antistatic wrist strap, ESD wrist strap, or ground bracelet is an antistatic device used to prevent electrostatic discharge (ESD) by safely grounding a person working on electronic equipment.

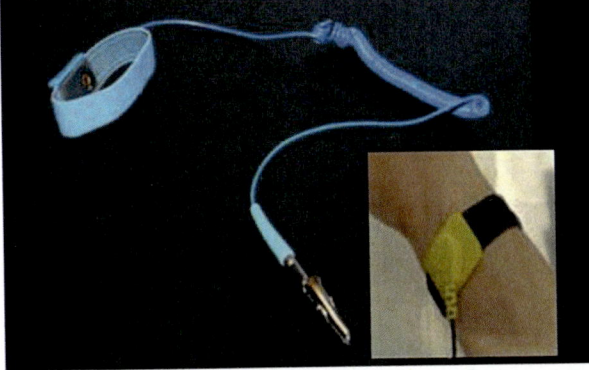

Antistatic Wrist Strap

It consists of a stretchy band of fabric with fine conductive fibers woven into it. The fibers are usually made of carbon or carbon-filled rubber, and the strap is bound with a stainless steel clasp or plate. They are usually used in conjunction with an antistatic mat on the workbench, or a special static-dissipating plastic laminate on the workbench surface.

Hand Gloves

You are not just protecting your hand from possible burns or brushes. it also protect the cellphones from scratches and possible electrostatic discharge. A cotton cloth made glove is essential to use.

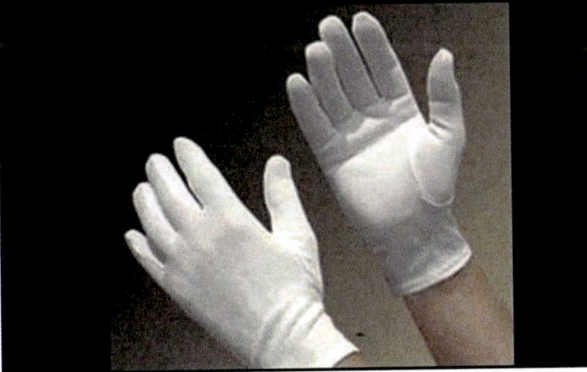

Hand Gloves

Safety Handling with Rework and Soldering Stations

Rework and soldering Station is a hot surface devices and can cause fire instantly and extreme burns on

skin when improperly handled.
Always Observe and Set it in proper heat and air flow amounts.

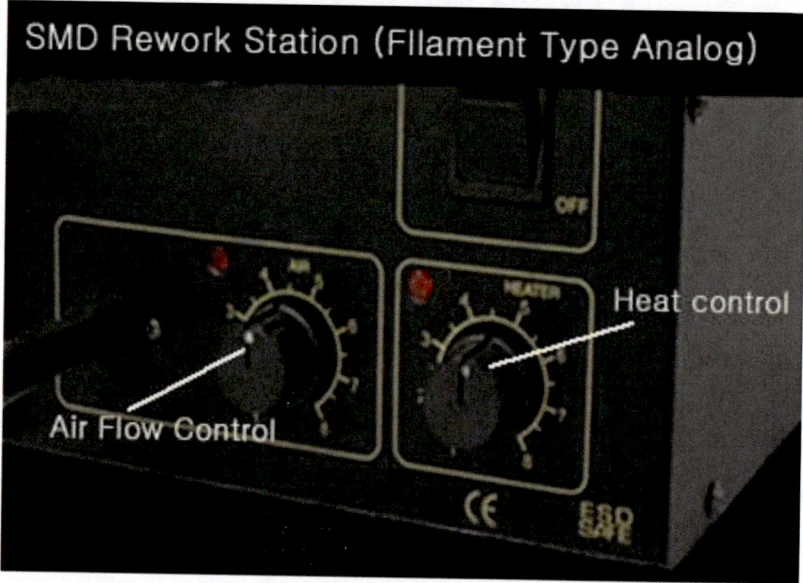

SMD Rework Station (FIlament Type Analog)

Heat control

Air Flow Control

Secure a safe place on your table where the rework station is located. Avoid inplacing it that people may pass or standing by especially kids.

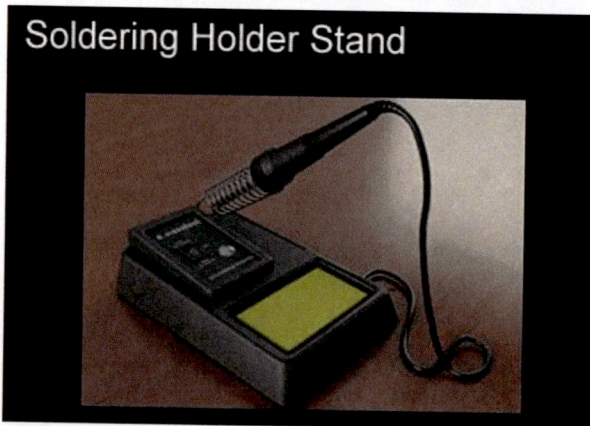

Soldering Holder Stand

Always shut it off when not in use and place unto the holder stand to avoid risk of fire and skin burns.

Safety Handling of a Multitester

a multitester may damaged easily when improperly handled. always check ranges when checking voltages and currents. The depletion yoke of the analog meter may be bust out when overdrive by a current to it.

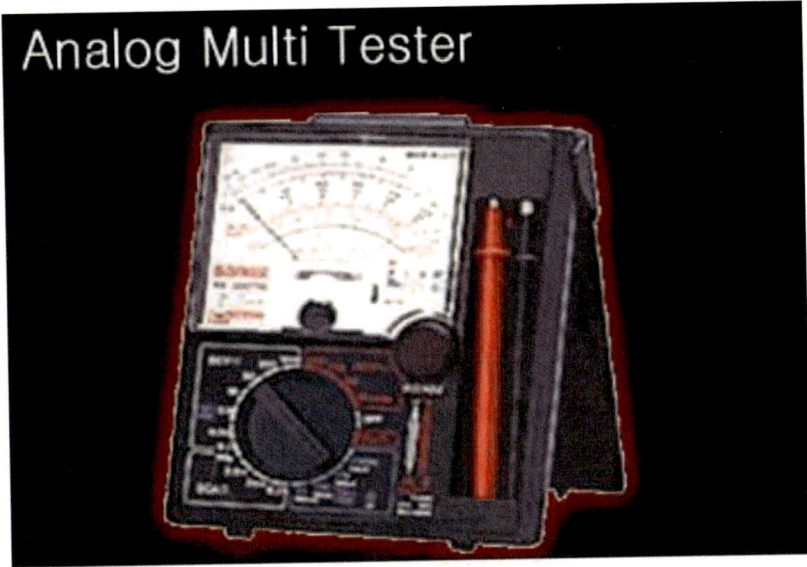

Analog Multi Tester

Measuring Resistance

Set the multimeter to Ohms or Resistance (turn meter on if it has a separate power switch). Understand that resistance and continuity are opposites. The multimeter measures resistance in ohms, it can not measure continuity. When there is little resistance there is a great deal of continuity. Conversely, when there is a great deal of resistance, there is little continuity. With this in mind, when we measure resistance we can make assumptions about continuity based on the resistance values measured. Observe the meter indication. If the test leads are not in contact with anything, the needle or pointer of an analog meter will be resting at the left most position. This is represents an infinite amount of resistance, or an "open circuit"; it is also safe to say there is the no continuity, or path between the black and red probes. Careful inspection of the dial should reveal the OHM scale. It is usually the top-most scale and has values that are highest on the left of the dial (a sideways "8" for infinity) and gradually reduce to 0 on the right. This is opposite of the other scales; they have the lowest values on the left and increase going right.

Measuring Voltage Ac-DC

Set the meter for the highest range provided for AC or DC Volts. Many times, the voltage to be measured has a value that is unknown. For this reason, the highest range possible is selected so that the meter circuitry and movement will not be damaged by voltage greater than expected.

Measuring Current by Ampere

Set the meter to the highest AC or DC Amp range supported. If the circuit to be tested is AC but the meter will only measure DC amps (or vice-versa), stop. The meter must be able to measure the same mode (AC or DC) Amps as the voltage in the circuit, otherwise it will indicate 0.

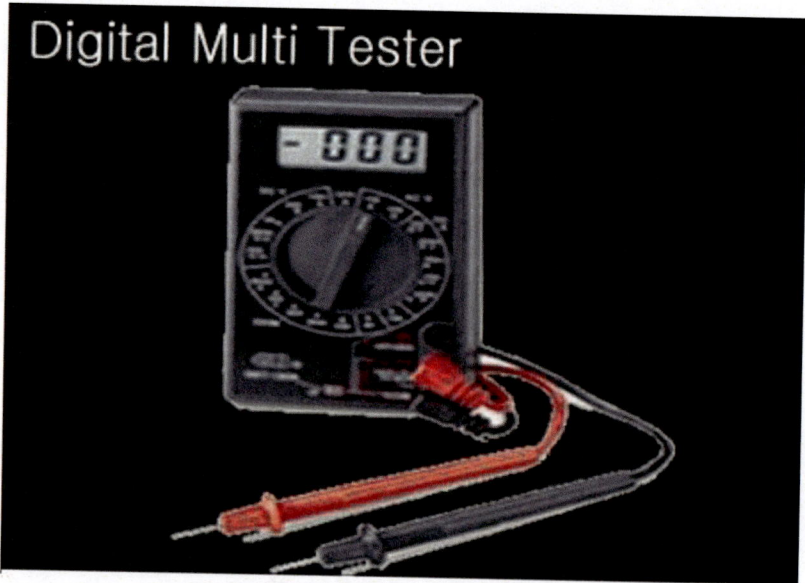

Be aware that most multimeters will only measure extremely small amounts of current, in the uA and mA ranges. 1 uA is .000001 amp and 1 mA is .001 amp. These are values of current that flow only in the most delicate electronic circuits, and are literally thousands (and even millions) of times smaller than values seen in the home and automotive circuits that most homeowners would be interested testing. Just for reference, a typical 100W / 120V light bulb will draw .833 Amps. This amount of current would likely damage the meter beyond repair. A "clamp-on" type ammeter would be ideal for the typical homeowner requirements, and does not require opening the circuit to take measurements (see below). If this meter were to be used to measure current through a 4700 ohm resistor across 9 Volts DC, it would be done as outlined below:

Safety Handling of a Power Supply
Power supply may also damaged and cause damaged to a component..

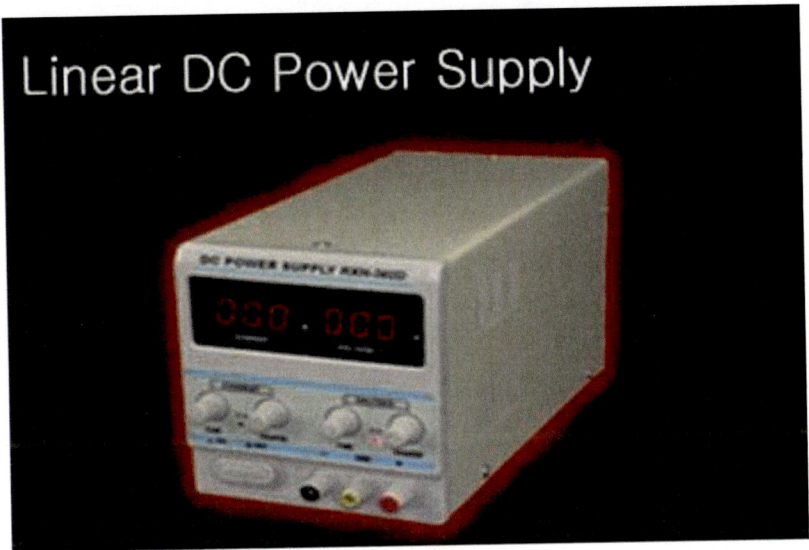

Always set it and determine the correct amount of Voltage range to avoid risk of blowing out any electronic parts.

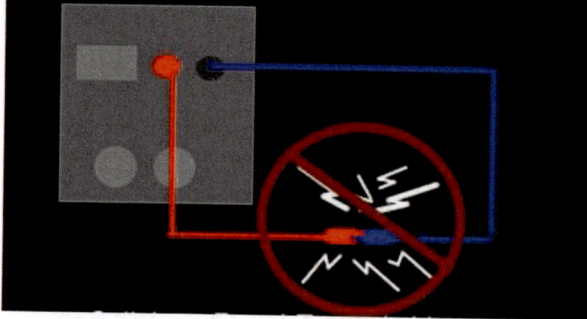

Avoid Shorting the two tips

Do not short the two alligator clips because the power supply will heat up and may busted out the protection fuse.

How To Use and Read a Multimeter

Using a multimeter is quite bit difficult for the first time especially the analog type one unlike the digital which is more convenient to use for beginners.

Every multimeter have its own user manual accompanied when you purchased it at any electronics store in your areas, and each one varies on how each circuits designed but there's always only one thing in common,

a Multimeter is is used to measure voltages AC or DC, currents and resistance, continuity and electronics components.

Maybe this only a take brief explanation on how to use a multimeter,
I have an example copy around here using my Sanwa analog multimeter which is made from Japan.

PARTS OF A MULTIMETER

- Frontal panel and the name of each part

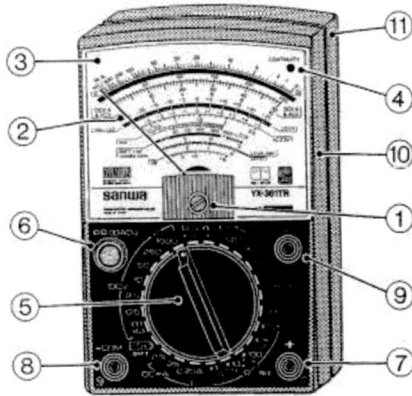

1.) Indicator Zero Connector	7.) Measuring Terminal +
2.) Indicatot Pointer	8.) Measurin Terminal - COM
3.) Indicator Scale	9.) Series Terminal Capacitor OUTPUT
4.) Continuity Indicating	10.) Panel
LED (CONTINUITY)	11.) Rear Case
5.) Range Selector Switch knob	
6.) 0-ohms adjusting knob	
/0- centering meter	
(NULL meter) adjusting knob	

EXPLANATION ABOUT THE SCALE

How to Use the Tester

● Meter scale plate

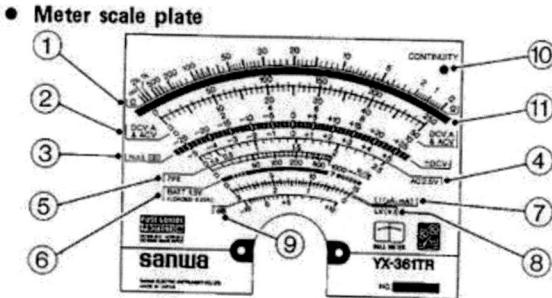

1.) Resistance (OHMS) scale
2.) DCV, A scale and ACV scale
   (10V or more)
3.) 0-centerig (NULL) +/- DCV scale
4.) ACV 2.5 (AC 2.5V) exclusive scale
5.) Transistor DC amplification factor
   (hFE) scale
6.) 1.5 baterry test (BATT 1.5V)
7.) OHMS range terminal to terminal current
   (Li) scale)
8.) OHMS range terminal to terminal voltage
   (LV) scale
9.) Decibel (dB) scale
10.) Continuity Indicating LED
11.0 Mirror: To obtain most accurate readings,
the mirror is deviced to make operator eyes, the indicator pointer, and the indicator pointer reflexed to
the mirror put together in line.

How to Measure Resistance

Multimeter with selector set to "Ohms". This meter only has a single Ohms range.Multimeter with
selector set to "Ohms". This meter only has a single Ohms range.
Set the multimeter to Ohms or Resistance (turn meter on if it has a separate power switch). Understand
that resistance and continuity are opposites. The multimeter measures resistance in ohms, it can not
measure continuity. When there is little resistance there is a great deal of continuity. Conversely, when
there is a great deal of resistance, there is little continuity. With this in mind, when we measure
resistance we can make assumptions about continuity based on the resistance values measured.

Observe the meter indication. If the test leads are not in contact with anything, the needle or pointer of an analog meter will be resting at the left most position. This is represents an infinite amount of resistance, or an "open circuit"; it is also safe to say there is the no continuity, or path between the black and red probes. Careful inspection of the dial should reveal the OHM scale. It is usually the top-most scale and has values that are highest on the left of the dial (a sideways "8" for infinity) and gradually reduce to 0 on the right. This is opposite of the other scales; they have the lowest values on the left and increase going right.

Connect the black test lead to the jack marked "Common" or "-"

Connect the red test lead to the jack marked with the Omega (Ohm symbol) or letter "R" near it.

Set the range (if provided) to R x 100.

Hold the probes at the end of the test leads together. The meter pointer should move fully to the right. Locate the "Zero Adjust" knob and rotate so that the the meter indicates "0" (or as close to "0" as possible). Note that this position is the "short circuit" or "zero ohms" indication for this R x 1 range of this meter. Always remember to "zero" the meter immediately after changing resistance ranges.

Replace batteries if needed. If unable to obtain a zero ohm indication, this may mean the batteries are weak and should be replaced. Retry the zeroing step above again with fresh batteries.

Measure resistance of something like a known-good lightbulb. Locate the two electrical contact points of the bulb. They will be the threaded base and the center of the bottom of the base. Have a helper hold the bulb by the glass only. Press the black probe against the threaded base and the red probe against the center tab on the bottom of the base. Watch the needle move from resting at the left and move quickly to 0 on the right.

Change the range of the meter to R x 1. Zero the meter again for this range. Repeat the step above. Observe how the meter did not go as far to the right as before. The scale of resistance has been changed so that each number on the R scale can be read directly. In the previous step, each number represented a value that was 100 times greater. Thus, 150 really was 15,000 before. Now, 150 is just 150. Had the R x 10 scale been selected, 150 would have been 1,500. The scale selected is very important for accurate measurements. With this understanding, study the R scale. It is not linear like the other scales. Values at the left side are harder to accurately read than those on the right. Trying to read 5 ohms on the meter while in the R x 100 range would look like 0. It would be much easier at the R x 1 scale instead. This is why when testing resistance, adjust the range so that the readings may be taken from the middle rather than the extreme left or right sides.

Test resistance between hands. Set the meter to the highest R x value possible. Zero the meter. Loosely hold a probe in each hand and read the meter. Squeeze both probes tightly. Notice the resistance is reduced. Let go of the probes and wet your hands. Hold the probes again. Notice that the resistance is lower still. For these reasons, it is very important that the probes not touch anything other than the device under test. A device that has burned out will not show "open" on the meter when testing if your fingers provide an alternate path around the device, like when they are touching the probes. Testing round cartridge type and older style glass automotive fuses will indicate low values of resistance if the fuse is lying on a metal surface when under test. The meter indicates the resistance of the metal surface that the fuse is resting upon (providing an alternate path between the red and black probe around the fuse) instead of trying to determine resistance through the fuse. Every fuse, good or bad, will indicate "good".

How to Measure Voltage

Set the meter for the highest range provided for AC Volts. Many times, the voltage to be measured has a value that is unknown. For this reason, the highest range possible is selected so that the meter circuitry and movement will not be damaged by voltage greater than expected. If the meter were set to the 50 volt range and a common U.S. electrical outlet were to be tested, the 120 volts present could irreparably damage the meter. Start high, and work downward to the lowest range that can be safely displayed. Insert the black probe in the "COM" or "-" jack.

Insert the red probe in the "V" or "+" jack.

Locate the Voltage scales. There may be several Volt scales with different maximum values. The range chosen the selector knob determines which voltage scale to read. The maximum value scale should coincide with selector knob ranges. The voltage scales, unlike the Ohm scales, are linear. The scale is accurate anywhere along its length. It will of course be much easier accurately reading 24 volts on a 50 volt scale than on a 250 volt scale, where it might look like it is anywhere between 20 and 30 volts.

Test a common electrical outlet. In the U.S. you might expect 120 volts or even 240 volts. In other places, 240 or 380 volts might be expected. Press the black probe into one of the straight slots. It should be possible to let go of the black probe, as the contacts behind the face of the outlet should grip the probe, much like it does when a plug is inserted. Insert the red probe into the other straight slot. The meter should indicate a voltage very close to 120 or 240 volts (depending on type outlet tested). Remove the probes, and rotate the selector knob to the lowest range offered, that is greater than the voltage indicated (120 or 240). Reinsert the probes again as described earlier. The meter may indicate between 110 and as much as 125 volts this time. The range of the meter is important to obtain accurate measurements. If the pointer did not move, it is likely that DC was chosen instead of AC. The AC and DC modes are not compatible. The correct mode MUST be set. If not set correctly, the user would mistakenly believe there was no voltage present. This could be deadly. Be sure to try BOTH modes if the pointer does not move. Set meter to AC volts mode, and try again. Whenever possible, try to connect at least one probe in such a way that it will not be required to hold both while making tests. Some meters have accessories that include alligator clips or other types of clamps that will assist doing this. Minimizing your contact with electrical circuits drastically reduces that chances of sustaining burns or injury.

How to Measure Current Amperes

Determine if AC or DC by measuring the voltage of the circuit as outlined above.
Set the meter to the highest AC or DC Amp range supported. If the circuit to be tested is AC but the meter will only measure DC amps (or vice-versa), stop. The meter must be able to measure the same mode (AC or DC) Amps as the voltage in the circuit, otherwise it will indicate 0.

Be aware that most multimeters will only measure extremely small amounts of current, in the uA and mA ranges. 1 uA is .000001 amp and 1 mA is .001 amp. These are values of current that flow only in the most delicate electronic circuits, and are literally thousands (and even millions) of times smaller than values seen in the home and automotive circuits that most homeowners would be interested testing. Just for reference, a typical 100W / 120V light bulb will draw .833 Amps. This amount of current would likely damage the meter beyond repair. A "clamp-on" type ammeter would be ideal for the typical homeowner requirements, and does not require opening the circuit to take measurements (see below). If this meter were to be used to measure current through a 4700 ohm resistor across 9 Volts DC, it would be done as outlined below:

Insert the black probe into the "COM" or "-" jack.

Insert the red probe into the "A" jack.

Shut off power to the circuit.

Open the portion of the circuit that is to be tested (one lead or the other of the resistor). Insert the meter in series with the circuit such that it completes the circuit. An ammeter is placed IN SERIES with the circuit to measure current. It cannot be placed "across" the circuit the way a voltmeter is used (otherwise the meter will probably be damaged). Polarity must be observed. Current flows from the positive side to the negative side. Set the range of current to the highest value.

Apply power and adjust range of meter downward to allow accurate reading of pointer on the dial. Do not exceed the range of the meter, otherwise it may be damaged. A reading of about 2 milliamps should be indicated since from Ohm's law I = V / R = (9 volts)/(4700 Ω) = .00191 amps = 1.91 mA.

If you're measuring the current consumed by the device itself, be aware of any filter capacitors or any element that requires an inrush (surge) current when switched on. Even if the operating current is low and within the range of the meter fuse, the surge can be MANY times higher than the operating current (as the empty filter capacitors are almost like a short circuit). Blowing the meter fuse is almost certain if the DUT's (device under test) inrush current is many times higher than the fuses rating. In any case, always use the higher range measurement protected by the higher fuse rating (if your meter has two fuses), or just be careful.

How to Check Basic Electronic Components

How to Check Basic Electronic Components Using a Multi-Meter

Basic electronic components such as resistors, capacitors, diodes and transistors are widely used in any electronic devices and gadgets. Knowing how to conduct a test on this components using a multimeter would give you an idea on how to trouble shoot and repair any defective cellphones or electronic equipments at home. Below are some basic D.I.Y. regarding proper testing of this components using a multimeter.

How to Check Resistors?

Read the indicated code value indicated in Schematic Diagram then select the Ohm-scale within but not way below the indicated value. A resistor is good if its resistance is close to the indicated value. Tolerance should be considered with the ohmmeter reading. While, no resistance reading at all on the ohmmeter scale settings means that the resistor is open. A zero resistance reading on all ohmmeter scale settings means that the resistor is shorted.

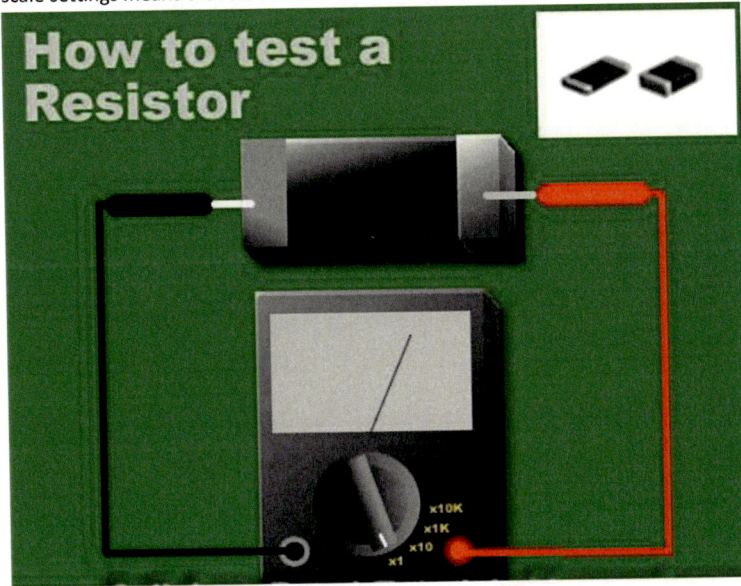

How to test a Resistor

How to Check Capacitors?

In most cases, a capacitor fails due to the deterioration of the dielectric material between its plate.Defective capacitors can have an internal shorted terminals, excessive leakage and degradation of capacitance meter. For an electrolytic capacitor (capacitors with polarity), short the terminal capacitor to discharge it prior to testing.

To test a capacitor, set the multimeter to Rx10 or Rx1K scale. Connect the tester negative probe to the capacitor positive terminal and the positive probe to the negative terminal.

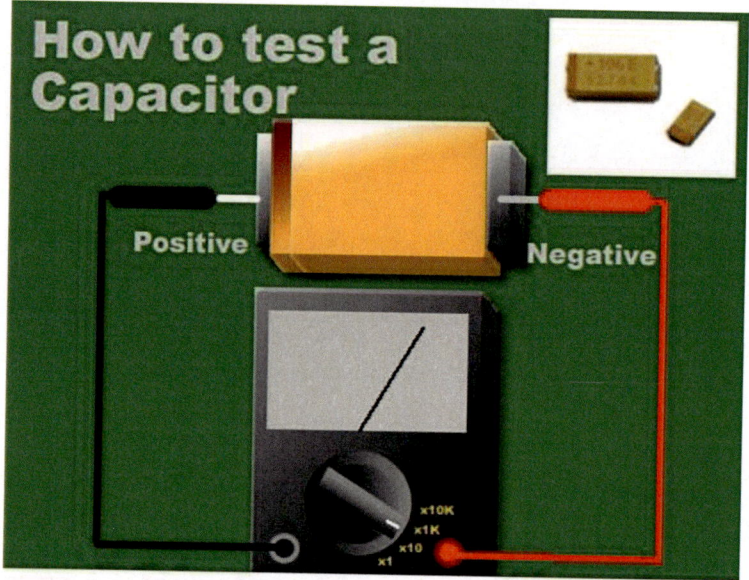

How to test a Capacitor

Positive

Negative

x10K
x1K
x10
x1

A good indication for electrolytic capacitor shows the meter needle deflecting towards zero and moves back again to infinite resistance position.

For ceramic, Mylar and other capacitor with a capacitance with less than 1.0 uF, the meter will not deflect at all.

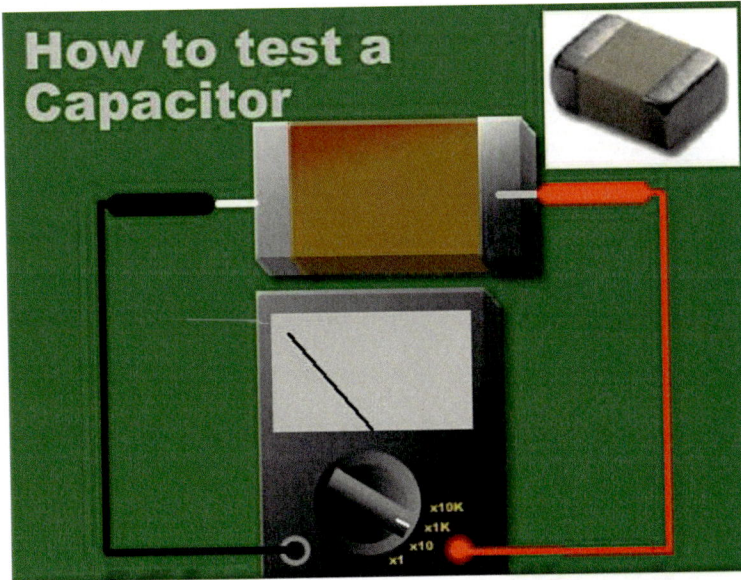

How to test a Capacitor

A defective indication for an electrolytic capacitor shows that the meter will rest on zero and remain stationary at a point which is an indication that the capacitor is shorted.

How to Check Diodes?

Set the multimeter knob to any of the resistance position (x1, x10, x1K or 10K ohm).Connect the positive probe to the anode and the negative probe to the cathode. Then connect the positive probe to the cathode and the
negative probe to the anode of the diode. A good indication in the first procedure will show the meter deflected very little or may not deflect at all.

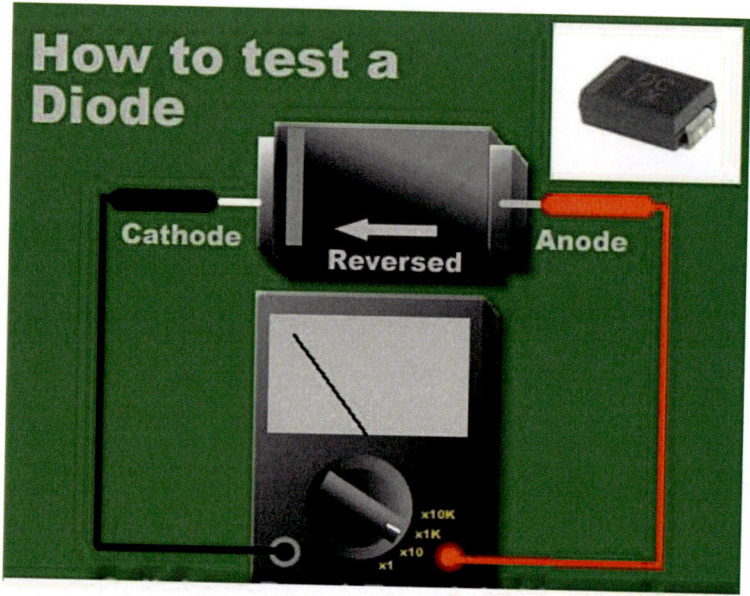

How to test a
Diode

Cathode

Reversed

Anode

×10K
×1K
×10
×1

And in the second procedure, the meter will deflect towards zero.The actual resistance reading is the forward resistance of the diode.

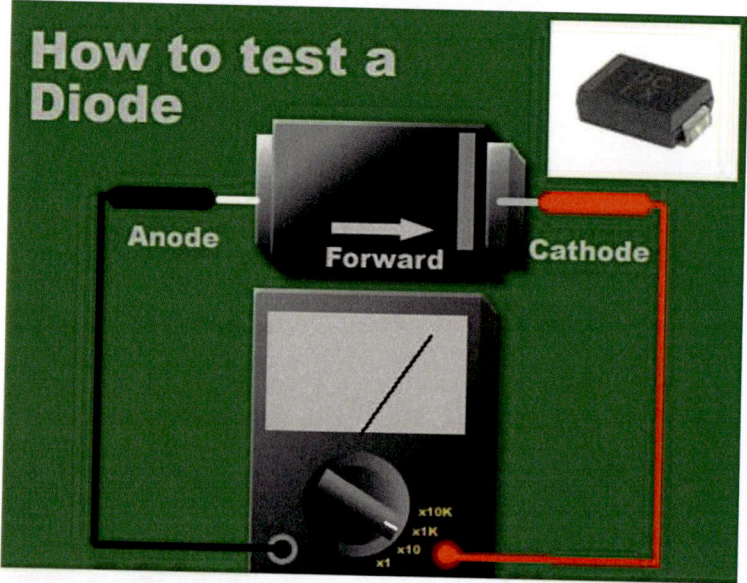

How to test a
Diode

Anode

Forward

Cathode

×10K
×1K
×10
×1

A defective indication shows that the meter won't deflect at all even when the probes are reversed. Or the meter deflects at the same time or almost the same resistance reading for both steps.

How to Check Transistors:

Bipolar transistors are usually checked out of a circuit by means of an ohmmeter. When it is desired to check for the resistance across the transistor emitter and collector, NPN or PNP, ohmmeter probes may be connected either way. A good transistor will show above a reading above 1000 ohm.

How to determine if it is NPN or PNP transistor?

To determine the correct terminal of the transistors, set the range selector to x 1 or 10 ohm.Connect the positive probe to the emitter and the negative probe to the base of the transistor. Note the reading interchange the connection of the probes to the leads of the transistor.

Base your conclusion on the table:

POSITIVE PROBE TO: -----NEGATIVE PROBE TO: -----RESISTANCE READING-- CONCLUSION:
  Emitter------- --   Base---------- Less than 150 ohm ------Transistor is NPN
  Base -------------Emitter --------Infinity ----------------Transistor is NPN

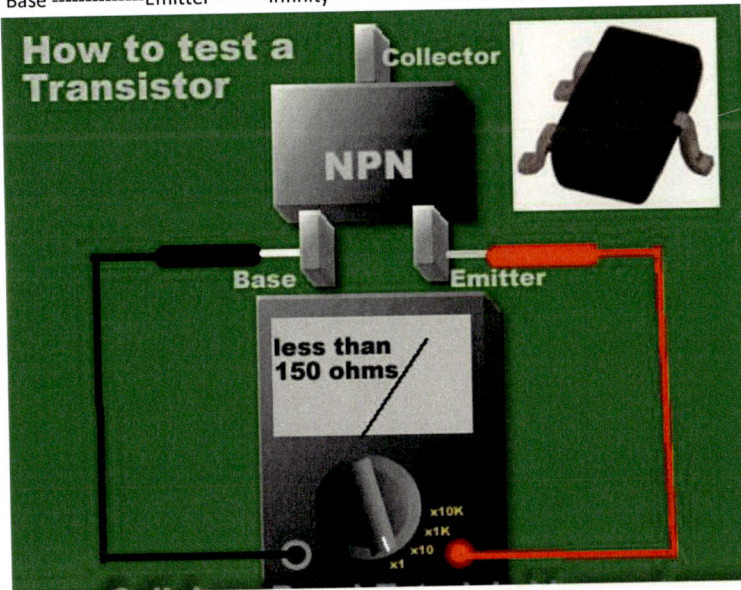

POSITIVE PROBE TO: NEGATIVE PROBE TO: RESISTANCE READING: CONCLUSION:

-Emitter------------Base ---------Infinity ---------------- Transistor is PNP

Base -------------- Emitter --- - Less than 150 ohm ------- Transistor is PNP

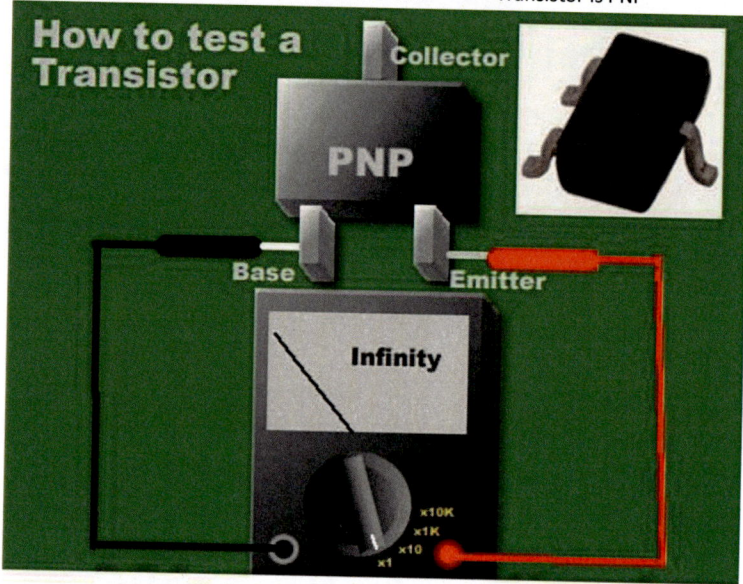

Some defective indications of transistors: Resistance between any pair of the terminals is less than 10 ohms, means that the transistor is shorted. Resistance between base and emitter or base collector for both the forward and reverse application of ohmmeter probes is infinity (meter needle don't deflect), means that the transistor is open. Transistors overheats (except power transistors) during normal operating condition means that the transistor is shorted.

How to Check an LED (Light Emitting Diode)

Set the Muti-meter to x1 connect the positive probe to cathode and the negative probe to anode. The good and working LED will then light up or glow, a busted LED will not.

How to test a
LED Light emitting diode

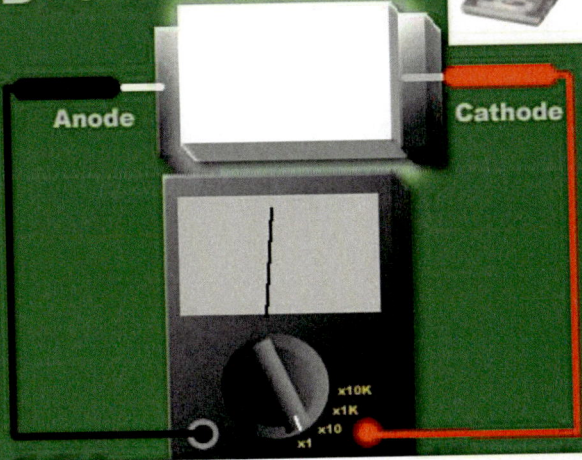

Anode

Cathode

×10K
×1K
×10
×1

How to Check a Coil?

Set the multimeter to X1 a good and working coil have a reading approximately point to zero ohms, without any reading means the coil is open or busted.

How to Check a Fuse?

A blown SMD Fuse is not visible to our naked eye, just set the multi-meter to x1 and put both test probe to both end side of the fuse. A full reading here to zero or continuity check is full. without any reading means the fuse is already busted.

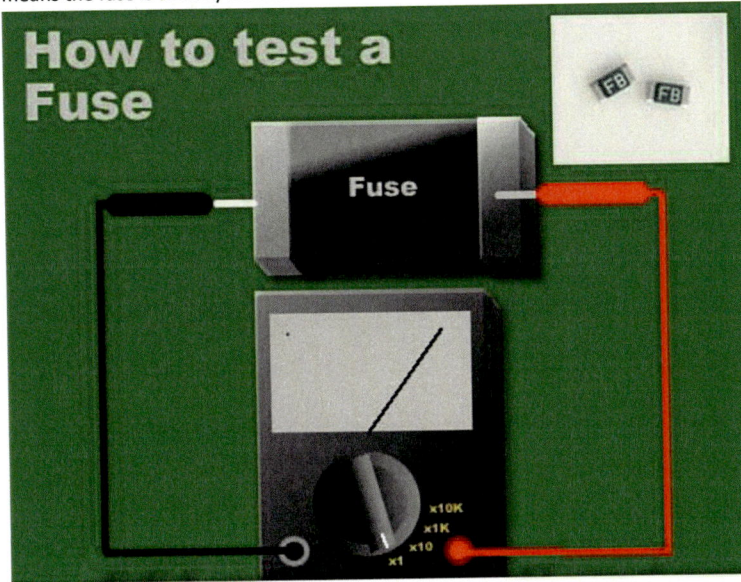

How to Check IC chips (Integrated Circuits)?

IC Chips is hard to determine faulty by using only a multi-meter, some advance equipment like the one that the manufacturer used during their productions. However; you can determine a faulty chips by some few experiences when it comes to troubleshooting, One techniques is that by comparing two same components from one another. like for example; if one chips is suspected to be faulty, then by replacing it with a good and working same chips, you can now determine if the said chips got a problem. It is a trial and error method at first; but as long as your experience and knowledge skills increases, you can determine it more quickly and accurately.

PART 05

How to Read Cellphone's Schematic Diagrams

Schematic Diagram is a layout of symbols and connection of every electronic components circuit where serve as a guide on how the circuit function or work.

Reading Schematic Diagrams is not a hard task to do, schematic diagrams is a big help to cellphone-repair

especially when working on or tracing lines and finding where a particular components mounted on a PCB board.

Such schematic diagrams is very useful and very important guide in every cellphone technician. It is equivalent to a handbook.

Learn how to read it. At first you might think that it is hard to do so, You are not going to be an experts and master in cellphone repair as long as you don't know how to read it. Many among cellphone repairman exist nowadays that do not have any knowledge about reading it. They always rely on finding free solutions over the internet and forums. Those people who give free solutions are those people who knows how to read a schematic diagram. Now here's your chance to learn and do not rely unto others, and be an expert and master troubleshooter when it comes to hardware problems.

Okay here's a step on how to read a schematic diagrams.

1. You need to download service **Schematic Diagrams**, as many or complete package in every cellphone products. each unit of a product have specific service diagrams.

2. You need to download <u>Adobe Acrobat Reader</u> so that you can open the schematic file which is in PDF format.

Now assuming that you already have those I've mention above; Let's try to open up one file like for example we are going to open a schematic diagram of Nokia N70.

here's what it looks like when scrolling down all the pages.
Let's take a little brief on each page for simple understanding..

A. page 1, In this page where you can find and Identify the whole assembly of the unit. this is also where to find the table of contents of the entire circuit's layouts.

Service Schematics

NOKIA N-70

Introduction

Exploded view and component disposal

RM-84

All measurements were made using following equipment:

Nokia repair SW	: Phoenix version 2005.12.5.90
Oscilloscope	: Fluke PM 3390A/B
Spectrum Analyzer	: Advantest R3267 with an analog probe
RF-Generator / GSM Tester	: Rhode & Schwarz CMU 200
Multimeter	: Fluke 73 Series II

While everyendeavor has been made to ensure the accuracy of this document, some errors may exist. If the reader finds any errors, NOKIA should be notified in writing.

Please send E-Mail to: training_care@nokia.com

Customer Care/ Service & Support Readiness / Content Cr
Copyright © 2005 NOKIA Only for training and service pu

B. page 2, In this page is a block diagram of an **RF and Baseband**: this is a basic explanation of the entire connection of a circuit. It was called a block diagram for it is being drawed into blocks.

What is a BASE BAND?

In telecommunications and signal processing, baseband is an adjective that describes signals and systems whose range of frequencies is measured from zero to a maximum bandwidth or highest signal frequency; it is sometimes used as a noun for a band of frequencies starting at zero. It can often be considered as synonym to lowpass, and antonym to passband, bandpass or radio frequency (RF) signal.

What is a RF?

Radio frequency (RF) is a frequency or rate of oscillation within the range of about 3 Hz to 300 GHz. This range corresponds to frequency of alternating current electrical signals used to produce and detect radio waves. Since most of this range is beyond the vibration rate that most mechanical systems can respond to, RF usually refers to oscillations in electronics circuits.

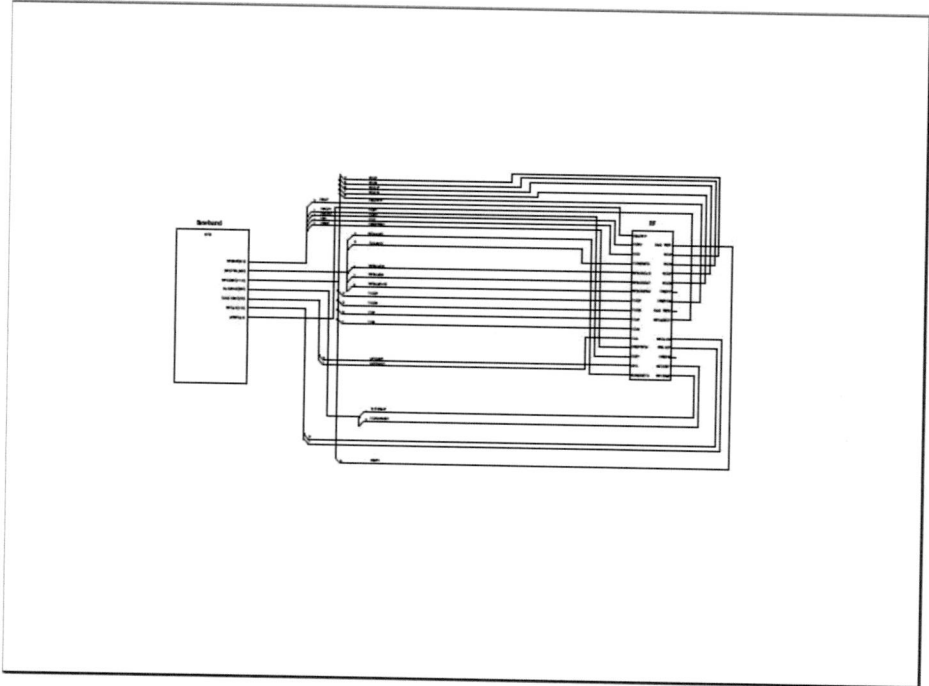

C. page 3, here we can find the **system connectors** and parts of the unit that correspond to the user or outer parts such us headset, charger and USB connection interfaces.

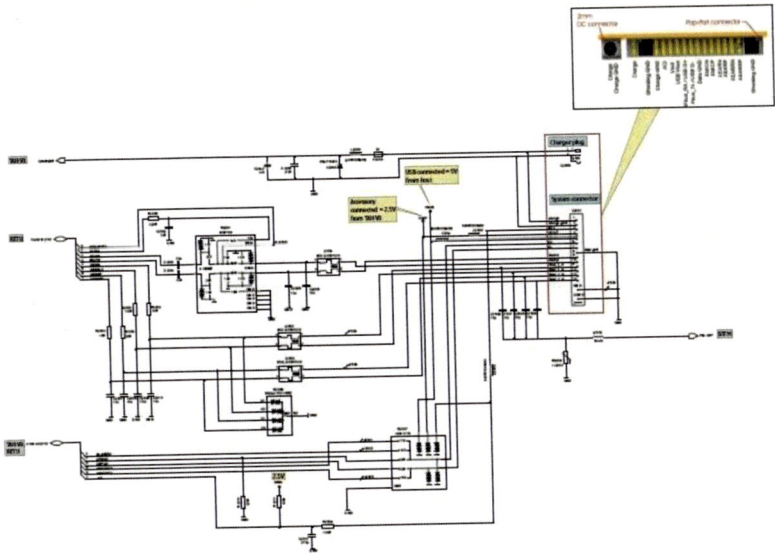

D. page 4, The **power management circuit**, **audio codecs and drivers** and the interfaces like the microphone, earpiece, mouthpiece, vibrator, sim-card, battery connections. This is the Power Supply Area of the entire circuits.

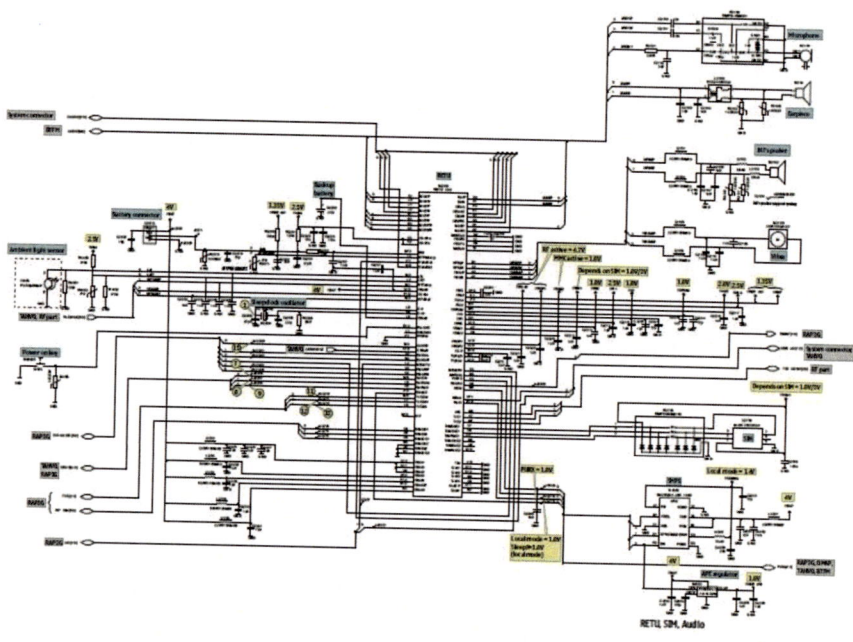

E. page5, Charging Control and Flash Interface Circuit.

F. page 6, This is the part of the circuit where the all application is being process, **Flash IC and memories**, this also where application and firmware are being stored.

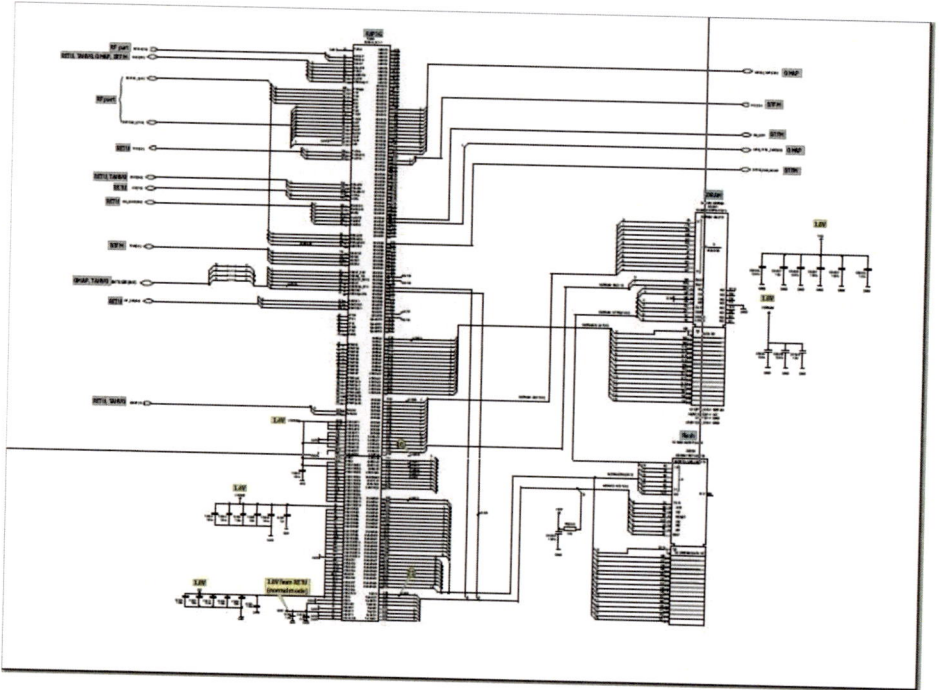

G. page 7, his the **Central processing of the unit (CPU)** like the personal computer (PC) cellphone also have a CPU to process applications and software.

H. page 8, A **Frequency Modulation (FM Radio)** circuit.

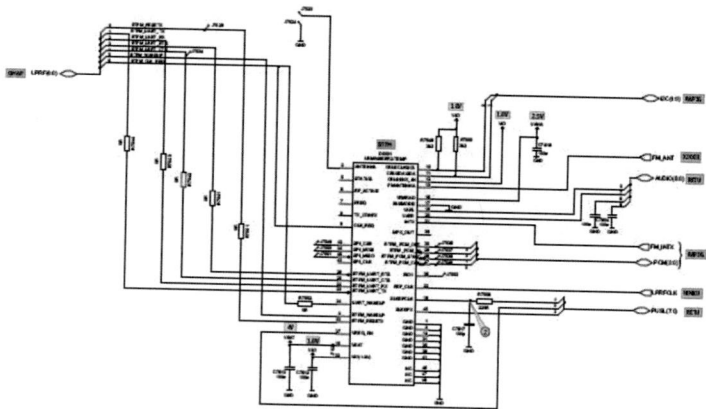

I. page 9,This page is the part of an LCD Display and Keypad circuit.

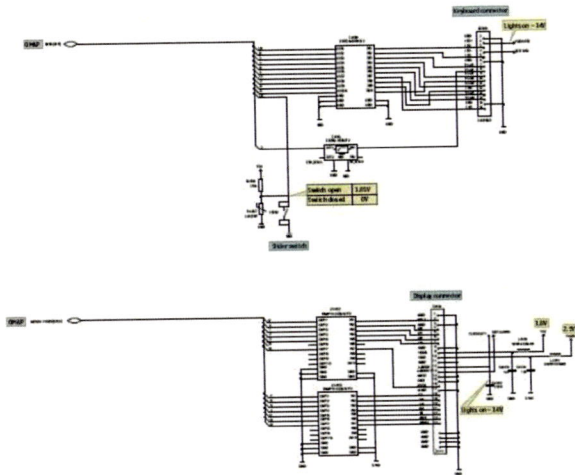

J. page 10, this is the RF components circuit, In this page the RF or the process of a network during Transmitting and Receiving Radio Frequency signals.

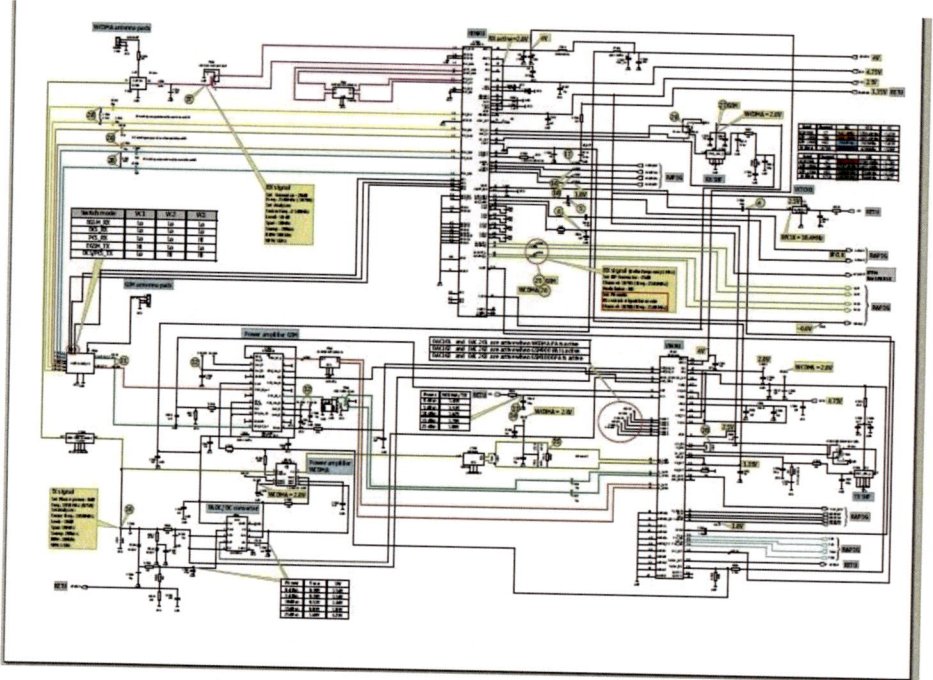

K. page 11, This the structure of the whole PCB Board and all the components mounted in the entire circuit.

this is also where pattern of test-points for check-up during production and servicing. at the right side is the pattern of waves of frequencies as a guide by using an oscilloscope, frequency generator and spectrum analyzer.

L. page 12, This is where the table of each and every components is mounted on the PCB board written in codes, like Rxxx - resistorr, Cxxx - Capacitor and etc.

The right side is the scale pattern of every components for quick and easy finding it.

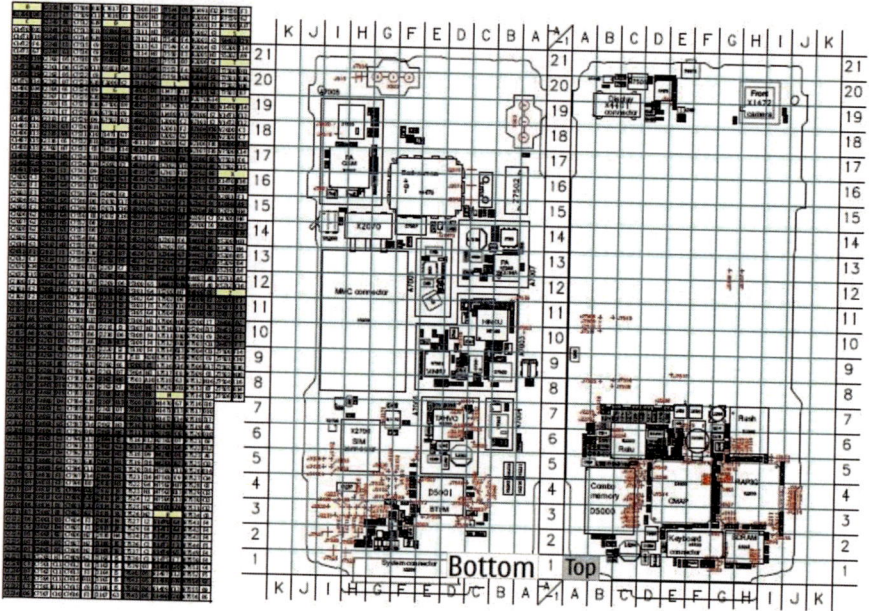

that was only the brief explanation of every pages of an Schematic Diagram. Further we will tackle on it even deeper.

How to Identify Component Symbols on Schematic Diagram

Identifying with Symbols on Schematic Diagram is very easy task, it's just like reading ABC's on English alphabet.

Since we are talking about mobile phone's circuit here, we are going to tackle only on its symbols being used herein, unlike in some major electronics components which have a lot of component symbols. Mostly, because Cellphone circuits have a lot of Integrated Circuit (IC) meaning the circuits is being compact into a smaller circuit to produce, and save a very small space to put a huge circuit connection into one tiny piece of circuits.

I have inserted the Layout of each component and how it's look's like mounted on a PCB (Printed Circuit Board) for better and easiest way of understanding.

Resistor

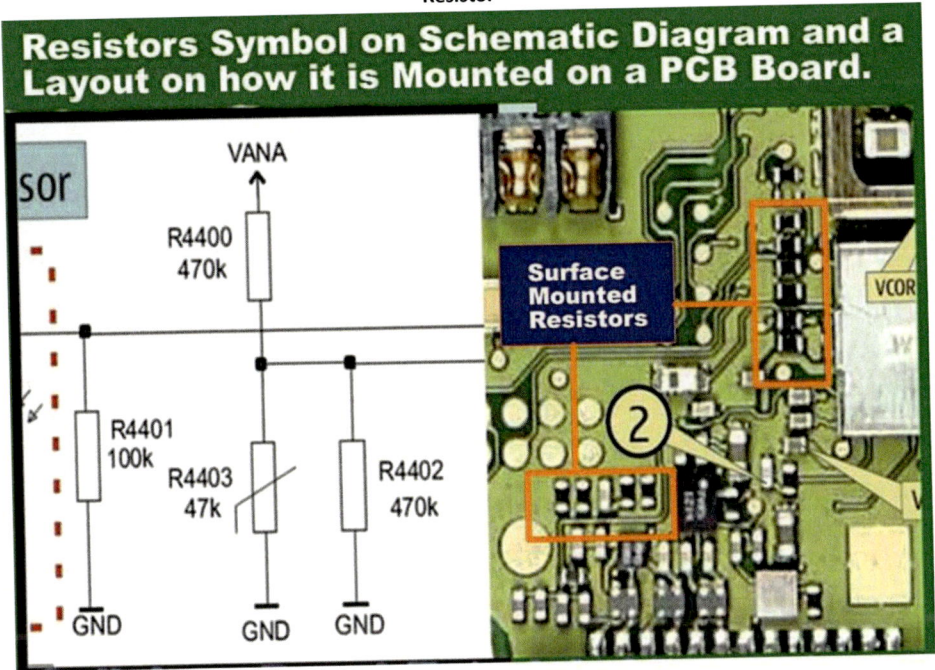

Resistors Symbol on Schematic Diagram and a Layout on how it is Mounted on a PCB Board.

Capacitor Symbol on Schematic Diagram and a Layout on how it is Mounted on a PCB Board.

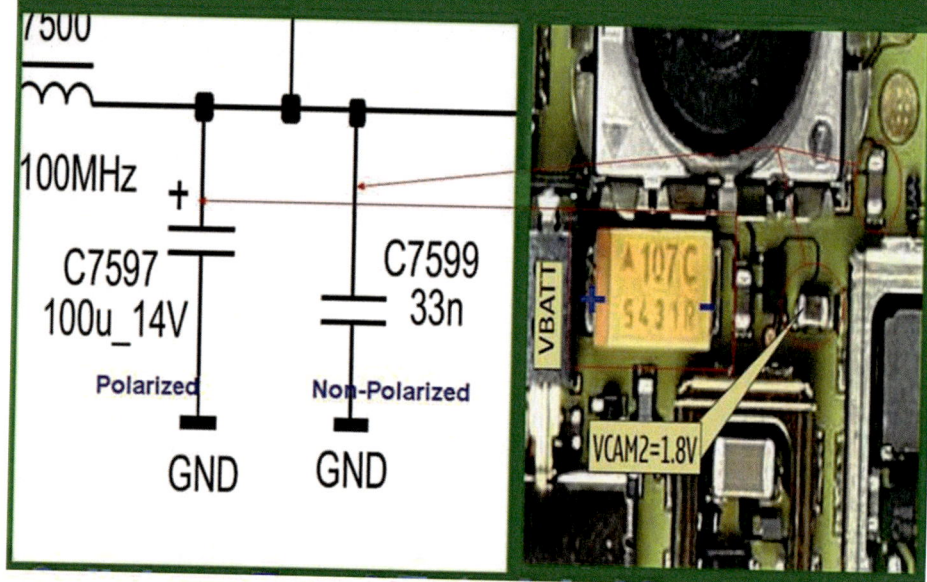

7500

100MHz

+

C7597
100u_14V

Polarized

GND

C7599
33n

Non-Polarized

GND

VBATT

A 107 C
5431R

VCAM2=1.8V

Transistor Symbol on Schematic Diagram and a Layout on how it is Mounted on a PCB Board.

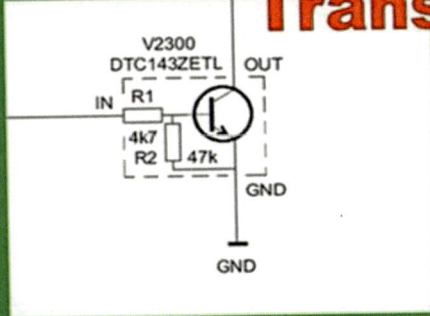

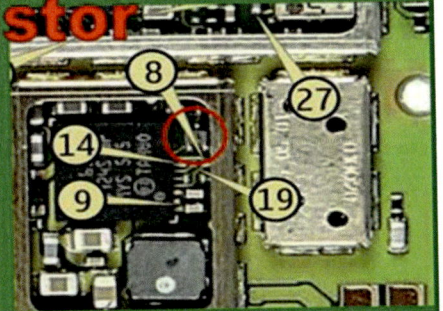

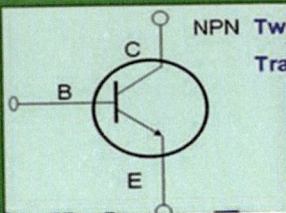

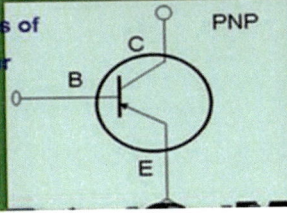

NPN Two types of Transistor

PNP

B = Base

C = Collector

E = Emitter

Diodes

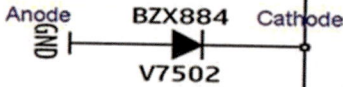

Diode Symbol on Schematic Diagram and a Layout on how it is Mounted on a PCB Board.

Diodes

Anode	BZX884	Cathode
GND ⊢	▶⊢	
	V7502	

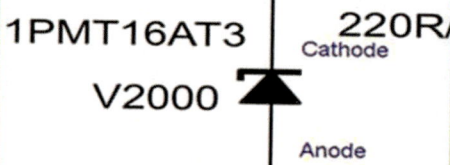

1PMT16AT3   220R/
                 Cathode

V2000

Anode

=GsM_Angel

Coils

Coil Symbol on Schematic Diagram and a Layout on how it is Mounted on a PCB Board.

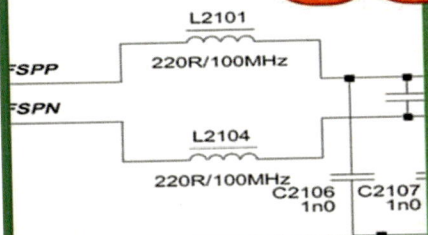

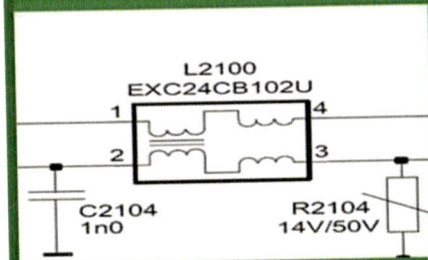

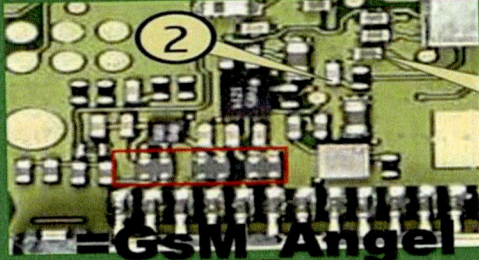

Fuse

Fuse Symbol on Schematic Diagram and a Layout on how it is Mounted on a PCB Board.

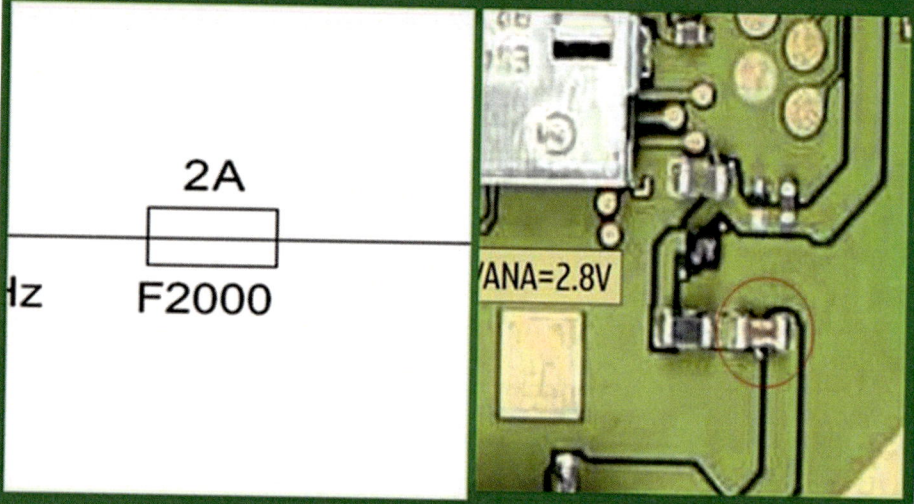

2A

F2000

Hz

/ANA=2.8V

Power Keys and Keypads , Mouthpiece, Earpiece and Ringtone Speaker

Electronics Interface Components Symbols

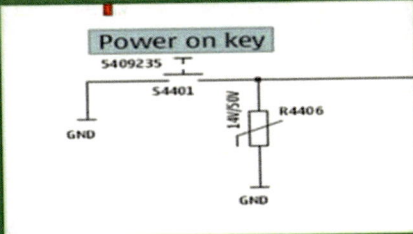

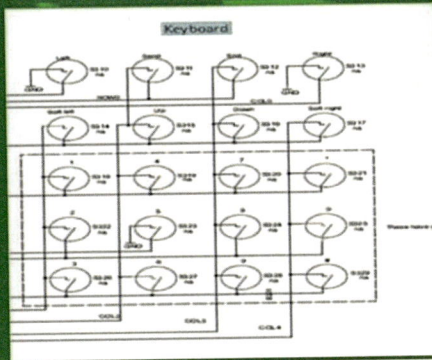

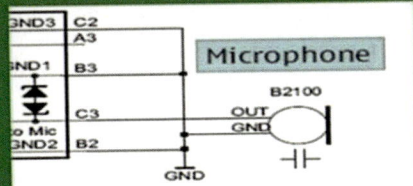

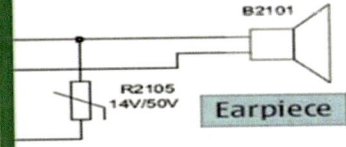

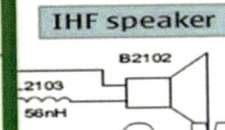

Power on key

S409235
S4401
14V/50V
R4406
GND
GND

Microphone

GND3 C2
       A3
GND1 B3
       C3
Mic   OUT
GND2 B2 GND
       GND
B2100

Keyboard

Earpiece

B2101
R2105
14V/50V

IHF speaker

B2102
L2103
56nH

=GsM_Angel=

Battery Cell

Button Cell Battery Symbol on Schematic Diagram and a Layout on how it is Mounted on a PCB Board.

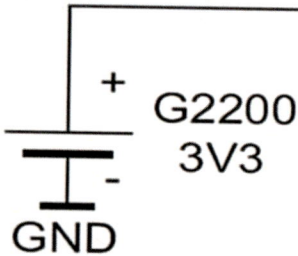

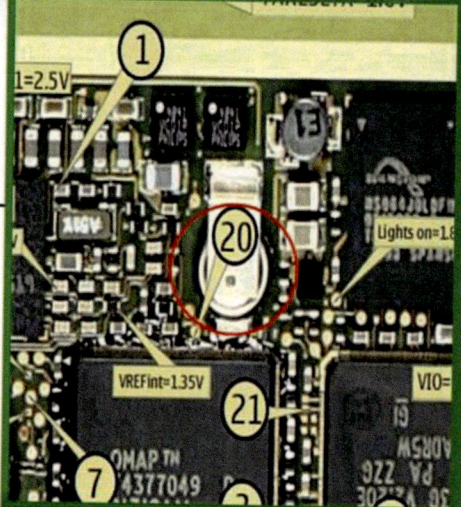

Clock Crystal Oscillator

Clock Crystal Oscillator Symbol on Schematic Diagram and a Layout on how it is Mounted on a PCB Board.

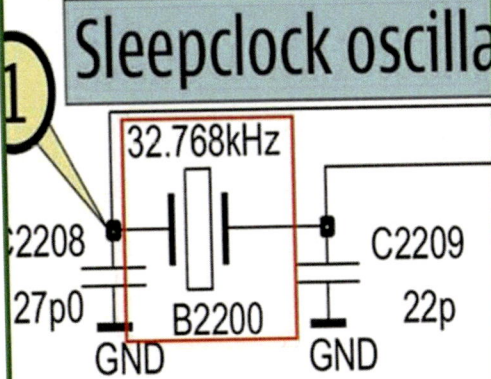

Sleepclock oscilla

32.768kHz

C2208
27p0
B2200
GND

C2209
22p
GND

VR1=2.5V
VRFC=1.8V
PURX=1.8V
VREFint=1.35

RF Filters

145

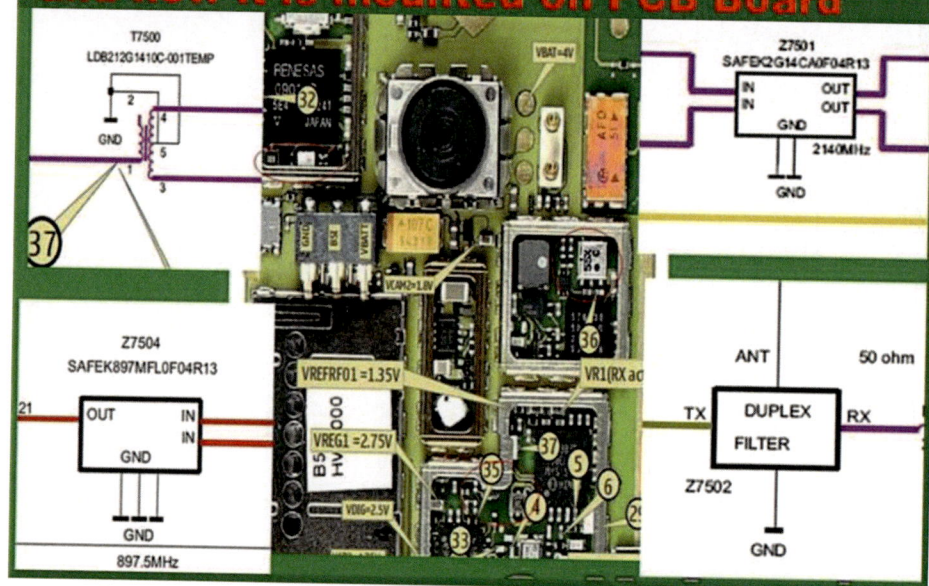

Electromagnetic Interference and Electrostatic Discharge Filters

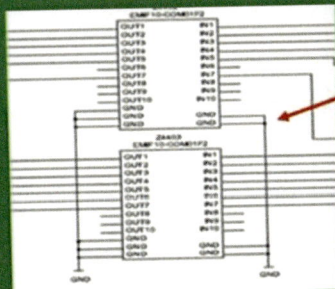

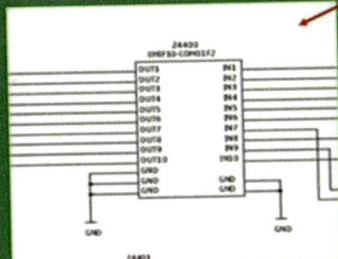

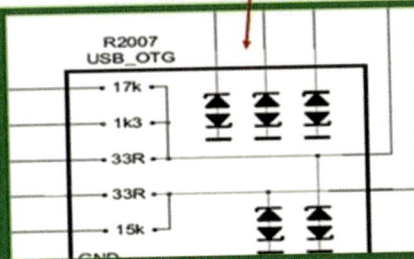

DC-DC Converters, Drivers and Regulators

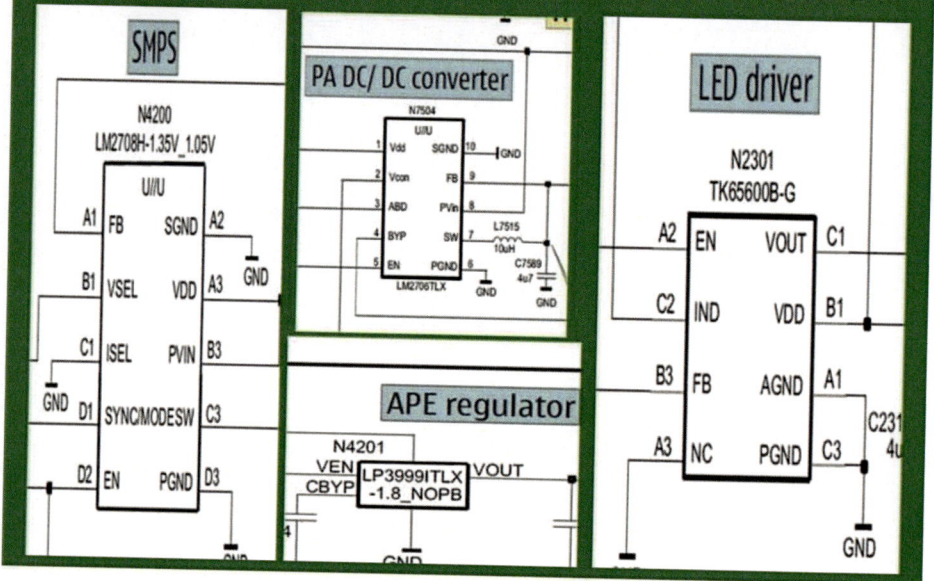

Integrated Circuit IC Chips

Integrated Circuits (IC's or Chips)

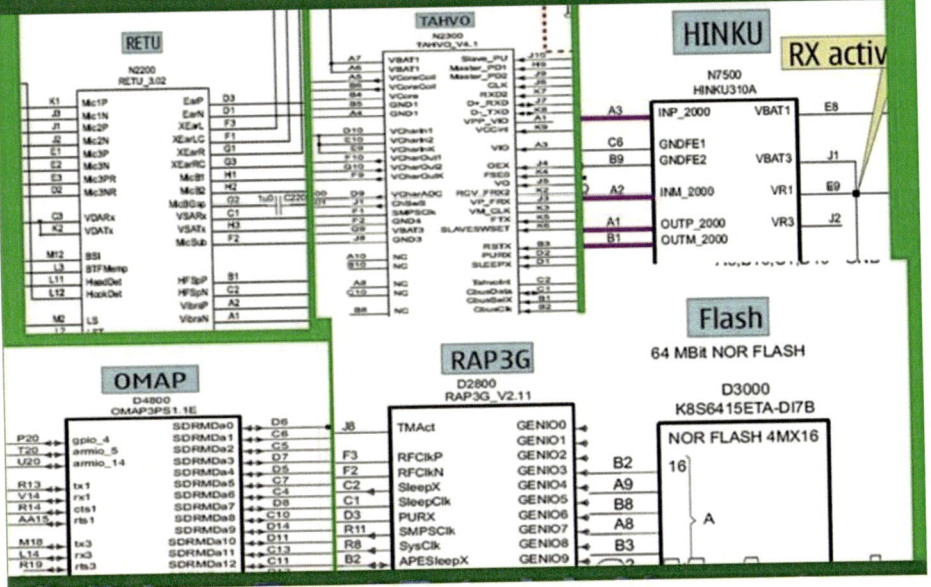

RETU
N2200
RETU_3.02

K1	Mic1P	EaP	D3
J3	Mic1N	EaN	D1
J1	Mic2P	XEarL	F3
J2	Mic2N	XEarLC	F1
E1	Mic3P	XEarR	G1
E2	Mic3N	XEarRC	G3
E3	Mic3PR	McB1	H1
D2	Mic3NR	McB2	H2
		McBGap	G2
C3	VDARx	VSARx	C1
K2	VDATx	VSATx	H3
		McSub	F2
M12	SSI		
L3	BTFMemp		
L11	HeadDet	HFSpP	B1
L12	HookDet	HFSpN	C2
		VibraP	A2
M2	LS	VibraN	A1

TAHVO
N2300
TAHVO_V4.1

A7	VBAT1	Slow_PU	
A6	VBAT1	Master_PD1	
A5	VCoreOut	Master_PD2	
B4	VCoreOut	CLK	
B5	GND1	RXD2	
A4	GND1	D_RXD	
		D_TXD	
D10	VCharIn1	VPP_VIO	
E10	VCharIn2	VCCI4	
C9	VCharInK		
F10	VCharOut1	VIO	
G10	VCharOut2		
F9	VCharOutK	OEX	
		FSEG	
D9	VCharADC	VIO	
J1	ChSel5	RCV_FRX2	
F1	SMPSCIk	VM_FRK	
F2	GND4	FTX	
F3	VBAT3	SLAVESWSET	
J8	GND3		
A10	NC	RSTX	
B10	NC	PURX	
		SLEEPX	
A8	NC		
C10	NC	Tahvolrit	
		CbusData	
B8	NC	CbusSelX	
		CbusClk	

HINKU
RX activ
N7500
HINKU310A

A3	INP_2000	VBAT1	E8
C6	GNDFE1		
B9	GNDFE2	VBAT3	J1
A2	INM_2000	VR1	E9
A1	OUTP_2000	VR3	J2
B1	OUTM_2000		

Flash
64 MBit NOR FLASH
D3000
K8S6415ETA-DI7B

NOR FLASH 4MX16

B2	16	
A9		
B8		A
A8		
B3		

OMAP
D4800
OMAP3PS1.1E

		SDRMDa0	D6	
P20	gpio_4	SDRMDa1	C6	
T20	armio_5	SDRMDa2	C5	
U20	armio_14	SDRMDa3	D7	
		SDRMDa4	D5	
R13	tx1	SDRMDa5	C7	
V14	rx1	SDRMDa6	C4	
R14	cts1	SDRMDa7	D8	
AA15	rts1	SDRMDa8	C10	
		SDRMDa9	D14	
M18	tx3	SDRMDa10	D11	
L14	rx3	SDRMDa11	C13	
R19	rts3	SDRMDa12	C11	

RAP3G
D2800
RAP3G_V2.11

J8	TMAct	GENIO0	
		GENIO1	
F3	RFClkP	GENIO2	
F2	RFClkN	GENIO3	B2
C2	SleepX	GENIO4	A9
C1	SleepClk	GENIO5	B8
D3	PURX	GENIO6	A8
R11	SMPSClk	GENIO7	
R8	SysClk	GENIO8	B3
B2	APESleepX	GENIO9	

How to Identify Resistor's Symbols and Layout

Resistor Component's Symbol and Layout

The symbol of a Resistor, as you can see that it is being label started with letter **"R"** meaning for Resistance and followed by a **"Mounted Code"**, that code is the number of that resistor for easy identification and search reason on the whole structure of a PCB board. Then, also ob-course the **Resistance Value** for test and check up procedures, like for example **"R4400 = 47K"** it means that Resistor number 4400 connected on that particular circuit's value is 47K or 47000 ohms. In that way we can easily trace and test that component using a Multi-meter tester.

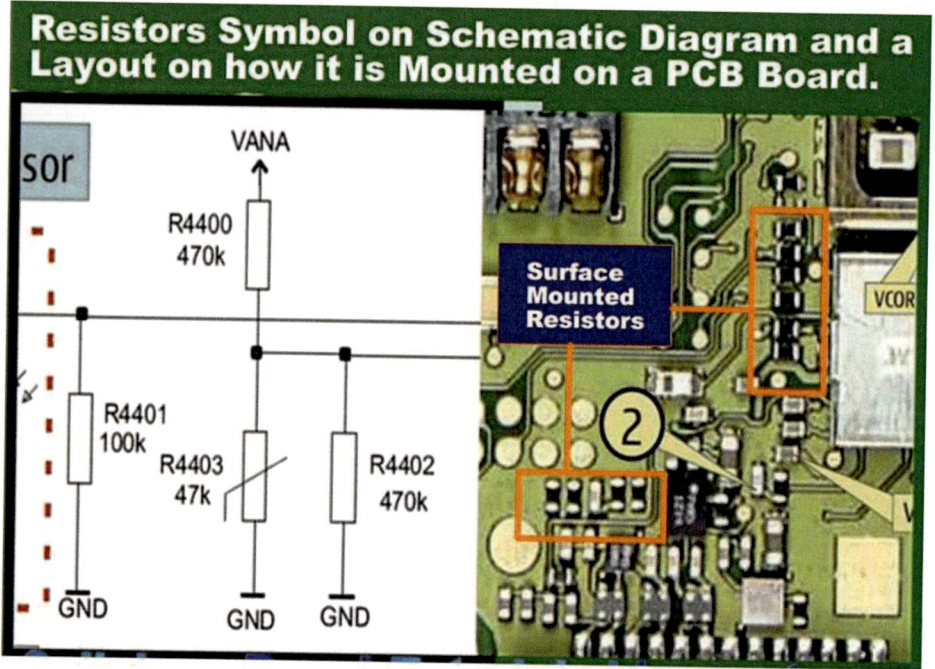

Resistors Symbol on Schematic Diagram and a Layout on how it is Mounted on a PCB Board.

There are two types shown in here, The first one is **Fixed Resistor** and the other one with a line across to it is called **Thermistor or Thermal Resistor.**

Thermistor or Thermal resistor is a variable Resistor, meaning it's resistance value is changeable. Thermal defines to heat temperature, it is being change by a current or voltage flowing across to it. It also have a capability to shut off when a voltage or current drive it to a maximum temperature level. While the **Fixed Resistor**, remains steady to it's resistance value.

How to Identify Capacitor's Symbols and Layout

Identifying Capacitors Symbol and Layout

There are two types of capacitors, the **Polarized** and the **Non-polarized**. The Polarized is indicated with **"+" positive** and **"-" negative**, meaning this cannot be change into its mounting position from a certain connection of a circuit polarity, The "+" positive is for the voltage supply line B+ only and the " - " negative is for the grounding lines. The capacitor will blown up if putting it into a non desired polarity position.

Non-polarized capacitor is a non-polar or without polarity meaning its position can be change without damaging it.

In Schematic Diagram it is stated as letter "C" stands for Capacitance then a mounting code and Capacitance value.

Capacitor Symbol on Schematic Diagram and a Layout on how it is Mounted on a PCB Board.

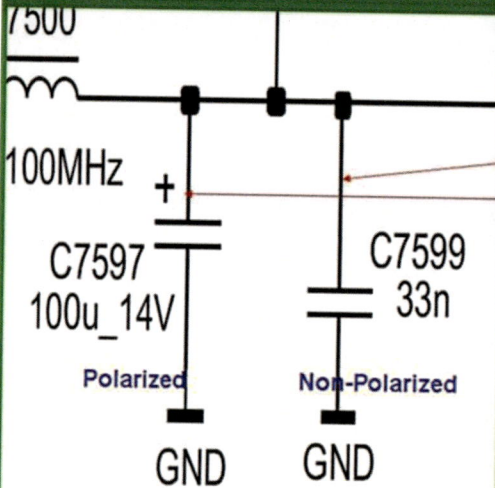

The Polarized indicated with desired maximum voltage value. like for example
C7597 1000mF_14V ,
the "14V" is the desired maximum voltage for that said capacitor.
While the Non-polarized labeled without desired voltage.
example: C2567 22pF

How to Identify Transistor's Symbols and Layout

Identifying Transistor's Symbol and Layout

There are two types of standard transistors, **NPN** and **PNP**, with different circuit symbols. The letters refer to the layers of semiconductor material used to make the transistor. Most transistors used today are NPN because this is the easiest type to make from silicon.

A transistor is a semiconductor device used to amplify and switch electronic signals.

The transistor is the fundamental building block of modern electronic devices, and its presence is ubiquitous in modern electronic systems.

It is labeled with letter "V" and then the mounting code and product code.

The leads are labeled base (B), collector (C) and emitter (E) in some schematics while in cellphone schematics is not, just be familiar with each leads.

What is a MOSFET?

Simple brief explanation, In mobile phones its is being used as a Switching circuit to the Camera Flash interface. It holds the large amount of voltage and then feed to camera flash light when it is being click to take a picture. That is why the Flash of the camera give a more bright light and speed in just a matter of blink of an naked eye..

The **metal–oxide–semiconductor field-effect transistor** (MOSFET, MOS-FET, or MOS FET) is a device used for amplifying or switching electronic signals.

A Power MOSFET is a specific type of metal oxide semiconductor field-effect transistor (MOSFET) designed to handle large amounts of power.

Its main advantages are high commutation speed and good efficiency at low voltages.

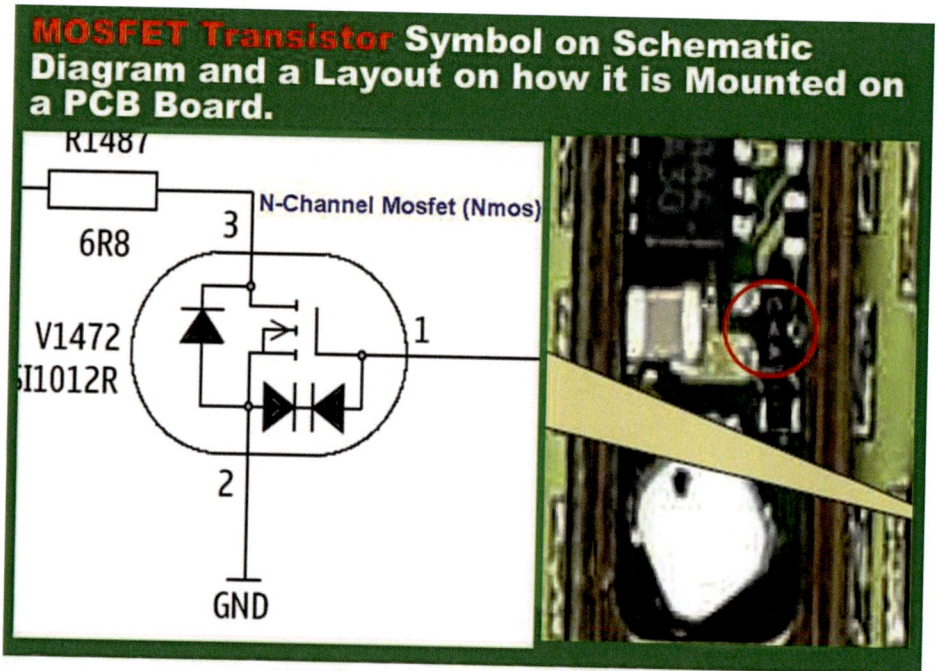

The power MOSFET is the most widely used low-voltage (i.e. less than 200 V) switch. It can be found in most power supplies, DC to DC converters and low voltage controller circuits.

There are many types Field effect transistor, this is the one is commonly used in mobile phone circuit.

How to Identify Diodes Symbols and Layout

Identifying Diode Symbol and Layout on Printed Circuit Board

There are many types of diodes, it is being used as a voltage and current rectifier,stabilizer,converter. In electronics, a diode is a two-terminal electronic component called **Anode** and **Cathode** that conducts electric current in only one direction.
The below picture shows a diode and a zener diode, A **Zener** diode is a type of diode that permits current not only in the forward direction like a normal diode, but also in the reverse direction if the voltage is larger than the breakdown voltage known as "Zener knee voltage" or "Zener voltage".
It is being labeled in letter "V" means voltage rectifier in a circuit the mounting code and the product code.

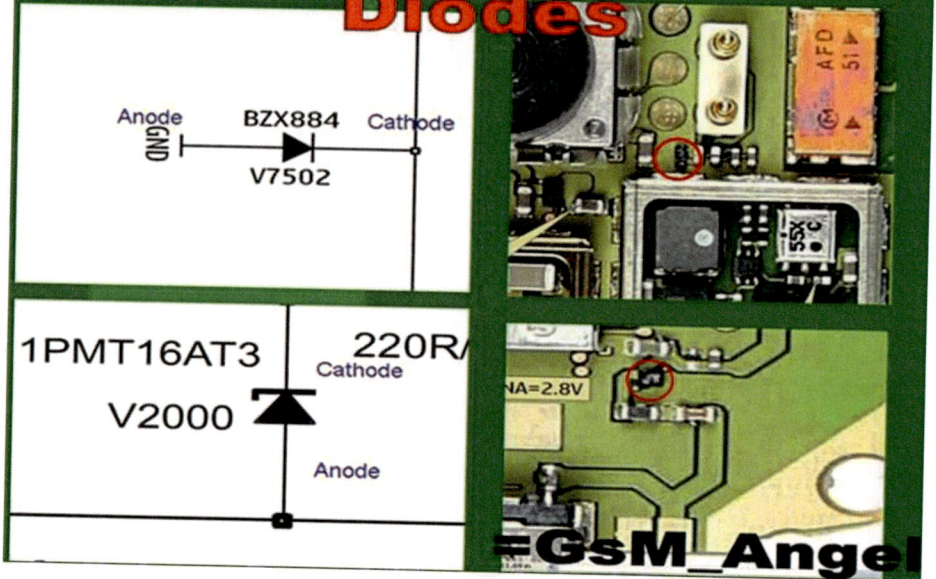

Diode Symbol on Schematic Diagram and a Layout on how it is Mounted on a PCB Board.

Diodes

Anode GND BZX884 Cathode
V7502

1PMT16AT3 220R/
V2000 Cathode
Anode

NA=2.8V

=GsM_Angel

A simple brief explanation,

Stabilize current and voltage - to maintain the flow of a current and voltage,

Rectifier - disallow unwanted current or voltage and purify it,

Converter - converts from AC voltage to DC voltage.

Light Emitting Diode

It is also a diode that can produce light. its like a light bulb.

A light-emitting diode (LED) is a semiconductor light source. LEDs are used as indicator lamps in many devices, and are increasingly used for lighting.

It also have Anode and Cathode terminal leads.

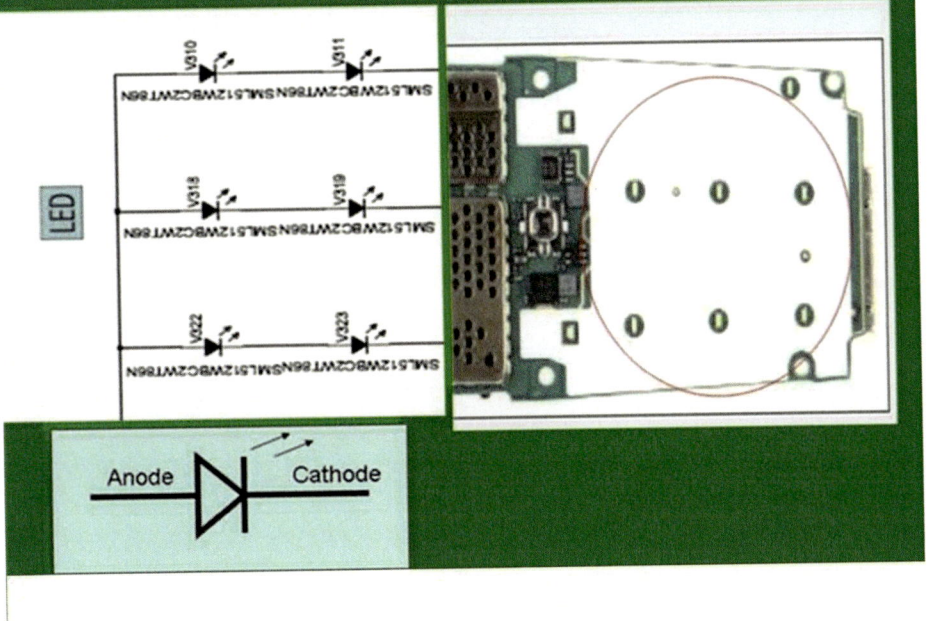

LED Symbol on Schematic Diagram and a Layout on how it is Mounted on a PCB Board.

Anode ▷◁ Cathode

The LED is based on the semiconductor diode. When a diode is forward biased (switched on), electrons are able to recombine with holes within the device, releasing energy in the form of photons. This effect is called electroluminescence and the color of the light (corresponding to the energy of the photon) is determined by the energy gap of the semiconductor.

PhotoDiode Photo Cell

A photodiode is a type of photodetector capable of converting light into either current or voltage, depending upon the mode of operation.

Meaning it has the ability to convert light energy into a voltage or current.

In mobile phone circuit it is being used as a sensor for a certain application of the device like for example, it switch the Camera Flash off when during daytime or when it detects that there is a light source on that certain area.

Photo Diode is widely used in a solar panels to produce free power energy from the sun light.

157

Photodiodes are similar to regular semiconductor diodes except that they may be either exposed (to detect vacuum UV or X-rays) or packaged with a window or optical fiber connection to allow light to reach the sensitive part of the device.

How to Identify Coil Symbols and Layout

Identifying Coil Symbols and Layout on Schematic Diagram.

The symbol of a coil (inductor) is just like a wave lines which emphasized that there is a winding component on that circuit which means that the coil is connected in there. In cellphone circuit many coil is being used in B+ voltage filtering to avoid saturated voltage and current.
coils are easy to identify in an schematic diagram for they are form into a wave line. It is labeled with

letter **"L"** which means Inductance.

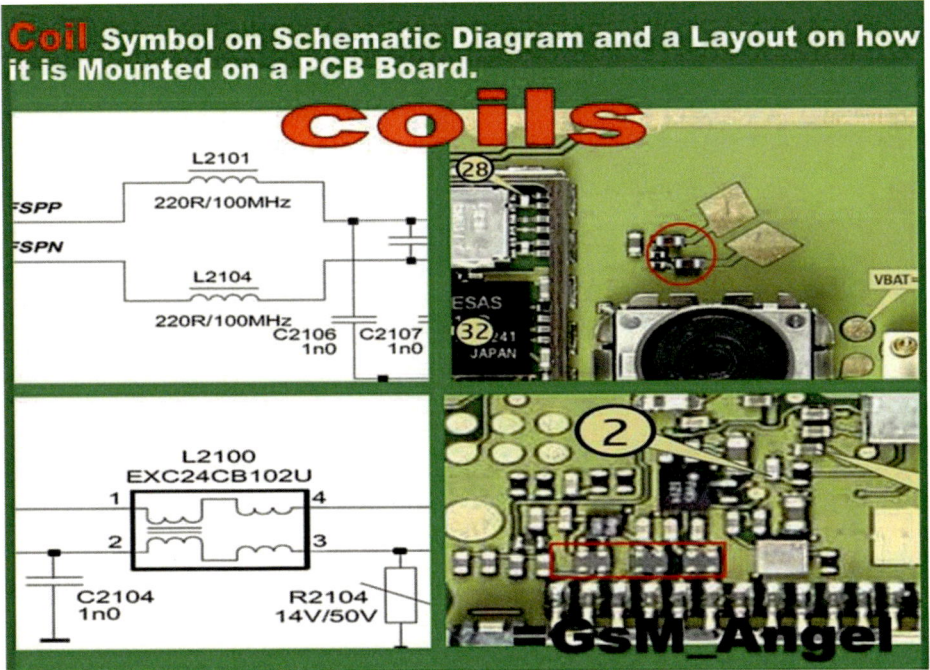

Coil Symbol on Schematic Diagram and a Layout on how it is Mounted on a PCB Board.

In cellphone circuit coils are also prone to be easily damaged like when it is being used in B+ line filtering. It will be blown out or end up busted if some short circuit occurs.

How to Identify Integrated Circuit Symbols and Layout

Identifying Integrated Circuit Symbols and Layout

Integrated circuits, also called "chips", are electronic circuits where all the components (transistors, diodes, resistors and capacitors) has been manufactured in the surface of a thin substrate of semiconductor material.

Integrated circuit is designed to save extra space on modern electronics.

In electronics, an integrated circuit (also known as IC, microcircuit, microchip, silicon chip, or chip) is a miniaturized electronic circuit (consisting mainly of semiconductor devices, as well as passive components) that has been manufactured in the surface of a thin substrate of semiconductor material. Integrated circuits are used in almost all electronic equipment in use today and have revolutionized the world of electronics.

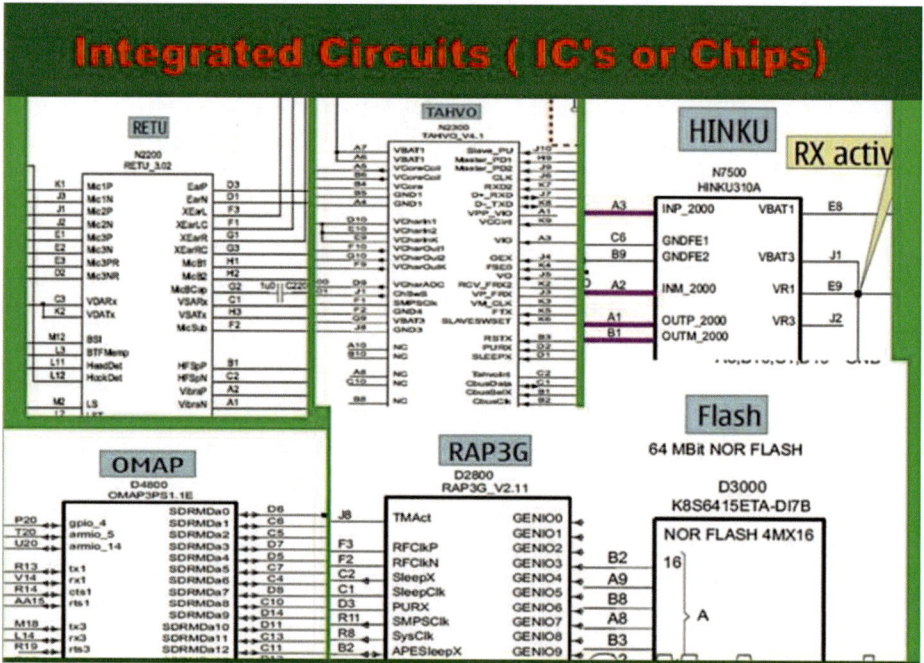

In mobile phones it is packed with each desired certain applications purpose like Power Management, Baseband Processor, Application Processor , Memory Storage, Audio Codecs, Bluetooth and Wi-Fi Ciruits.

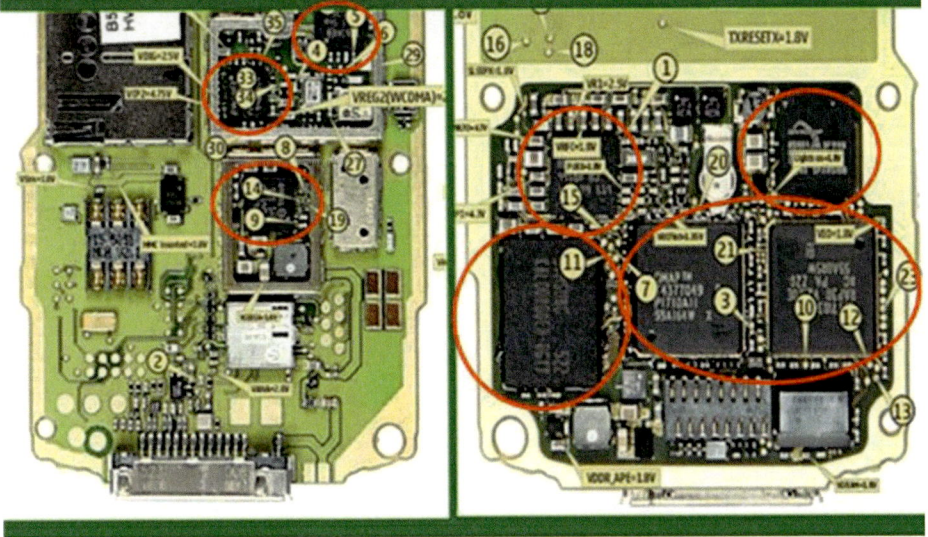

Some large pack chips composed of many circuits and certain application both in-place in one packaging. IC Chips are very delicate to handle with and troubleshoot if found faulty, it needs a little bit deep knowledge and understanding on how that chips works on a particular circuit. Experience is the best tool to handle with it.

How to Identify DC to DC Voltage Drivers, Regulators and Converters Symbols and Layout

Identifying DC to DC Voltage Drivers, Regulators and Converters Symbols and Layout

DC to DC Regulators and Converters are packed in a tiny BGA (ball grid array) chips.
It used to convert, regulate and drives a certain amount of current-voltage.
It has the ability to stabilize, reduce or step up a voltage that feeds towards it.

in mobile phones it has a digital signal that been able to switch it on and off.

like for example it switch the LED lamp that used to light up the Display Screen while the cellphone is in used status and turn it off when the cellphone is not in use or at the sleep mode.

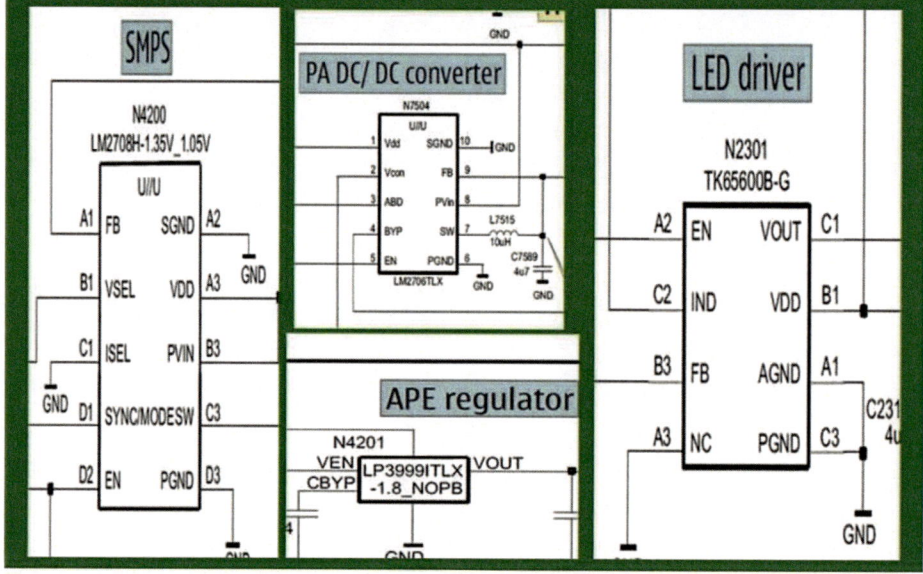

DC Voltage Regulator, Drivers and Converters

SMPS

N4200
LM2708H-1.35V_1.05V

U1/U

A1	FB	SGND	A2
B1	VSEL	VDD	A3
C1	ISEL	PVIN	B3
D1	SYNC/MODESW		C3
D2	EN	PGND	D3

GND

GND

PA DC/ DC converter

GND

N7504
U1/U

1	Vdd	SGND	10	GND
2	Vcon	FB	9
3	ABD	PVin	8
4	BYP	SW	7
5	EN	PGND	6

LM2706TLX

L7515
10uH
C7589
4u7
GND
GND

APE regulator

N4201
VEN
CBYP
LP3999ITLX
-1.8_NOPB
VOUT

GND

LED driver

N2301
TK65600B-G

A2	EN	VOUT	C1
C2	IND	VDD	B1
B3	FB	AGND	A1
A3	NC	PGND	C3

C231
4u

GND

There are various kind and designed of these said components which according to each every purpose to the circuit. Sizes and bumps leads also have may differ with each other.

Layout of DC Converters and Regulators

This chips may also damaged cause by a corrosive element or if a short circuit occurs.

How to Identify EMI-ESD Symbols and Layout

Identifying EMI-ESD Symbols and Layout on schematic diagram and PCB board

EMI-Electromagnetic Interference and **ESD-Electrostatic Discharge** is pack in tiny chips called by many technician as Crystal IC for it glows like a crystal glass.

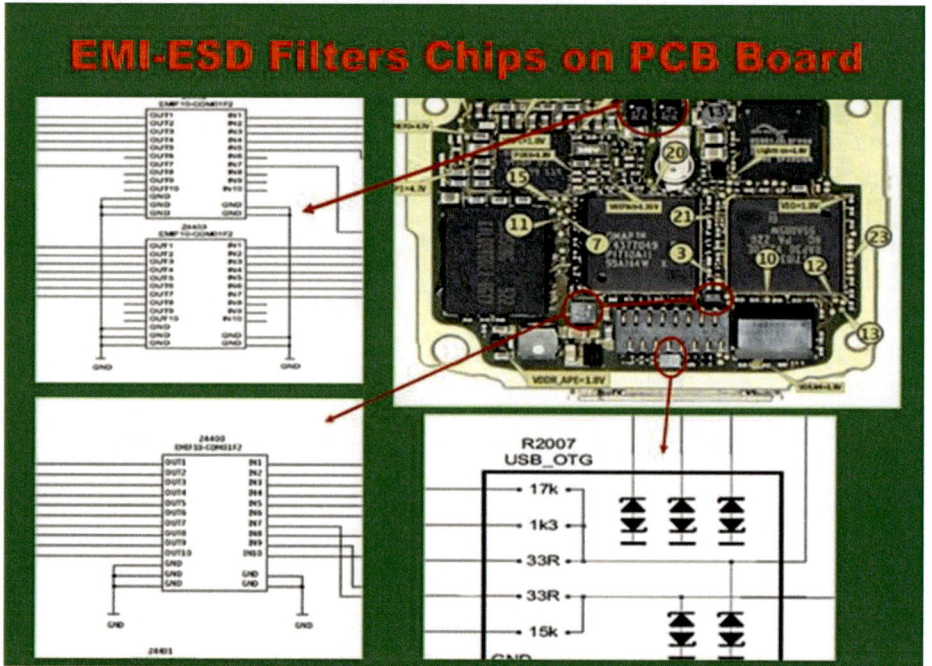

EMI-ESD filter are used to protect a certain circuit from hazardous Electromagnetic Interference and Electrostatic Discharge.

Electromagnetic Interference cause by elecromagnetic machines like like a chainsaw, an electric blower and other things that has high frequency levels.

Electrostatic Discharge (ESD)- a human body is a potential source of electrostatic and can cause damage, especially to semiconductor devices when touching it.

EMI-ESD Filters Chips Symbols

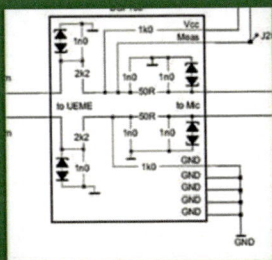

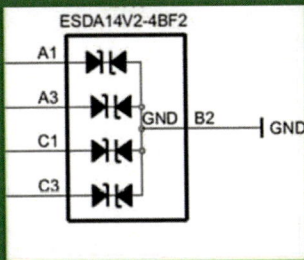

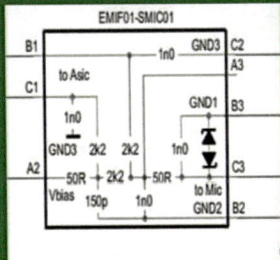

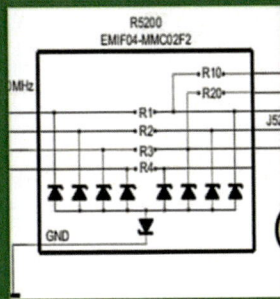

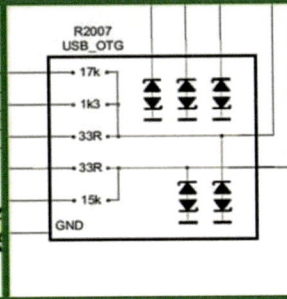

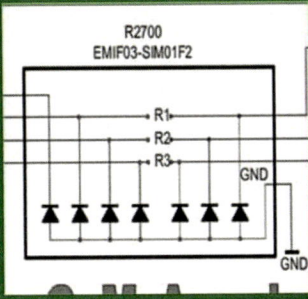

ESDA14V2-4BF2

EMIF01-SMIC01

R5200
EMIF04-MMC02F2

R2007
USB_OTG

R2700
EMIF03-SIM01F2

EMI-ESD Filters can be easily breakdown and busted when those two elements occurs. It often used in Keypads circuit, Display circuit, USB (Universal Serial Bus)Interface circuit, Removable Flash Memory Devices circuit and other Interface that is prone to ESD and EMI hazards.

How to Identify RF Filter Symbols and Layout

Identifying RF Filter Symbols and Layout

RF filters of all types are required in a variety of applications from audio to RF and across the whole spectrum of frequencies. As such RF filters form an important element within a variety of scenarios, enabling the required frequencies to be passed through the circuit, while rejecting those that are not needed.

The ideal filter, whether it is a low pass, high pass, or band pass filter will exhibit no loss within the pass band, i.e. the frequencies below the cut off frequency. Then above this frequency in what is termed the stop band the filter will reject all signals.

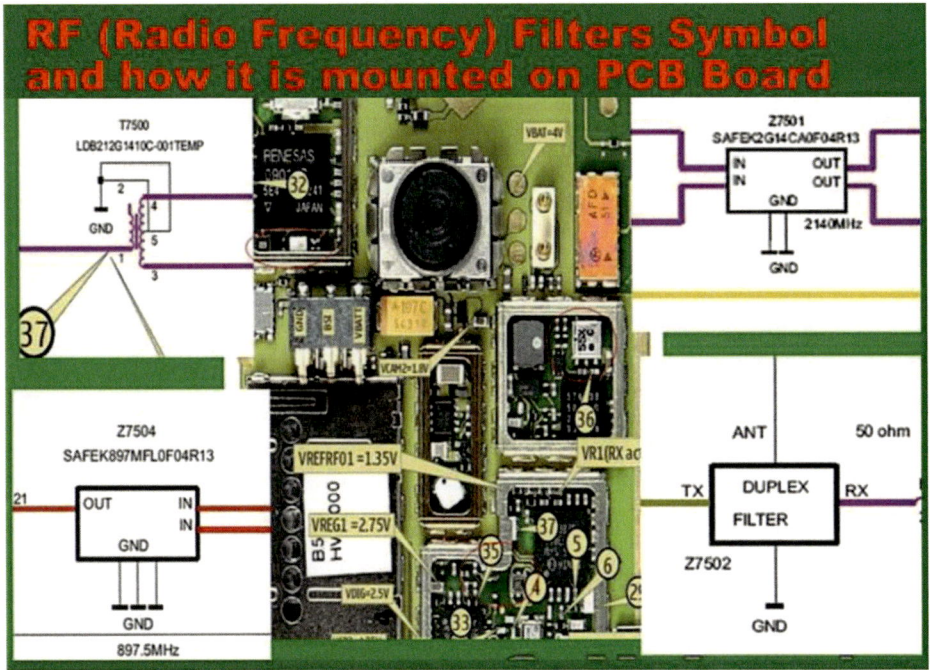

Basic types of RF filter

There are four types of filter that can be defined. Each different type rejects or accepts signals in a different way, and by using the correct type of RF filter it is possible to accept the required signals and reject those that are not wanted.

The four basic types of RF filter are:

* Low pass filter
* High pass filter
* Band pass filter
* Band reject filter

As the names of these types of RF filter indicate, a low pass filter only allows frequencies below what is termed the cut off frequency through. This can also be thought of as a high reject filter as it rejects high frequencies. Similarly a high pass filter only allows signals through above the cut off frequency and rejects those below the cut off frequency. A band pass filter allows frequencies through within a given pass band. Finally the band reject filter rejects signals within a certain band. It can be particularly useful for rejecting a particular unwanted signal or set of signals falling within a given bandwidth.

How to Identify Battery Cell Symbols and Layout

Identifying Battery Cell Symbols and Layout

A back up battery cell or button cell is being used in cellphones circuit to back up the digital clock crystal oscillator. It used to maintain the clock at its real time status.

Its like when removing the battery of the mobile phone wont reset the settings of the digital clock that is being installed on a phone. Some phones without battery back-up like the old ones need to reset again after removing and replacing the battery. Its a big help to a digital circuits such high tech mobile phones circuit.

A battery cell is have two lead terminal which is negative and positive voltage output.

The metal can case of this type of battery is its positive (+) terminal, and the negative (-) terminal is the cap.

The negative is connected to a ground lines of a circuit while the positive is feed to a clock oscillator circuit. It has low power output voltage range from 1.5 volts to 3.5 volts. In mobile phones used about 3.3voltage output.

They are compact and have long life. They are usually a primary single cell with a nominal voltage between 1.5 and 3 volts. Common anode materials are zinc or lithium. Common cathode materials are manganese dioxide, silver oxide, carbon monofluoride, cupric oxide or oxygen from the air. Mercuric oxide batteries were formerly a common battery type but have been withdrawn from marketing due to their mercury content.

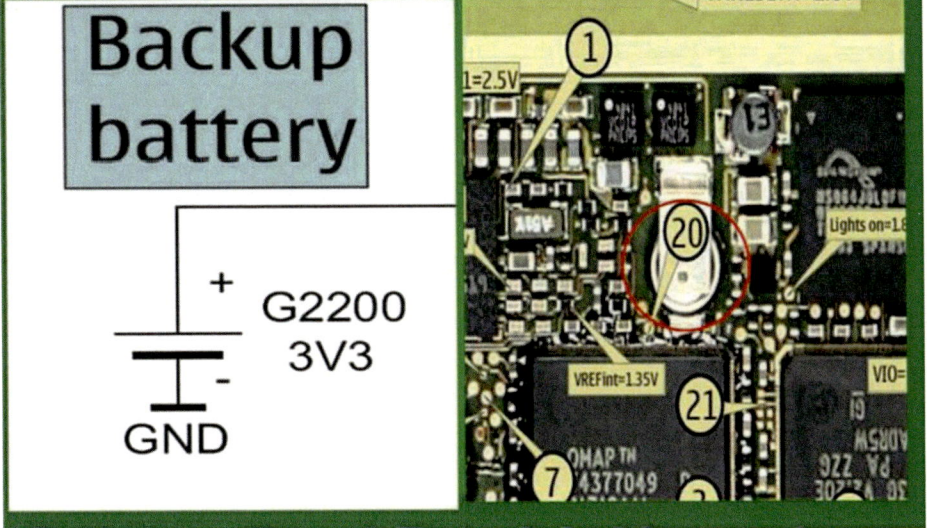

Button Cell Battery Symbol on Schematic Diagram and a Layout on how it is Mounted on a PCB Board.

A back up battery may also damaged when due to degradation, corrosion and losses its voltage when being shorted or by liquids like water;

A damaged battery cell can be easily notice when a leakage occurs, its liquid chemical will flow out and can cause damages to a nearby components.

In a mobile phones you can determine when the back-up battery is weak, when try to set the time of the clock, then power it off and by removing the battery for a while and put it back again, when the clock stayed at its time where you set, it means that back-up battery is still working but, if it ask you to set the clock again it means that the back-up battery is not working.

How to Identify Power Switch , Mouthpiece, Earpiece and Ringtones Speakers User Interface Symbols and Layout

Identifying User Interfaces Components such as Power Switch, Microphone, Earpiece and Ring-tone speakers and Layouts On Schematic Diagram

User Interface Components are those components
such as **power switch, keypads, vibrator**, a **micro phone** such as **mouthpiece, speakers** like **earpiece** and **ring tones speaker**. These components are also important to familiarized with, for these are commonly prone to be easily got damaged. when it comes to hardware troubleshooting, in Nokia service manual or Schematic diagram it is marked for easy guides while some other various mobile phone products was not.

In the symbols below the power switch labeled as power key, and also likewise the keypad component symbols that is a circle with two pointing lines insides labeled as keyboard.

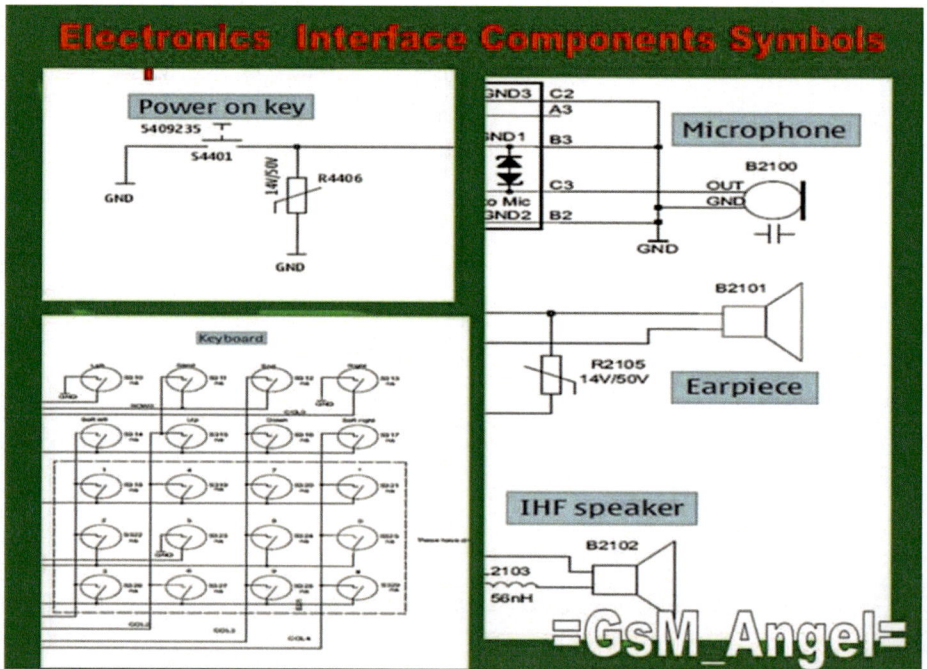

In mobile phones there is one microphone and two micro speakers being used; First is the microphone that receive the voice to transmit,

A cellphone microphones

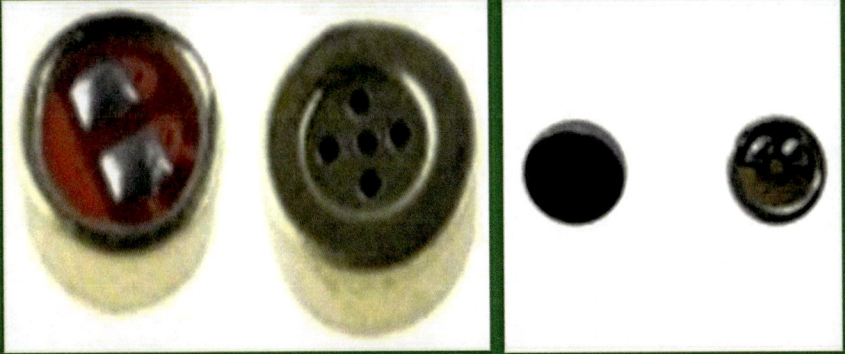

the two micro speakers are examples on the picture below,

A Cellphone Speakers Components

Earpice Speaker

Ringtone Speaker

the first one is for the hearing which is called the earpiece, that is the one that send the voice to hear, the second one is for the ring-tones speaker, it is that send the tones and tell that someone is calling or sending a message. Familiarizing the uses and works of these three micro speakers on a circuit is a big help for troubleshooting.

How to Identify Clock Crystal Oscillator Symbols and Layout

Identifying Clock Crystal Oscillator Symbols and Layout

Oscillator

An electronic component circuit that have the ability create real time clock signal. a vibrating crystal that made by so-called piezoelectric material produce a maintained and sustained frequency such as applied into real time clock like quartz wristwatches.. This one is being used to maintain the clock system in a digital circuit and maintain Radio Frequency transmitters and Receivers.

It labeled sleep clock oscillator or just clock oscillator in schematic diagrams.

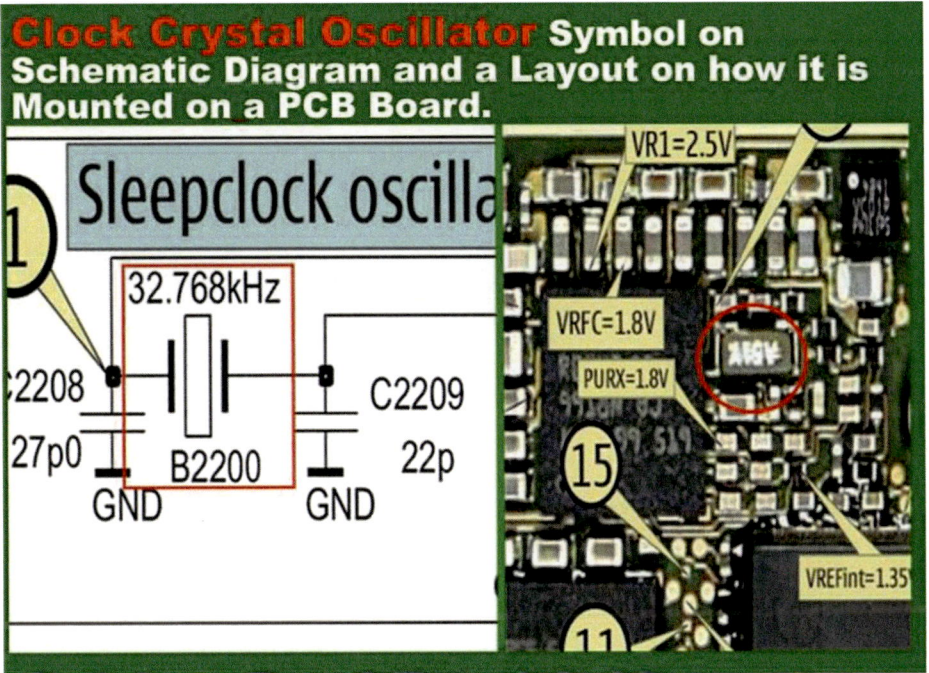

In Cellphones if the clock oscillator is faulty it results on not powering the phone. The phone is dead, because as stated above that oscillator supports on digital radio frequencies circuitry.

How to Identify Fuse Symbol and Layout

Identifying Fuse Symbols and Layout

Fuse

A fuse is the component used to protect from sudden arise of the desired amount of currents and voltages into a certain circuit. The fuse will be blown out if a certain circuit have a very low resistance or shorted. a Fuseo is made by a metal wire that can be easily busted if a high current or voltage will flow on it.

It is labeled letter "F" means a fusible device then a product code or number.

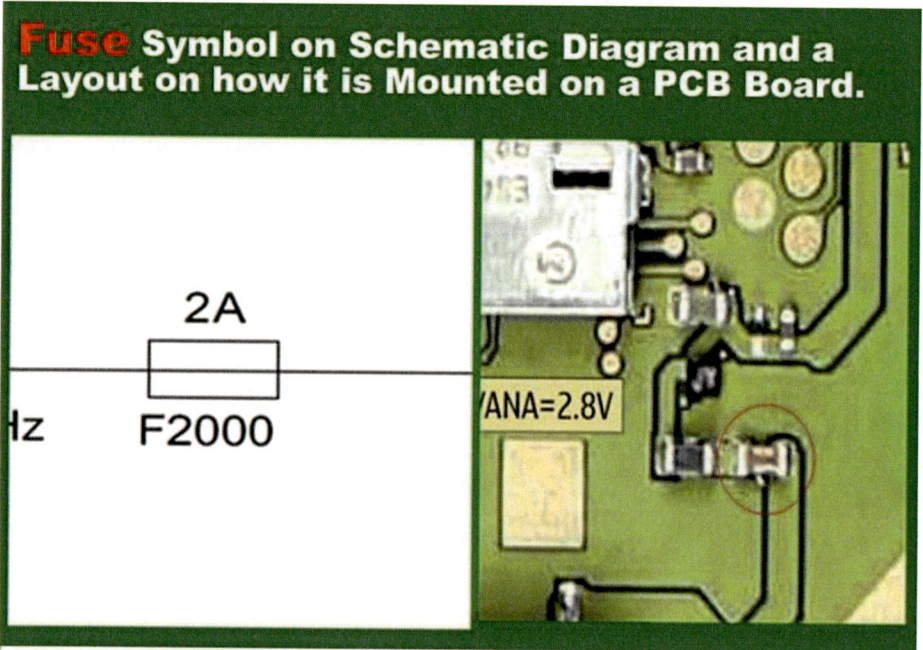

Fuse Symbol on Schematic Diagram and a Layout on how it is Mounted on a PCB Board.

A fuse is often used in a charging circuit of any mobile phones. The phone will indicate no charging reaction if a fuse is already blown.

How to Find Component Parts on PCB Board

A certain components parts is easy to find with an aide of schematic diagrams. In Nokia Phones finding it was been so easy for they provide a complete and accurate component data on their Schematic Diagrams. While other various mobile phone don't have. Some cellphone technicians find it hard to fix some of mobile phone products for they don't provide schematic diagrams to be available, but many experts and masters can do the job even without schematic diagrams. Experts can rely on their deep knowledge on electronics components and circuits, many of them where electronic engineers and also many of them where professionally skilled by experience and mastered for years. You can be one of them if you follow their instinct but before that they all started from scratch. We are all start from scratch.

Now, let's take up a very simple method on how to find certain electronic component's location where it is being mounted on a particular PCB Board layouts.
Here's an example of Nokia N70 schematic diagram, **Download it here** if you haven't a copy yet, and make sure you have **Adobe Reader** installed on your computer to be able to open it.
If you already have a copy of this schematic diagram, open it and scroll it down to the bottom page.
In the bottom page which is the last page you may found this **Component Finder Page**.

see picture below:

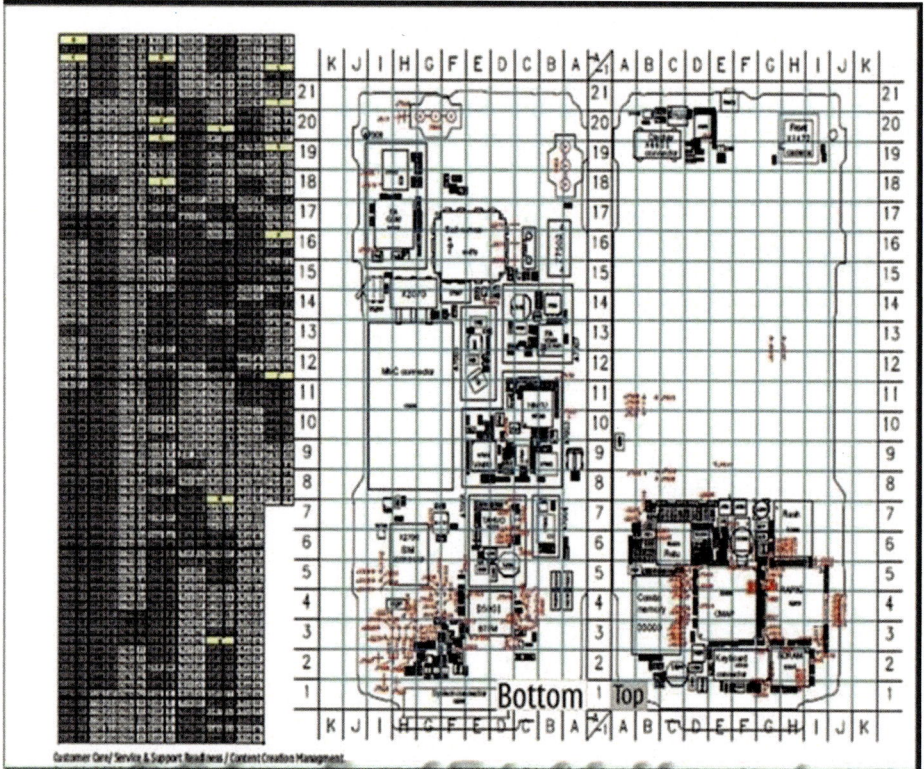

On the right side you may find the table of components which is listed in codes like for example, Resistors starts with letter "R" then "mounting code" . next to it on the left is the "**pattern codes**" which is means the spot point which is scaled by letters and numbers on the PC Board,

This are the certain component or parts number				This are the pattern numbers in a certain area of which where is that particular parts or component is located or mounted.											
B		C2235	D6	C7508	B10	C7617	F3	J3108	H3	J7544	D5	R1491	E12	R7558	F3
B2200	D6	C2237	E7	C7509	C11	C7618	F3	J3109	H3	J7545	E7	R2000	F3	R7559	G2
C		C2240	B2	C7512	G19	D		J3110	I5	J7546	E6	R2001	F3	R7560	A17
C1470	D15	C2241	G3	C7513	B11	D2800	H4	J3111	H3	J7547	D3	R2002	G3	S	
C1471	F18	C2242	E5	C7514	G19	D3000	H7	J3112	H3	J7548	F4	R2003	G3	S4401	E21
C1472	F6	C2243	I3	C7515	C9	D3001	H2	J3113	G3	J7549	C4	R2004	G3	S5200	I14
C1473	G7	C2244	G1	C7516	C9	D4800	E4	J3114	H3	J7550	E3	R2005	H3	S5202	A9
C1476	I19	C2300	D5	C7518	E9	D5000	B4	J3115	G5	J7551	D3	R2006	G2	T	
C1477	G19	C2301	D6	C7520	C11	D5001	D4	J3116	H6	J7553	F4	R2007	F1	T7500	D11
C1478	I19	C2302	D5	C7522	C9	F		J3117	G6	J7554	H20	R2009	G1	T7501	B10
C1479	E14	C2303	D7	C7523	G18	F2000	C2	J3118	G5	L		R2010	F1	T7502	H16
C1480	D14	C2304	C6	C7524	B9	G		J4800	D3	L1473	E11	R2011	G1	T7503	B7
C1481	D20	C2307	E7	C7525	G18	G2200	F6	J4802	D3	L1474	E7	R2070	G14	V	
C1482	D20	C2309	E5	C7527	B10	G7500	B9	J4803	D3	L1479	C15	R2071	E6	V1470	F14
C1483	E6	C2312	E7	C7528	B10	G7501	C9	J4805	D3	L1480	C15	R2100	F2	V1471	E13
C1484	E12	C2313	E7	C7529	D9	G7502	B7	J4806	D3	L2000	C2	R2101	E2	V1472	E12
C1485	E13	C2314	G7	C7530	B11	J		J4807	D3	L2001	F2	R2104	E19	V2000	C3
C1486	E13	C2315	G6	C7531	C10	J1471	G7	J4808	D3	L2002	G2	R2105	E19	V2300	C7
C1487	C15	C2316	C6	C7532	B11	J1472	F6	J4811	D7	L2003	G2	R2106	F18	V4400	B20
C1488	C15	C2700	H7	C7533	C8	J1473	E14	J4812	G5	L2100	E19	R2107	F18	V7500	C14

On the right side of the page is the layout of all of components with respective **codes** mark on it. Each component mounted in horizontal and vertical positions.

This is the layout of every parts or components mounted on a PCB BOARD.

Each parts or components was written into particular codes for an ease of locating it.

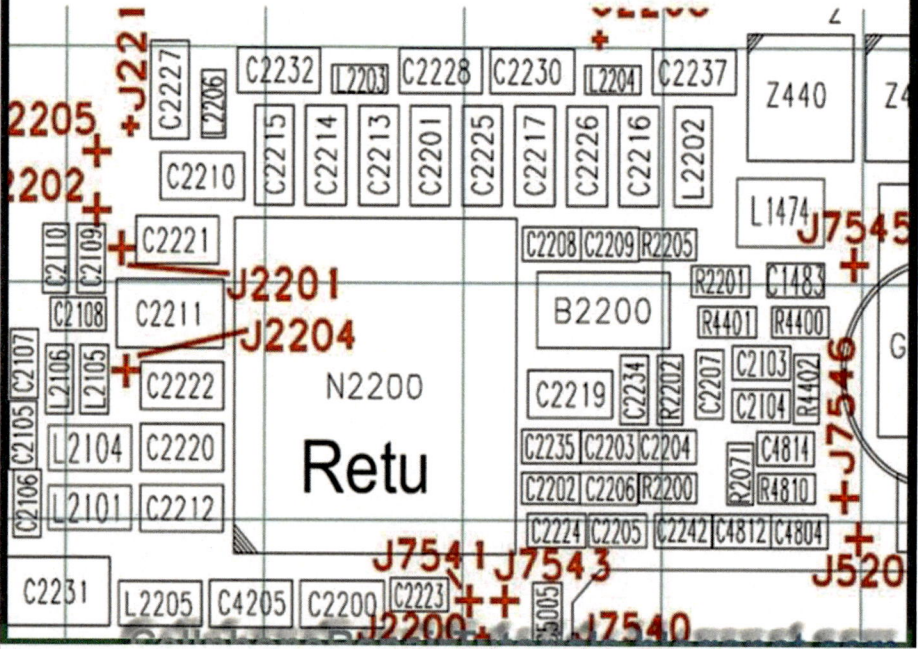

In both sides on the PCB layout is being scaled by letters and numbers, this is were the **pattern codes** from the first picture above being produce by combining the letter and number to make the mapping spot point.

The **spot point** of where these letter and number meets across each other, is the exact location where that certain component is being mounted.

The layout of the whole PCB BOARD which scaled and coded with letters and numbers to wrap a certain parts or components location in a particular circuit areas....

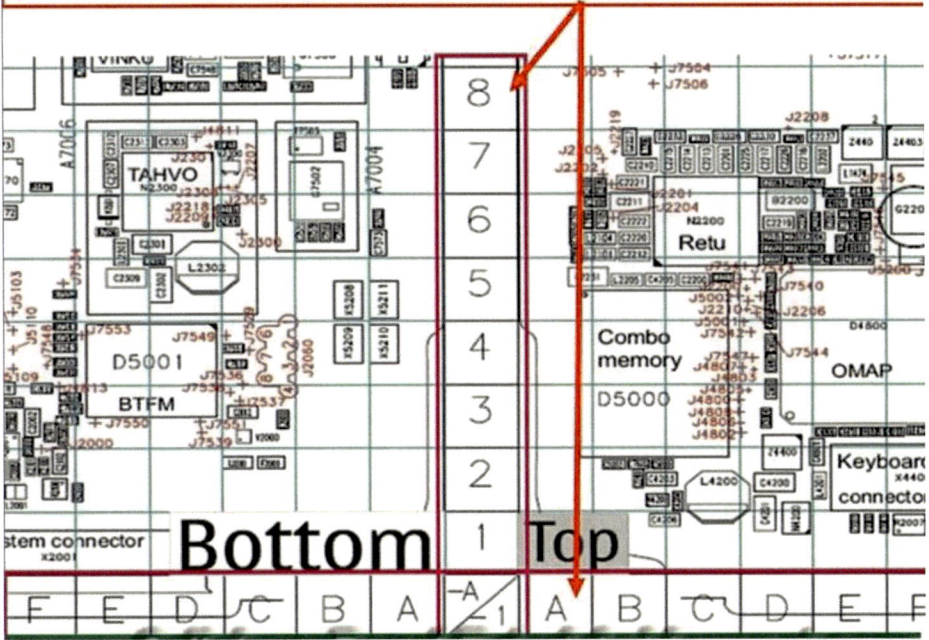

Now let's take a little bit exercise on how to use this methods..

Okay, assuming that we are looking for a certain components on a PCB board.

Let say that we are going to find the 2n2 valued capacitor on RF Section for that phone is having a problem of network signal.

now scroll up the page to RF Section which is on page 9 and find these two 2n2 (2.2nanofarad) valued capacitor *see guide picture below;* Just remember and get the **Mounting Code** for it is the code were going to use as a guide to to the component finder table of components.

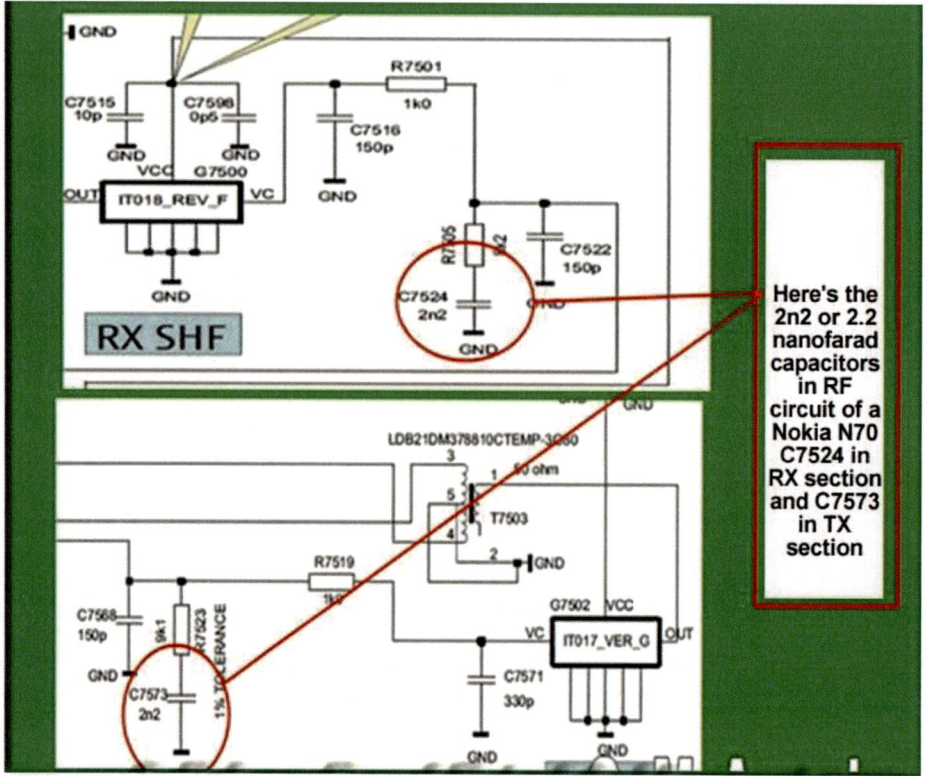

RX SHF

Here's the 2n2 or 2.2 nanofarad capacitors in RF circuit of a Nokia N70 C7524 in RX section and C7573 in TX section

Then after finding it scroll back to the Component Finder page Table of components, then find it on the lists of the components codes like "C7524 is on B9" and "C7573 is on A6"

1473	G7	C2244 G1	C7516 C9	D4800 E4	J3114 H3	J7550 E3	R2005 H3	S5202 A9
1476	I19	C2300 D5	C7518 E9	D5000 B4	J3115 G5	J7551 D3	R2006 G2	T
1477	G19	C2301 D6	C7520 C11	D5001 D4	J3116 H6	J7553 F4	R2007 F1	T7500 D11
1478	I19	C2302 D5	C7522 C9	F	J3117 G6	J7554 H20	R2009 G1	T7501 B10
1479	E14	C2303 D7	C7523 G18	F2000 C2	J3118 G5	J	R2010	T7502 H16
1480	D14	C2304 C6	C7524 B9	G	J4800 D3	L1473 E11	R2011 G1	T7503 B7
1481	D20	C2307 E7	C7525 G18	G2200 F6	J4802 D3	L1474 E7	R2070 G14	X
1482	D20	C2309 E5	C7527 B10	G7500 B3	J4803 D3	L1479 C15	R2071 E6	V1470 F14
1483	E6	C2312 E7	C7528 B10	G7501 C9	J4805 D3	L1480 C15	R2100 F2	V1471 E13
1484	E12	C2313 E7	C7529 D9	G7502 B7	J4806 D5	L2000 C2	R2101 E2	V1472 E12
1485	E13	C2314 G7	C7530 B11	J	J4807 D3	L2001 F2	R2104 E19	V2000 C3
1486	E13	C2315 G6	C7531 C10	J1471 G7	J4808 D3	L2002 G2	R2105 E19	V2300 C7
1487	C15	C2316 C6	C7532 B11	J1472 F6	J4811 D7	L2003 G2	R2106 F18	V4400 B20
1488	C15	C2700 H7	C7533 C8	J1473 E14	J4812 G5	L2100 E19	R2107 F16	V7500 C14
2103	E6	C3005 I1	C7567 E10	J2212 I3	J5102 F5	L7503 E10	R4810 E6	Z2001 F1
2104	E6	C3006 I2	C7568 E8	J2213 I3	J5105 G4	L7504 H19	R5100 G5	Z2003 E1
2105	A6	C3007 H1	C7569 G17	J2214 I3	J5106 H3	L7506 H18	R5200 I7	Z4400 D2
2106	A6	C3008 I2	C7570 E9	J2215 I3	J5107 H3	L7510 E10	R5204 I15	Z4401 G3
2107	A6	C4200 D2	C7571 B6	J2218 D6	J5108 F4	L7511 D10	R7501 C9	Z4402 E7
2108	B6	C4201 D1	C7573 A6	J2219 B7	J5109 F4	L7512 D10	R7503 C11	Z4403 F7
2109	B7	C4203 B2	C7575 E10	J2220 I3	J5110 F4	L7514 B13	R7504 C11	Z7500 F14
2110	A7	C4204 C2	C7577 E10	J2221 I4	J513 H20	L7515 C14	R7505 C9	Z7501 C10
2200	C5	C4205 B5	C7579 A13	J2300 C6	J5200 E5	L7516 G16	R7506 G17	Z7502 B16

The code of 2n2 capacitors in TX and RX circuits C7524 and C7573

The location in the pattern were it is being mounted on the part of the PCB Board the first one is in B9 and then the other one is in A6

the next thing again you have to do is to remember and get that code then proceed to the Component Layouts. and scale the spot point of "letter B and 9" then letter "A and 6" on the scaled on the opposite sides.

See picture below

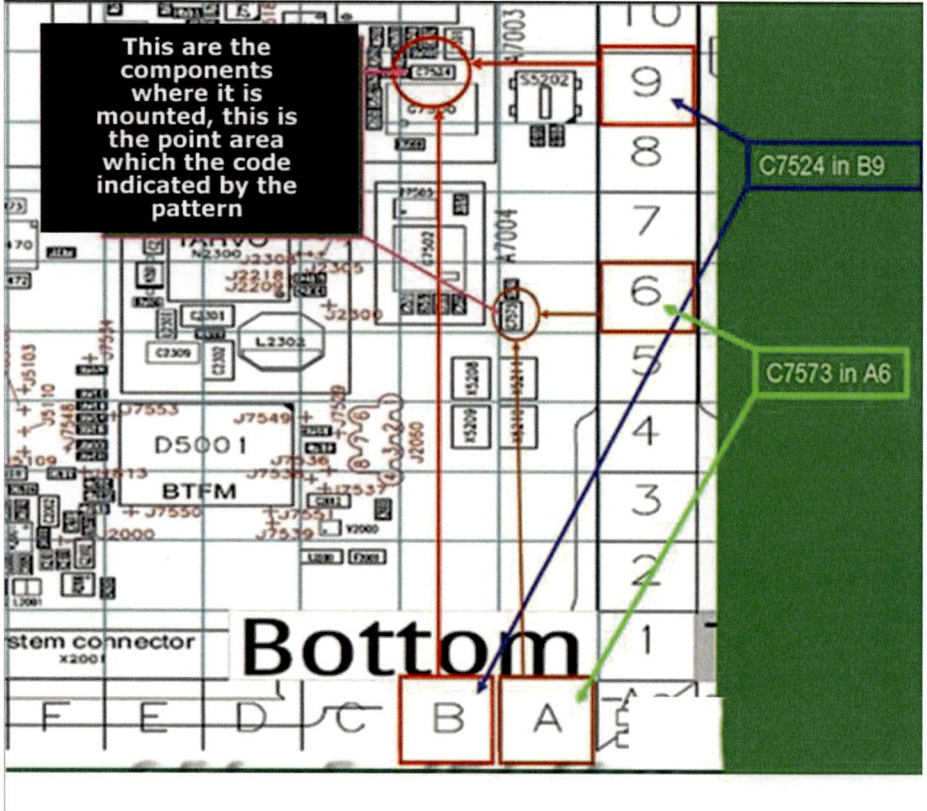

This are the components where it is mounted, this is the point area which the code indicated by the pattern

C7524 in B9

C7573 in A6

Bottom

The last part is to scroll it up on the whole component layout on the upper page 10 or on your PC board then spot and mark that component where it is being mounted.

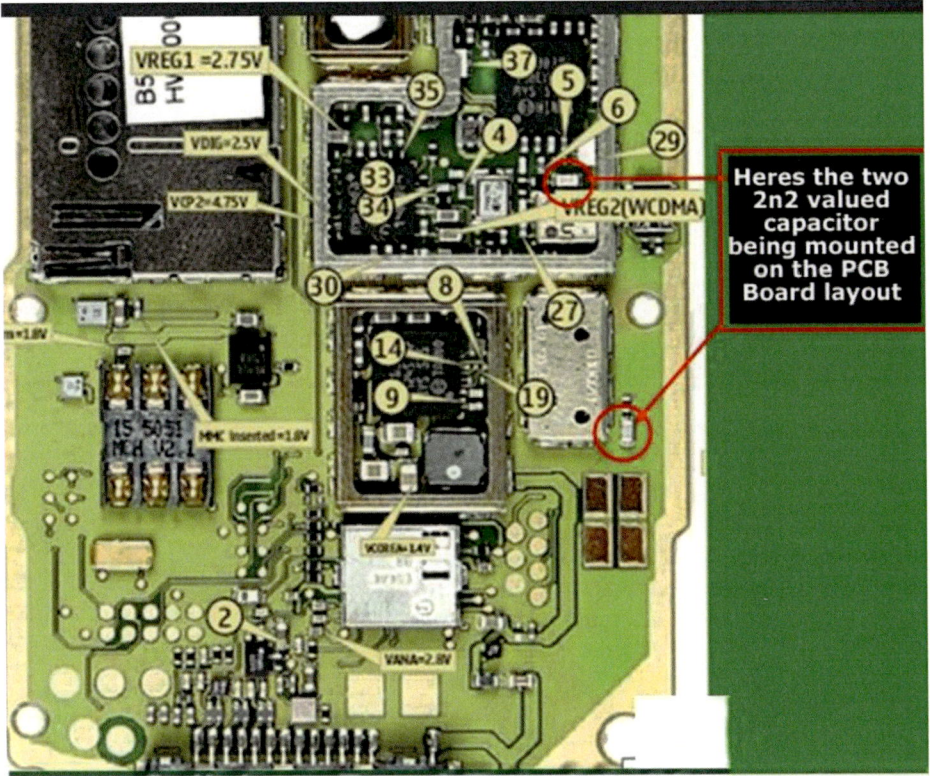

Heres the two
2n2 valued
capacitor
being mounted
on the PCB
Board layout

There you go you just found it! congratulation!

Practice it more often, so that you can be familiarize on each component or parts for that certain product. The more often you do it, the more chances you will mastered it. sooner, you can work it alone without even using the schematic diagram anymore.

PART 06

How To Solder SMD Components Manually by Hand

Proper Soldering and De-soldering Methods and Techniques on Surface Mount Components

Soldering is the process of using a metal alloy with a low melting temperature (solder) to Fuse the the electrical contacts of a component to the pads of a circuit board. Proper soldering maximizes the strength and conductivity of the connection. Poor soldering can result in weak connections, higher resistance that causes heat buildup at the connection, and possible failure of the component.

The type of components and the pads to which they will be attached dictate the appropriate soldering method. The correct amount and duration of heat to be applied is a function of the heat transfer characteristics of the component, the circuit board, the solder pads, the solder and flux, and the environment, in which the soldering takes place. For this reason, effective soldering requires reasonably controlled. Some experimentation is usually required to determine the optimal conditions for each application.

General Soldering Guides
All soldering applications require the following considerations:
* **Preparation** - Clean connections are essential to soldering. Clean connection maximize the ability of the solder to adhere uniformly to the joint surfaces ((welting).
* **Soldering Method** - The component type and size and your specific application determine the soldering method.
* **Materials Selection** - The component contacts, circuit board pads, solder, and flux materials must be compatible with soldering method.
* **Maximum Temperature** - The soldering materials and method determine the temperature profile. All components must be able to withstand the maximum exposure temperature of the soldering operation for specified time and duration.

Manual (Hand) Soldering Technique

While the amount of solder, and the amount and duration of heat to be applied are application-specific, the following general hand-soldering guidelines will lead to consistent and reliable solder connections. A hot air gun is proffered for even heat application and control. The following techniques applies to hand soldering of surface mount components using solder wires and soldering iron.

Preparation

Before beginning to the soldering process, identify the solder composition
and flux type. The solder type dictates the appropriate temperature of the soldering iron tips. Use small diameter wire solder for soldering small SMT components.

Select an appropriate size tip before heating the soldering iron for a fine work result. Clean the tip of any oxidation or contamination. Place a sponge soaked in cold water, nearby for frequent tip cleaning between soldering operations.

Clean the electronic component's contact/leads and the circuit board pads of any contamination or residue.

Hot Air Gun and Soldering Iron Temperature Settings

Hot air temperature tends to be variable when working on any SMD components various Mobile Phones Products used different kinds of solders, check the manufacturer recommendations for specific solder types. The solder manufacturer may only provide the melting temperature range, so you may have to experiment to determine the appropriate temperature.

The amount temperature on Hot Air gun commonly setting is between 250-350 degrees Celsius.
While soldering iron is between 200 to 280 degree Celsius.

This procedure covers the general guidelines for soldering surface
mount chip components. The following surface mount chip
components are covered by this procedure. While all of these components are different, the techniques for soldering are relatively similar

Chip Resistors

The component body of chip resistors is made out of alumna; an extremely hard, white colored material. The resistive material is normally located on the top. Chip resistors are usually mounted with the resistive element facing upwards to help dissipate heat.

Ceramic Capacitors

These components are constructed from several layers of ceramic
with internal metallized layers. Because metal heats up much faster than ceramic, ceramic capacitors need to be heated slowly to avoid internal separations between the ceramic and the metal layers. Internal damage will not generally be visible, since any cracks will be inside the ceramic body of the component.

NOTE

Avoid rapid heating of ceramic chip capacitors during soldering
operations.

Plastic Body

Another style of chip component has a molded plastic body that
protects the internal circuitry. There are a number of different types
of components that share this type of exterior package. The termination styles for plastic chip
component packages vary considerably.

MELF

MELF - Metal Electrode Face cylindrical components. These may be capacitors, resistors, and diodes. It
can be hard to tell them apart - since there is no universal coloring or component designators printed on
the component bodies.

Replacing SMD Component on Printed Circuit Board

De-soldering and Soldering Hand Method

TOOLS & MATERIALS

Cleaner
Flux
Microscope or
Magnifying Glass lamp
Solder
Soldering Iron with Tips
Rework Station Hot Air
Wipes
PROCEDURES TO REMOVE SMD COMPONENT
Add liquid flux to both terminal pad.

Apply
Flux

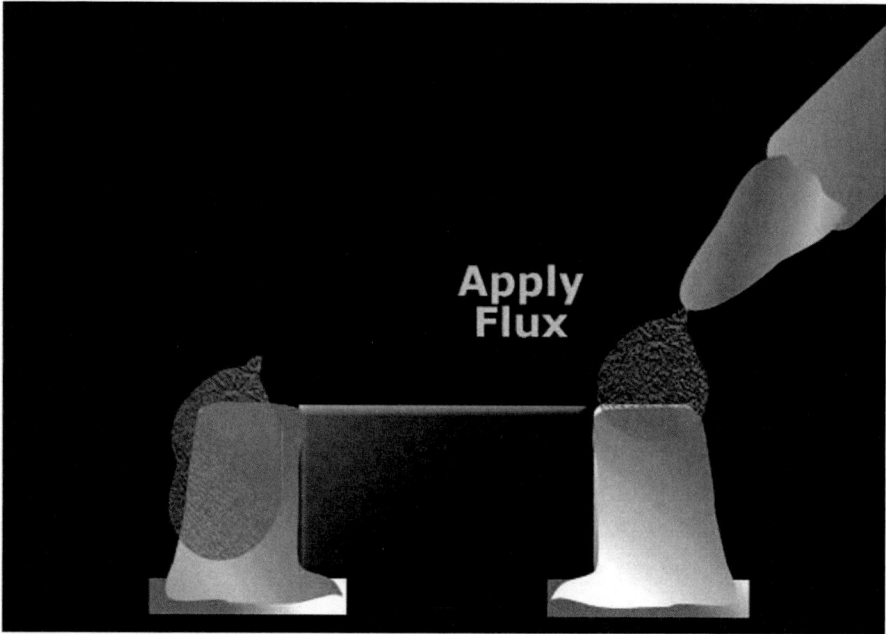

Apply Desired Amount of heat on both sides of the leads.

Apply
Heat

Melted
solder

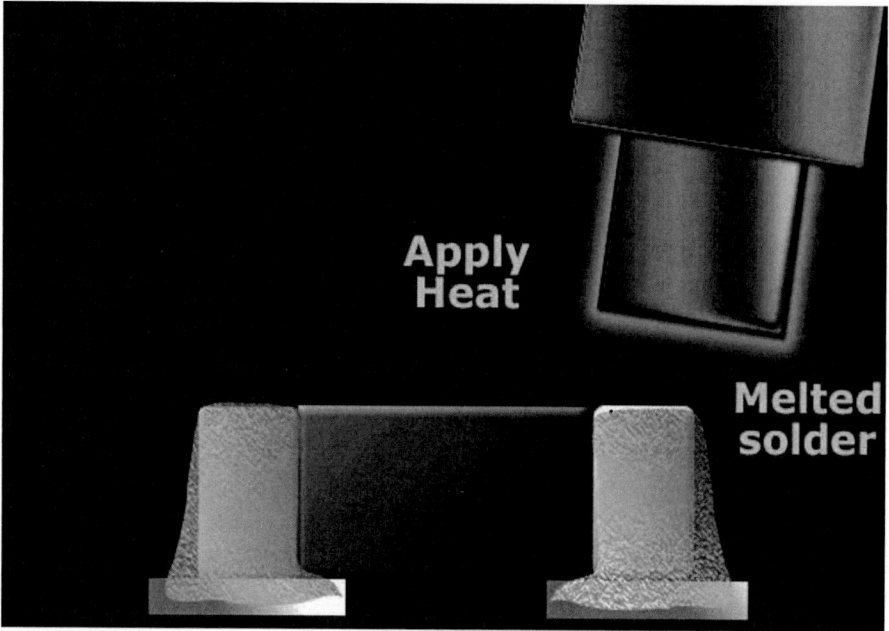

Use a Tweezer to hold the component and observed until the solder joint is melted.

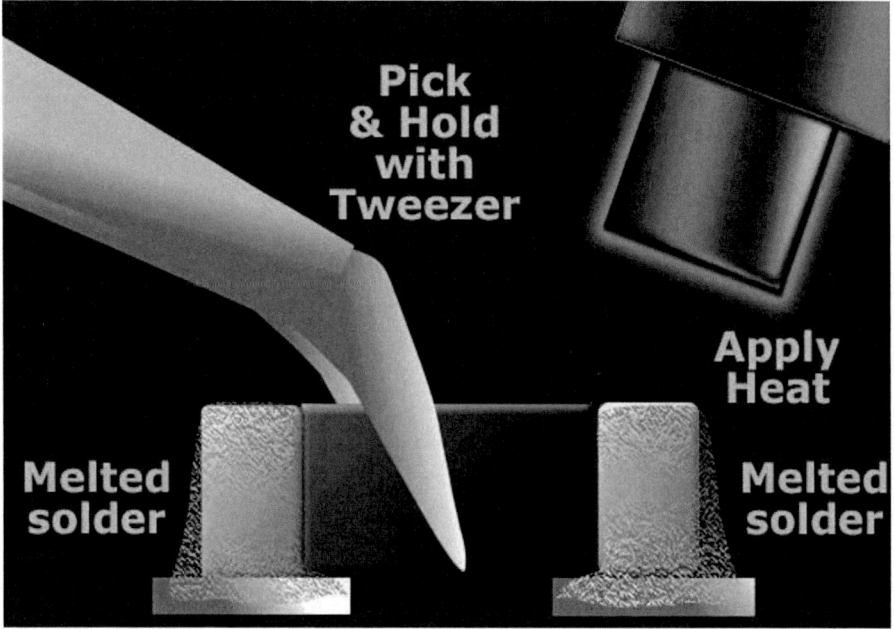

Slowly pull in upward direction, when solders are already melted. do not pull upward forcibly when the solder is not melted yet. You might end up lifted the the terminal surface pads.

Pull
Upward

Remove
upward

PROCEDURE TO REPLACE SMD COMPONENT

Clean the surface terminal pads with cleaning kits.
Removed remaining old solders by using solder wick

Clean the solder terminal with wick until all remaining solder removed

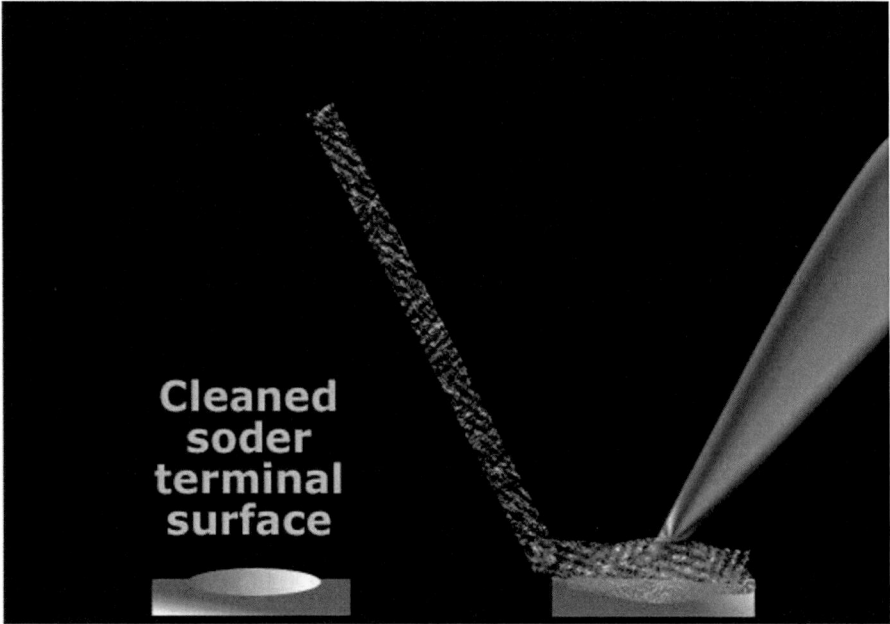

Cleaned
soder
terminal
surface

When the pads is cleaned, Apply adequate amount of flux into the pads.

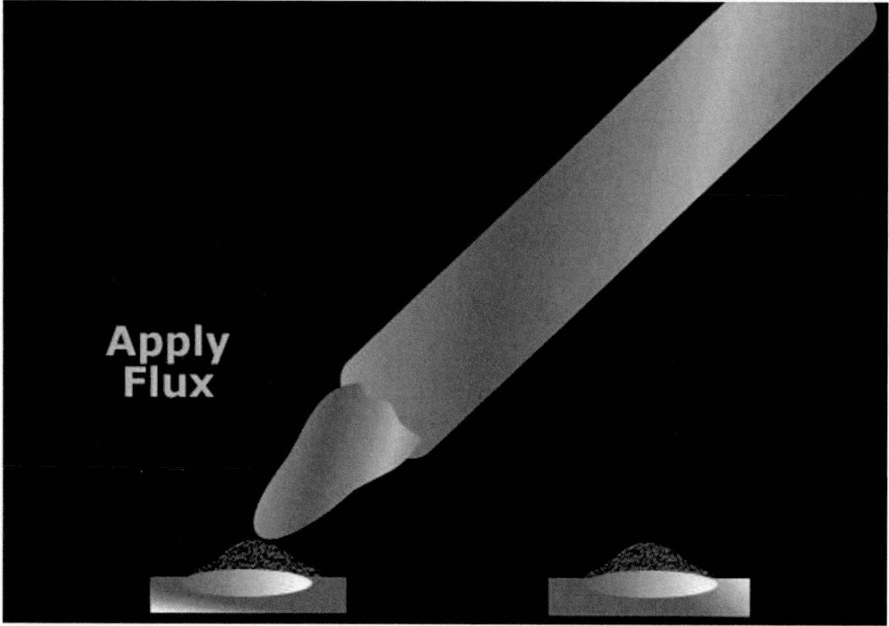

Apply Flux

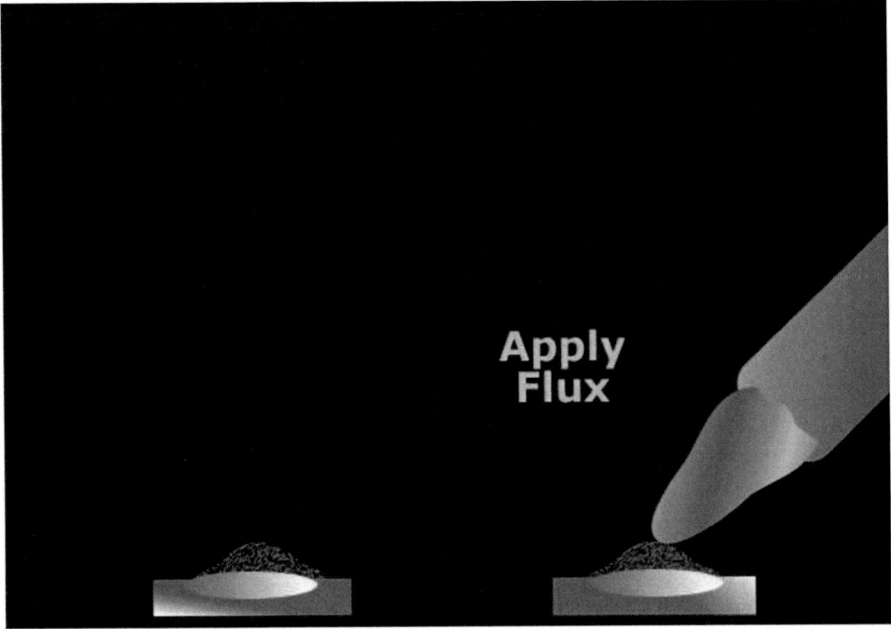

Apply
Flux

Then apply both pads with fresh solder with desired heat controlled soldering iron.

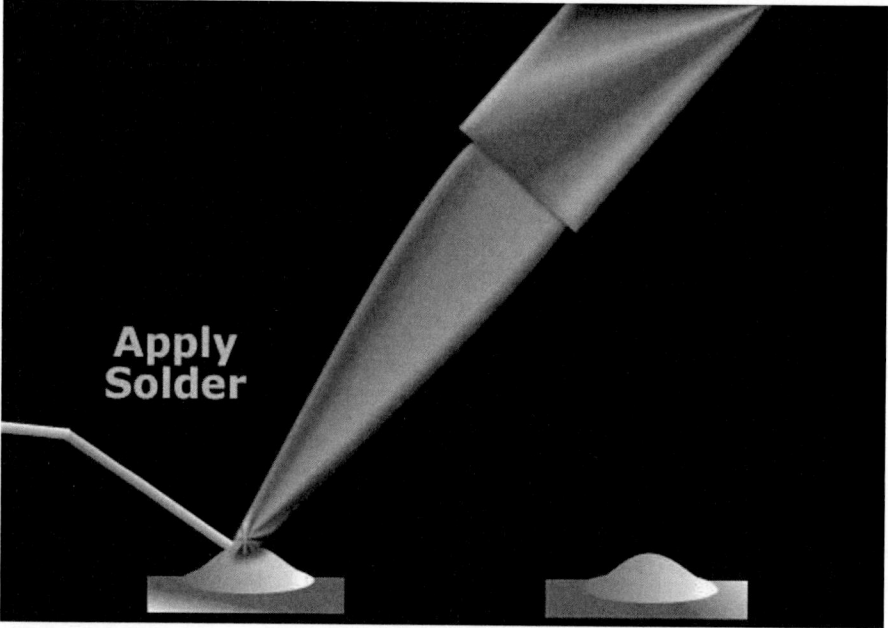

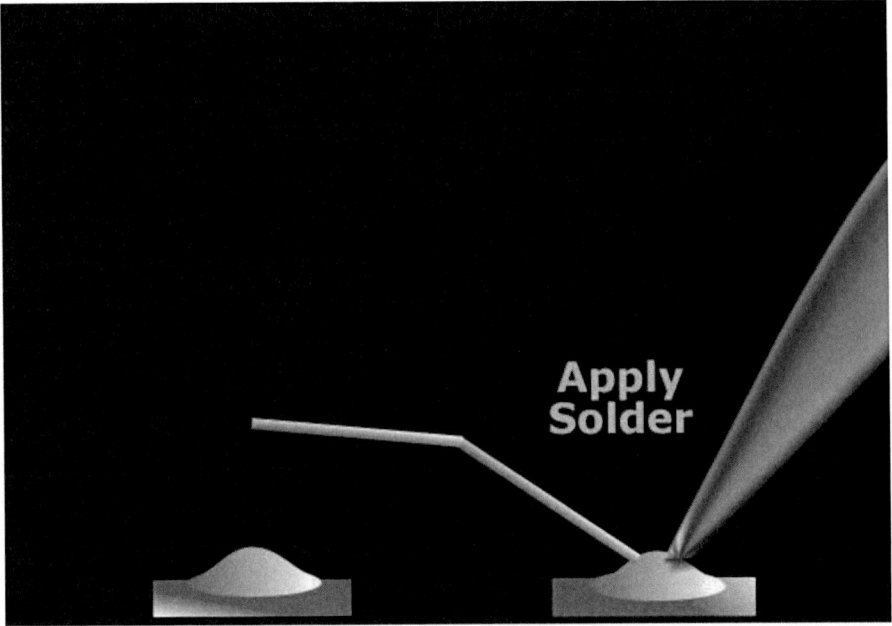

Apply Solder

Place the component in position and hold it steady with a tweezers so that the hot air won't push the component out of alignment.

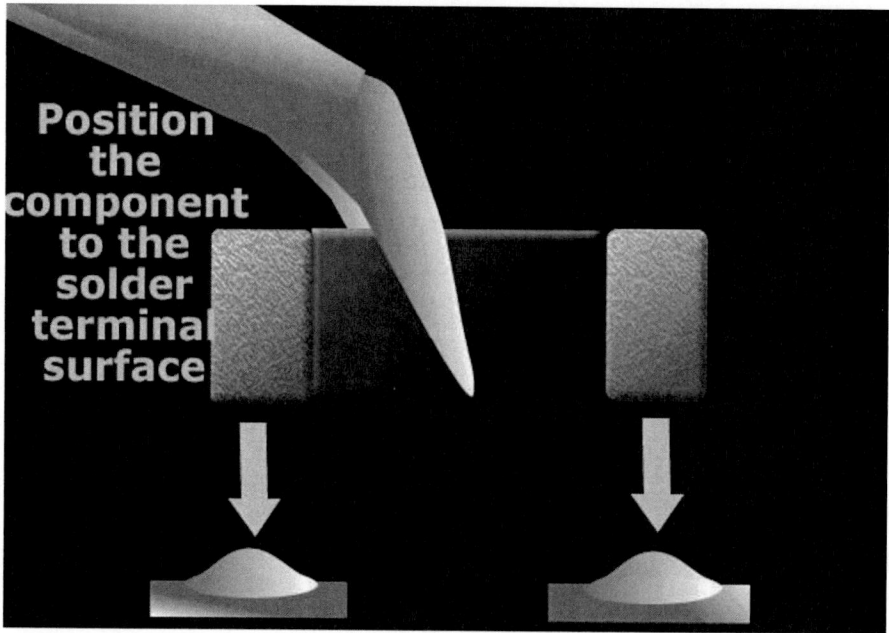

Position the component to the solder terminal surface

Tack it down and apply heat

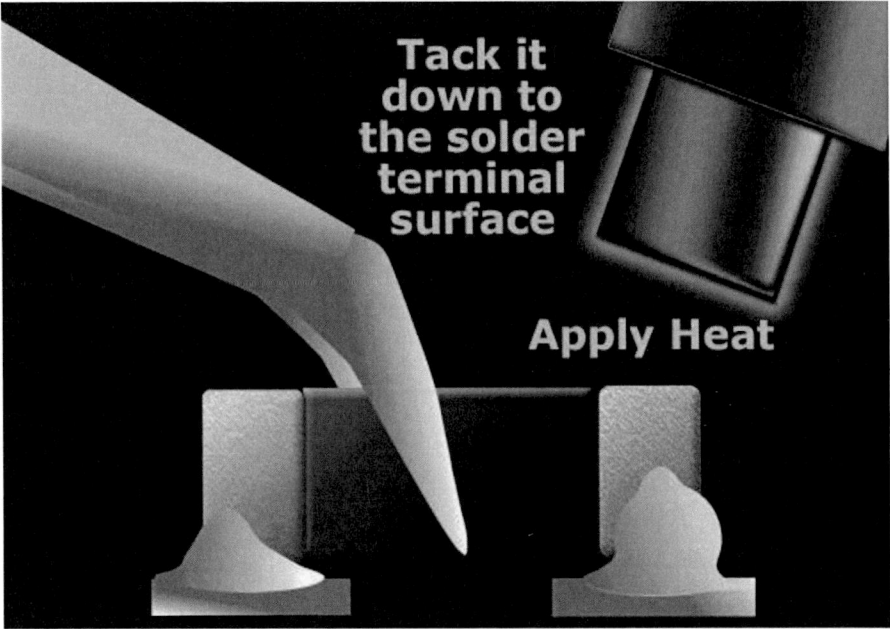

Tack it down to the solder terminal surface

Apply Heat

Wait a moment for the solder to solidify both leads terminal.

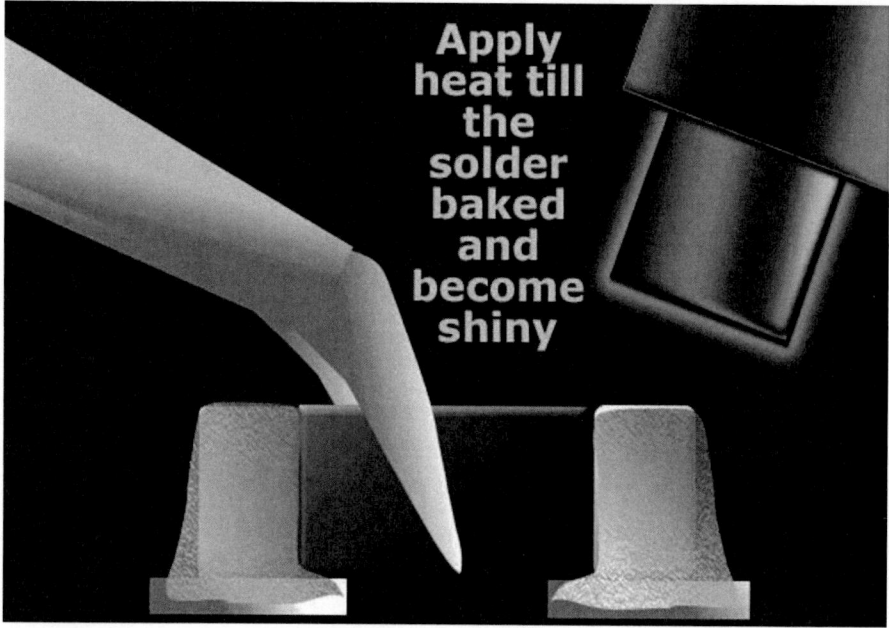

Apply heat till the solder baked and become shiny

Remove heat and hold the SMD components with tweezer until the heats out and cool.

Remove
Heat
wait
until it
heats
out

Cleaned the surrounding areas with cleaning kit.

Finish Product

You can practice by doing this with an old and non working cellphone PC Board. The more you do practice the more you will master it. Also observed and always become familiar of Hot air and soldering iron temperature settings. In my experience various type of cellphones solders have different melting point of the solder leads. There are too soft and there are also hard soldered leads to removed.

How to Reball BGA Chips of a Mobile Phones Manually by Hand

Reballing Ball Grid Array (BGA) Chips in mobile phones manually by hand

Reballing BGA chips tends to need and have a good steady hand, since most cellphone technician applied it manually by hands. It also requires good practice and experimentation before proceeding to reball any chips in mobile phones, because there are chips in mobile phones that can be easily damaged if you are not so familiar of doing it as well. like the CPU's and the Application processor chips are very vulnerable and can be easily damaged when applying non recommended heat on it. I advice that spending much time to practice it with non working PC board and chips is a good way to start. To put thing straight up, in real life there are technician that are good re-baller and some have poor skills on it. that is what I observe mostly when attending many forums on the Internet. The truth is by practicing doing it is the key to enhance re-balling chips skills.

Re-balling Chips Methods

. Prepare the proper Tools -You need to prepare also proper reballing kits and a cleaning kits for further cleaning the PC board.

. A good and controlled hot air temperature, You need to refer to manufacturers manual for proper temperature settings.

Identifying Spare Parts on Mobile Phones Handsets

As part on this tutorials, A good technician must also learn how to identify spare parts and how each particular parts works on cellphone handsets. Familiarizing each
Now various brands and models of every mobile phone products although have the same parts but differs on each sizes and technical specs. Others also are compatible with each other..

The Following are the most common types of spare parts you can find inside mobile phones handsets.

* **Battery**
* **Battery Connector**

* Antenna
* LCD
* LCD Frame
* Camera Module
* Plug-in Connector
* Flex Cable Wires
* Navigator/Joystick/Trackball
* Touch Screen Panel
* Microphone
* Speaker
* Buzzer/Ringer
* Keypad Membrane
* Simcard Connector
* On/Off Switch
* Vibrator
* Back Housing
* Housing

BATTERY-

A battery is used to provide power supply to the PCB circuits and components. There Are various types of Batteries in each particular mobile phone products, and varies to each sizes and specifications. Manufacturers coded each particular packaged according to sizes and where specified product to use. The standard battery Voltage Range is 3.7V and is made of rechargeable **Lithium Ion**.

Battery Connectors

This the interface where the battery connects and supply the voltage to the cellphones main circuitry or PC Board. Old models used 4 pin which lead to four battery output sources such as +(positive) -

(negative) BSI (battery status indicator) and Btemp (Battery Temperature)
The latest designs consists of only three pins, The + (positive) - (negative) and BSI (battery status indicator) the Btemp is diminished and still in cellphone circuitry included.

Antenna's

Antennas are used to intercepts and boost network signals, without it the phone will hardly connects to service providers and results network signal lost.
Antennas also consists of many types and sizes and varieties. It varies according to how each manufacturers designs. It is made of thin brass or stainless metal mounted on a plastic packaging.

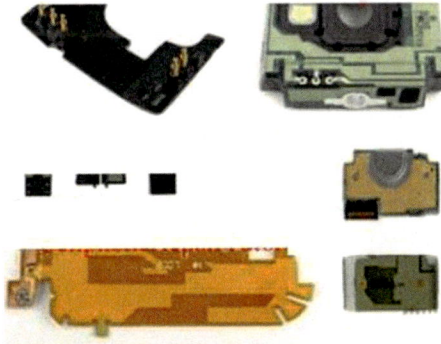

LCD

Liquid Crystal Display(LCD) is the component that visualize the operation of a mobile phone handset. It is made of glass with tiny crystal fixel that imitate the light source that has programmed to display certain information such as text and images.

207

LCD also comes from wide range of specifications older LCD are called monocrome which only display one certain color. The later designs where multicolored and displays rich text and images. The higher the fixel amount on a certain LCD the higher the picture resolution of images can displays.

Camera Module

Camera Modules is the component used to capture and store images, also comes in different specifications and packaging. Examples of these modules are shown below.

Plug-in Connectors

Plug in connectors are interfaces used in charging or by charger plugging, USB and data cables. Various mobile products also have different plug-in connectors designs.

Flex Cable Wires

These are wires that is made into a flat thin wires used as an interface to connect from one circuit or components to another. It is called "Flex" means Flexible others also called it a "ribbon wire"

Joystick and Trackball

this a component parts which is used to navigate certain features on a mobile phones. It is commonly navigate "UP","DOWN","LEFT","RIGHT","MENU","ENTER" keys.

Touch Screen Panels

Touch screen panels are made of flat thin glass which is designed with high capacitive or capacitance value. It navigates everywhere on LCD screen by just using a finger to or a stylus pen to switch trough certain feature on a mobile phone handsets.

Microphone

A microphone also known as "mouthpiece"is the component used to intercepts and imitates human voice and sounds to sends to particular receiver or caller. Cellphone microphone are small and have different forms of packaging.

Speaker

Speakers are the components that are used to hear someone talking when a call is made, without it you cannot hear the other persons voice calling at you. It is called an "earpiece by most common Technicians.

Buzzers and Ringers

These are also speakers that can generate high audible sound louder than Earpiece speakers. It amplifies the ringtones or voice or music more audibly.

Keypads Membrane

This are made of tiny round metals that acts as a switch in a row of letters and numbers characters on keypads mattress.

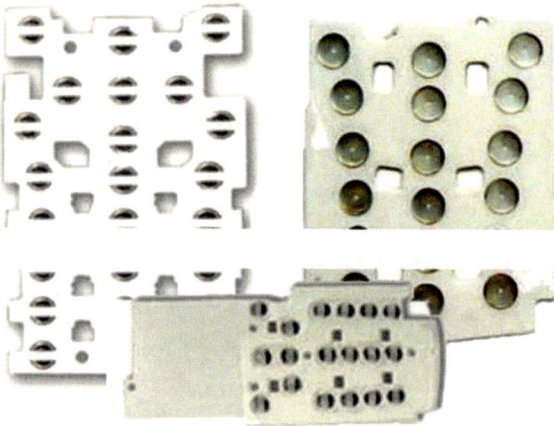

SIM Card Connectors

This is an Interface that acts as a holder and connects the Sim card to the PC board circuits.

ON and OFF Switch

It is made of tiny metal that conducts connectivity when press. It is being used as a power on and off, Volume control switch and camera shutter switch on various mobile phones.

Vibrator

it is made of a tiny motor that conduct vibration when in active mode. It has been attach an unbalance tiny metal on its tip, that is why it creates vibration when the motor rotates.

Other Parts

More Parts like LCD Frames, ON and OFF rubber buttons, Metal frames, Screws, Back housing, Face plates are also plays vital role on mobile phones packaging.

Some Parts may I have not included here, for some are just so rare in some mobile phone products.

PART 07

Understanding Major Integrated Circuits (IC) on Mobile Phones

Power Management IC
Application Processor
Flash IC
RAM IC

What is Power Management IC, How Does it supply power voltage to a Mobile Phones circuit

Power Management IC is a power IC, that manage, control and distribute and Supply Power voltages from the battery source to other corresponding circuits or chips.

It is highly designed to convert, regulate, stabilize current and voltages that flow across unto it.

A power supply IC Chips can divide and multiply certain voltage from one desired voltage source to any desired power output voltages.

Which is for example a battery voltage source amounts at 3.7voltsDC while other components chips or circuit only requires the amount of 1.8volts, This 1.8volts is the amount of voltage is what the power management IC are going to convert.

A block diagram below shows a brief details on how power supply IC converts and distribute certain desired

voltage from a battery power source to other corresponding circuits or components.

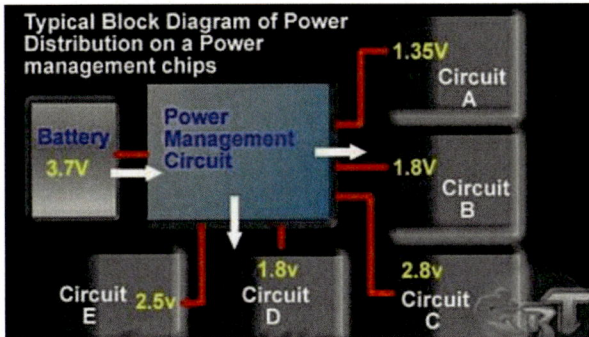

Typical Block Diagram of Power Distribution on a Power management chips

In a typical schematic diagram like in Nokia mobile phones, certain output supply power voltages were labeled as how much the amount of each output to supply power voltages to another circuits or components.

A failure of a power management IC to gain this following output voltage is also a failure to other corresponding components or circuits to work.

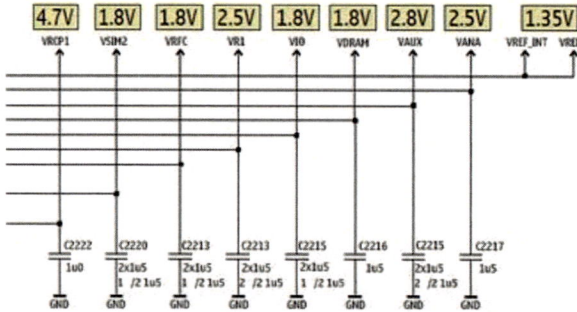

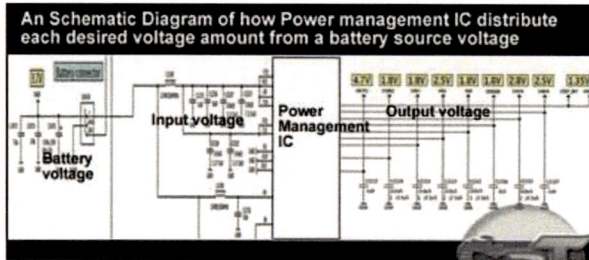

4.7V	1.8V	1.8V	2.5V	1.8V	1.8V	2.8V	2.5V	1.35V
VRCP1	VSIM2	VRFC	VR1	VIO	VDRAM	VAUX	VANA	VREF_INT VREF

C2222	C2220	C2213	C2213	C2215	C2216	C2215	C2217
1u0	2x1u5	2x1u5	2x1u5	2x1u5	1u5	2x1u5	1u5
		1 /2 1u5	1 /2 1u5	2 /2 1u5	1 /2 1u5		2 /2 1u5
GND	GND	GND	GND	GND	GND	GND	GND

An Schematic Diagram of how Power management IC distribute each desired voltage amount from a battery source voltage

A picture below is an example layout of a power management IC mounted on a printed circuit board.

216

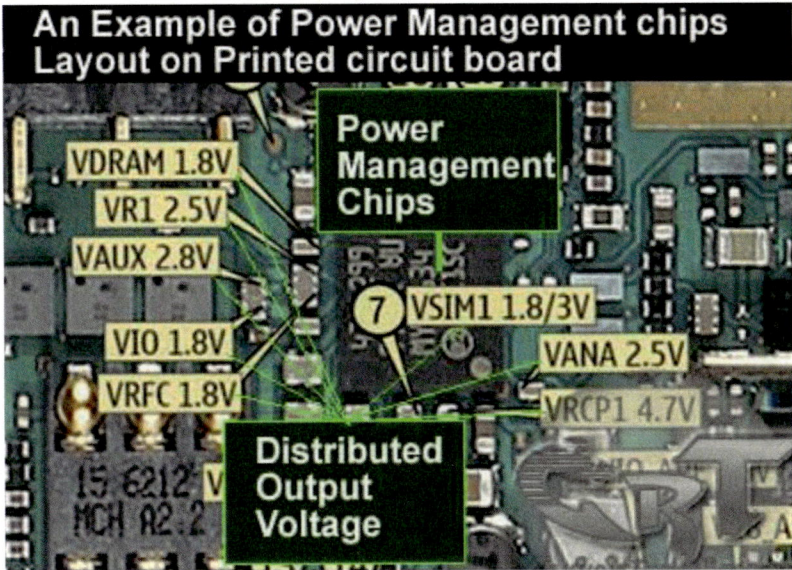

An Example of Power Management chips Layout on Printed circuit board

VDRAM 1.8V
VR1 2.5V
VAUX 2.8V
VIO 1.8V
VRFC 1.8V

Power Management Chips

7 VSIM1 1.8/3V
VANA 2.5V
VRCP1 4.7V

Distributed Output Voltage

A deep familiarization of how this chips works including its whole operation within a circuitry of mobile phones is also a powerful tool in troubleshooting hardware problem issues on a mobile phones.

What is An Application Processor in Mobile Phones Circuit Do

An application processor is a central processing unit (CPU) like the one installed on personal computer. It is the brain and controls all kind of data and information any application in mobile phones circuit. It is microprocessor integrated circuit (IC) chip.

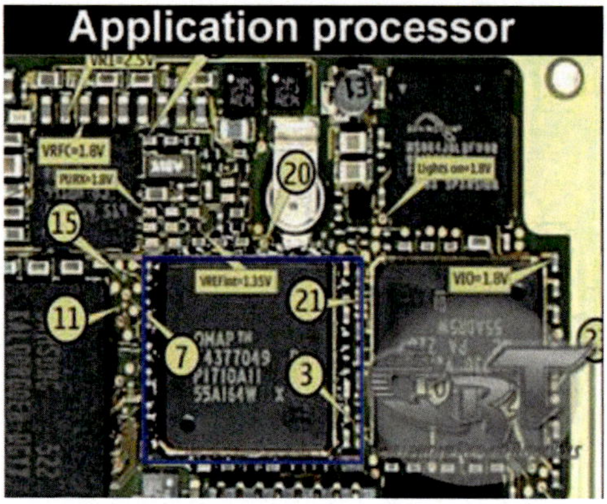

Application processor

LCD controller, camera interface, serial interfaces, memory interface,USB controller, bluetooth and wifi controller,and more. are controlled by an the application processor.

Blockdiagram

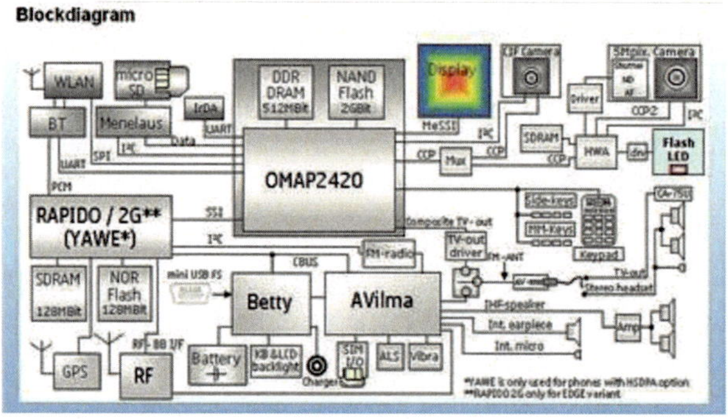

Here's an example of an application processor block diagram below, on how this kind of IC works on mobile phones circuit. This kind of an application is commonly used on Nokia latest designed of mobile handsets. The description of this application processor below will help us understand how does this certain IC work.

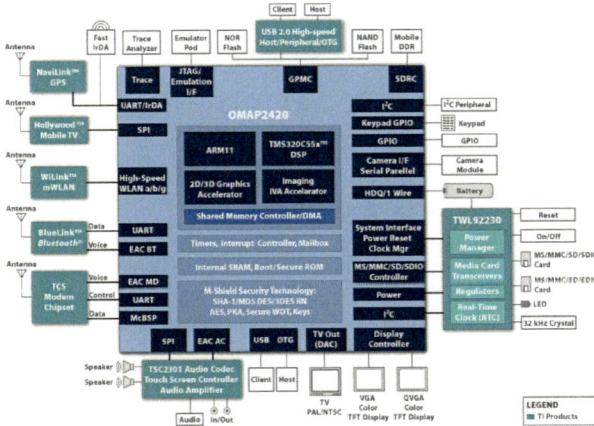

OMAP2420 Processor block diagram with labels including: Client, Host, USB 2.0 High-speed Host/Peripheral/OTG, Fast IrDA, Trace Analyzer, Emulator Pod, NOR Flash, NAND Flash, Mobile DDR, NaviLink™ GPS, Trace, JTAG/Emulation I/F, GPMC, SDRC, Antenna, UART/IrDA, I²C, I²C Peripheral, Hollywood™ Mobile TV, SPI, Keypad GPIO, Keypad, OMAP2420, GPIO, GPIO, WiLink™ mWLAN, ARM11, TMS320C55x™ DSP, Camera I/F Serial Parallel, Camera Module, High-Speed WLAN a/b/g, 2D/3D Graphics Accelerator, Imaging IVA Accelerator, HDQ/1 Wire, Battery, Shared Memory Controller/DMA, BlueLink™ Bluetooth® Data Voice, UART, EAC BT, Timers, Interrupt Controller, Mailbox, System Interface Power Reset Clock Mgr, TWL92230, Power Manager, Reset, On/Off, MS/MMC/SD/SDIO, Antenna, Internal SRAM, Boot/Secure ROM, MS/MMC/SD/SDIO Controller, Media Card Transceivers, MS/MMC/SD/SDIO Card, TCS Modem Chipset, Voice, EAC MD, M-Shield Security Technology: SHA-1/MD5 DES/3DES RN AES, PKA, Secure WDT, Keys, Power, Regulators, Card, Control Data, UART, McBSP, I²C, Real-Time Clock (RTC), LED, 32 kHz Crystal, SPI, EAC AC, USB OTG, TV Out (DAC), Display Controller, Speaker, TSC2301 Audio Codec Touch Screen Controller Audio Amplifier, Client, Host, TV PAL/NTSC, VGA Color TFT Display, QVGA Color TFT Display, LEGEND TI Products, Audio In/Out

OMAP2420 Processor

The OMAP2420 processor is a single-chip applications processor that supports all cellular standards, and complements any modem or chipset and any air interface. It is intended for high-volume wireless handset manufacturers and is not available through distributors. The OMAP2420 includes the benefits of the OMAP 2 architecture's parallel processing, giving users the ability to instantly run applications and operate multiple functions simultaneously without quality of service compromises. The OMAP2420 includes an integrated ARM1136 processor (330 MHz), a TI TMS320C55x™DSP (220 MHz), 2D/3D graphics accelerator, imaging and video accelerator, high-performance system interconnects and industry-standard peripherals.

Graphics

The OMAP2420 processor embeds Imagination Technologies' POWERVR MBX™ graphics core, making it the first applications processor to support OpenGL ES® 1.1 and OpenVG™, providing superior graphics performance and advanced user interface capabilities. TI is enabling sophisticated and dynamic images with "smart pixel" technology offered via OpenGL ES 1.1. This unique technology allows each pixel in an image to be programmed individually, giving developers the power to create rich effects with cinematic realism. Users will now experience "life-like" facial features, advanced reflection effects and multi-textured backgrounds in the mobile environment.

Multimedia enhancements made in the OMAP2420 include an added imaging and video accelerator for higher-resolution still capture applications, multi-megapixel cameras and full-motion video encode and decode with VGA resolution of 30 frames per second. An added TV video output supports connections to television displays for displaying images and video captured from the handset. 5-Mb internal SRAM also boost streaming media performance. Access to the OMAP Developer Network also provides an extensive range of programs and media components that manufacturers can use for differentiating and delivering products to market fast.

Key Features:

- Dedicated 2D/3D graphics accelerator at 2 million polygons per second
- Added imaging and video accelerator enables high-resolution still image capture, larger screen sizes and higher video frame rates
- Supports high-end features including 4+ megapixel cameras, VGA-quality video, high-end interactive gaming functionality and analog/digital TV video output
- 5-Mb internal SRAM boosts streaming media performance
- Software compatibility with previous OMAP processors
- Parallel processing ensures no interruptions or degradation of service with simultaneously running applications
- Optimized power management companion chip, TWL92230 12 mm x 12 mm, 325-ball MicroStar BGA™, 0.5-mm pitch

What is NAND and NOR Flash Memories

There are two types of flash memory, **NOR** and **NAND**. The names refer to the type of logic gate used in each memory cell. (Logic gates are a fundamental building block of digital circuits). NOR flash memory was first introduced by Intel in 1988. NAND flash was introduced by Toshiba in 1989

The two chips work differently. NOR flash is faster, but it's also more expensive and takes longer to erase and write new data. NOR is most often used in mobile phones. NAND has significantly higher storage capacity than NOR. It has found a market in devices to which large files are frequently uploaded and replaced. MP3 players, digital cameras and USB drives use NAND flash.

NAND Flash is a special form of Flash memory. Flash memory is a memory technology that keeps data even when the power supply is cut off; this is known as a non-volatile memory type. Flash memory can be read pretty fast, but writing to Flash memory is pretty slow compared to many other -volatile-memory technologies such as SRAM or DRAM. Flash also has a limited number of write-cycles; manufacturers typically specify something in the area of 10,000 writes for the lifetime of the part. NAND Flash is faster than regular Flash, although the general characteristics still hold.
Flash memory is widely used in digital cameras, portable MP3 players, USB (Flash) sticks, and many other devices.

NOR flash memory is a type of non-volatile storage technology that does not require power to retain data.
NAND devices are accessed serially, using the same eight pins to transmit control, addressing and data. NOR flash memory supports one-byte random access, which allows machine instructions to be retrieved and run directly from the chip, in the same way that a traditional computer will retrieve instructions directly from main memory. NOR flash has an SRAM interface that includes enough address pins to map the entire chip, enabling for access to every byte stored within it.

Some devices use both NAND and NOR. A pocket PC, for instance, may use embedded NOR to boot up the operating system and a removable NAND card for all its other memory or storage requirements.

What is RAM IC ? how does it work on mobile phones handsets

Random access memory (RAM) is used in mobile phones circuit to store memory data. It is made of millions of transistors and capacitors that being packed into integrated circuit (IC)
Transistors and capacitors are paired to create a memory cell, which represent a single bit of data. The capacitor holds the bit data of information, a 0 or a 1. The transistor acts as a switch that lets the control circuitry on the memory chip read the capacitor or change its state. In most cases common form of mobile phones memory is a Dynamic random access memory (DRAM)
The opposite of RAM is Serial Dynamic Random access memory (SAM). SAM stores data as a series of memory cell that can only be access sequentially. If the data is not in the current location each memory cell is check until the needed data is found.

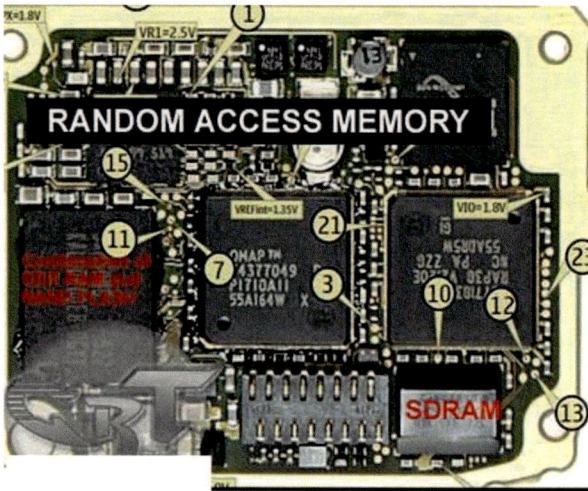

SDRAM

SDRAM stands for Synchronous Dynamic Random Access Memory. DDR is short for "DDR SDRAM" and stands for Double Data Rate. Nowadays to avoid misunderstandings SDRAM is often specified as SDR SDRAM and SDR stands for Single Data Rate by analogy with DDR. Therefore, the main difference between SDR and DDR memory the doubled speed: DDR can transfer data at roughly twice the speed of SDRAM.

DRAM. Dynamic Random Access Memory is used to temporarily store information on mobile phones. DRAM is made up of many cells and each cell is referred to as a bit. A cell contains a capacitor and a transistor. Since computer machine language is made up of 1s and 0s, it has the value of one when active and zero when inactive.

SDRAM or Synchronous Random Access Memory is the result of DRAM evolution. This type of memory synchronizes the input and output signals with the system board. Its speed ratings are in MHz. SDRAM was introduced in 1996 and is still used today. SDRAM transmits every clock count at a specific time. DDR RAM (or Double Data Rate Random Access Memory) does the same but it does so twice every clock count. This makes DDR RAM twice as fast as SDRAM.

PART 08

LIQUID DAMAGE

Types of liquid damage: Toilet, fresh, salt, food

Tools used in treatment

Chemicals used in treatment

Let's face it, we've all experienced it before, leaving your cell phone on a wet countertop, spilling a drink on it, dropping your phone in the pool, or better yet the toilet (you'd be surprised how often it happens). Inevitably, lots of cell phones suffer accidental water damage, and for those of you that don't already know, cell phone water damage requires immediate attention!

If you wait too long, the damage may be too severe to be repaired. Since are Iphone's, smart phones, and blackberry's are our lifelines, and because are cell phones are NOT covered under warranty for any kind of water damage. You are going to want to read over these 10 useful tips on what to do when dealing with water damaged electronics –you never know when it may come in handy!

Cell phone water damage of any kind can be extremely destructive to your phone. Why is water damage so serious? Water contact of any kind can be detrimental to your phone, as it can short circuit or erode your phone's electronic components and interior functions. Believe it or not you are better off dropping your phone in the toilet then in the pool or hot tub (I am guilty of this one). The reason why is due to corrosive chemicals that can vastly harm your cell phone.

Highly Corrosive Damage:

Salt water pools and ocean water contains a great amount of salt, which makes it highly corrosive. Due to this corrosivity, damage happens very quickly when your phone comes into contact with salt water.

Chlorine pool water and bromyime (hot tub water) contains a high amount of chemicals, which are also very corrosive. Chlorine and other pool chemicals quickly destroy your phone's electronic components and can cause irreparable damage if not treated immediately.

Believe it or not, tap water can sometimes be fairly corrosive because it still contains chemicals (such as mineral deposits and other substances) that can be dangerous to your phone. Although the chemicals are only minorly corosive, are minimal and do not deteriorate your phone as quickly as others.

However, in whichever way your phone receives water damage, water damage to your cell phone can sometimes be unrepairable. A very scary thought. Although it sometimes can be repaired and taken care of (or at least with minimal damage) if it is treated urgently and by following these ten simple tips…

1. DO NOT turn on your device! And Remove The Battery Immediately!

Do NOT turn your water damaged cell phone on! This will cause it to circulate, short out, and could cause <u>permanent</u> irreversible damage. Naturally, in a sudden urgent state of panic most people tend to do this to see if their phone is still functioning –this is a big mistake! No matter what you do, do not turn on your phone because it will wet and fry the circuit board and you will just have lost what little hope was left in recovering the device. Removing the battery immediately will ensure that there is no source of power for the cell phone and can hopefully prevent damage from following through the circuits.

2. Let The Device Air Dry

Not only will removing your battery reduce the chances of damaging the devices circuits, it also allows the water within the phones interior to evaporate and hopefully get rid of any hidden water out from the little nooks and crannies. Remember to separate your battery from your phone and let it dry separately, also remove your memory card and SIM and lay them out as well. These cell phone sidekicks should NOT be in your phone while its drying.

CAUTION: Do NOT use a heated blow dryer, or any source of extreme heat! Let's face it – extreme heat damages electronics. Adding heat to a water damaged cell phone can only increase the damage and corrosion. And although your phone may seem to be dry, the inside circuit board may still be wet. You can however select 'cool' mode on your dryer, this way heat will not damage your phone.

3. Use Air To Force Out Water

Ideally you want to remove as much water as possible from inside the phones shell. Buy a pressurized air-can or use an air-pressure machine and try to blow out the internal water out of the phone. It saves time, and it's a good way to get as much water out faster. Another way to air dry is to put your phone on the ACC and let it air dry for about a day or two. Any cool vent that doesn't produce a lot of heat is acceptable.

4. Use Rice or a Bheestie Bag To Absorb The Moisture

Water damaged phones are such a common problem that there are products available specifically designed to help dry all sorts of electronics damaged by water. Products like the Bheestie Bag promise to dry out any electronic device, however they aren't all that cheap, and there is no guarantee your phone will work properly. But, in comparison to buying a new mobile phone it could be money very well spent. There are plenty of electronic retailers and online stores that sell Bheestie Bags, look it up to find out.

Now, a cheaper way of doing this is using dry rice. Since rice absorbs moisture, placing a water damaged device in a sealed zip lock bag with dry rice will allow the moisture to be absorbed, it will be drawn out from the phone and absorbed by the surrounding rice (you should leave the phone in the rice bag overnight to give it enough time to absorb the moisture, if not longer, because you want to be safe). Silica gel can also do the same trick (you'll usually find them in the pockets of new purses and bags), however it's highly unlikely you'll have enough stashed away somewhere for a electronic emergency. So your best bet is sticking to rice.

5. Be Patient With The Drying Process

You are going to have to wait awhile. When something is wet, it seems logical that heat would dry it. After all, isn't this the principle we follow with our clothing, our hair etc? Well, that rule doesn't apply to electronics so keep the hair dryer away from your mobile. The oven or dryer are not good options either, just in case you were thinking of those alternatives. Heat damages electronics – end of story!

6. Put It Back Together -Give It A Try!

If you've tried any or all of the above tips for drying out your water damaged phone, put the components back together and give it a try. Remember to test out the phone's functions. Just because it's turned on doesn't mean it's fully operational. If your phone still isn't working to your satisfaction, try the tips below.

7. Find Replacement Parts

If only parts of the phone have suffered water damage, either your phone provider or a private electronic supplier might be able to identify and sell the parts required to get the mobile working again. I suggest to google small electronic stores in your area, they usually will try to repair it for half the price. Sending your phone in to the provider could take over a month to get fixed.

8. Send It To The Manufacturer

If you've tried everything else and your phone still just won't work, put the wet cell phone in a ziplock bag and send it back to your cell phone manufacturer. Many devices have at least a one year manufacture warranty on them. However, don't get your hopes up because electronic warranty is usually determinate by water damage. If you actually look inside your cell phone, there should be a water damaged sticker that turns red when tampered by liquid, so they will know. Yet, they might be able to take a look at it and give you a better idea of how damaged the device is, and whether it is worth repairing. Many times they can repair it by replacing parts or working their magic, but expect to get a fairly hefty bill for their repair work, you just might be better off buying a brand new phone. Repairs can get expensive!

9. Dry It With Alcohol

This is one ***hypothesis*** that you should try only as a very last resort. One desperate method is to drench a swab in alcohol and mop it around your device. You should only do this with rubbing alcohol (not the drinking type) to help remove any water that might have found its way into hidden spots on the phone that air drying might not reach. Let's make this COMPLETELY clear: this is a <u>risky</u> option that has the potential to ruin your phone, but if you have nothing else to loose then give it a go. But don't say I didn't warn you. Therefore, Only attempt this if you have no other option, have a backup of your data and do not care if the phone is permanently damaged! I have never tried it myself and don't think I ever would. But it is a theory I came across.

10. Buy A New Phone

Sorry, but when all else fails, get a new phone. If you're on a term contract, try and negotiate with your cell phone provider and see if you might be eligible for a plan renewal or any discounts or upgrades. Even if you are not eligible for an upgrade, threaten to leave them for another service provider, be smart! You'll be surprised how easily they can adjust the system. If you're not willing to do that, Ebay and other online electronic retailers have a lot of decent deals on electronics.

Now obviously these devices do not come cheap and they really are our lifelines when used for business and personal enjoyment. You should try to get into the habit of backing up your phone on a monthly basis. Remember to get a screen protector, case, and phone skin for your cell phone as they help protect your phone's shell. Of course, your best option for preventing water damage is to prevent it from happening altogether, but seeing as we can't turn back time I hope you find these tips useful. If I had done research on this topic sooner I may have saved myself a couple of cell phones over the years. Be smart with your smart phone. Remember to try to always keep your phone far away from liquid and water. Don't leave it beside your drink, or beside the ledge of the pool, and always check for wet counter tops because accidents happen. But when they do, hold on to your nerves, and remember these steps to get that device dried out!

Top 10 DIY Repairs and Upgrades to Make Your Smartphone Last Forever

You can never save your phone from every drop, spill, scratch, and crash you encounter during its life. Heck, even a year of wear and tear can take its toll on any phone. Instead of paying hundreds of dollars for a new device every time yours breaks, here are 10 repairs and upgrades you can perform yourself at home. P

10. Fix a Loose Charging Port with a Toothpick

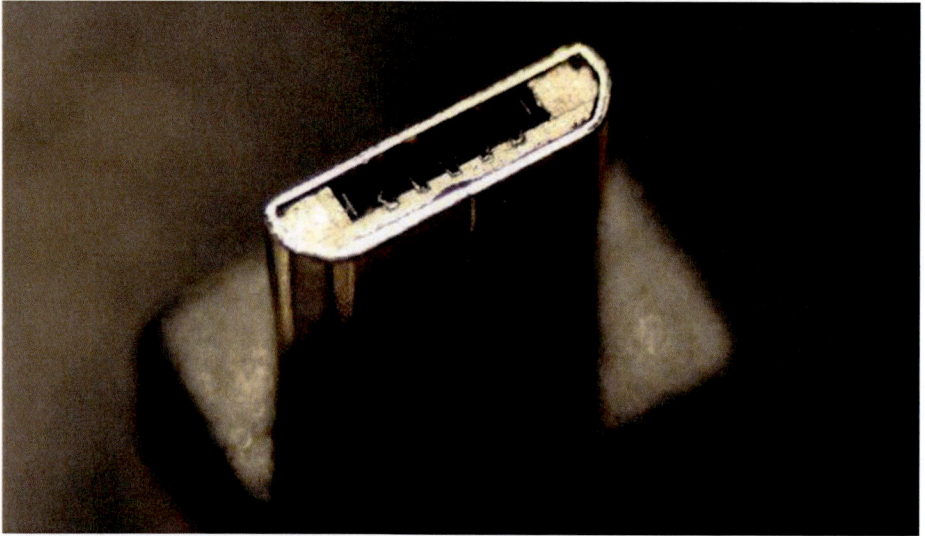

When you buy a new phone or tablet, you may notice that the micro-USB charging and data port is a pretty snug fit. Over time, that fit gets looser and looser, and if some of your gadgets don't even hold their connector plugs firmly anymore, the fix may be as easy as taking a sharpened toothpick and cleaning out the area around the connector.

I will explains that one of his devices didn't even firmly grip the USB connector anymore, and it would fall out with the slightest movement. He thought he would have to pop it open and try to secure the plug itself, but the fix was much simpler: over the years, the port had accumulated lint and dirt from regular use, and all he needed was a thin, sharpened toothpick (small enough to get in there, and made of wood as to not conduct electricity) to clean the gunk out

After a good cleaning (and you can see the amount of crud he scraped out at the link below,) the fit wasn't as snug as new, but it was much better than it had been in years. I had a hard time believing something so simple would work so well, so I tried it too with my old OG Motorola Droid, and sure enough, after I cleaned out what was hiding in there, USB connections were much firmer. Simple, easy, and hopefully it'll help some of your USB devices as well.

9. Get Buggy Speakers Working Again buggy with a cotton swab

It's a fairly common problem: you plug in headphones to your iPhone (or in my case, it was an iPod Touch) and the speaker works just fine for

Similar to the charging port, your headphone jack can also get gunked up with lint and other debris from your pockets. When that happens, your phone can have problems switching from headphones to speaker when you don't have your headphones plugged in. There's no need to open up your phone or take it in to get fixed. Just stick a cotton swab down the headphone jack to clear it out and it should be good as new.

It's a fairly common problem: you plug in headphones to your iPhone (or in my case, it was an iPod Touch) and the speaker works just fine for alerts and phone calls, but pull out the headphone cable and the device won't play through the speaker at all. The fix is actually surprisingly simple: just grab a cotton swab, pull off some of the cotton, and get up in there. P

The real problem is that some debris or moisture has shorted out the contact that switches from headphones to speaker inside the headphone jack not that the speaker itself is busted. Cleaning it out with a swab is a quick fix to what could be an expensive repair if you left it to Apple. We're willing to bet the same issue happens with some Android phones too, so it's worth keeping in mind even if you don't have an iPhone or iPod Touch.

How to fix the iPhone speaker problem (water damage)

Problem: The iPhone speaker works fine when headphones are plugged into it. However, as soon as the headphones are removed, there is no sound emitted from the iPhone. In other words, the iPhone speaker doesn't work. My phone wouldn't ring and I couldn't hear any sound from the iPhone. This happened to my phone after it was water damaged.

Solution: Find a q-tip. Insert the q-tip into the headphone jack of the iPhone. Swivel the q-tip around for a bit and clean the inside of the headphone jack. Once I did this, the problem was magically fixed!

How to fix the iPhone with water damage problem

you can attempt to fix it by putting the phone in a container of uncooked rice. The rice soaks up most of the moisture from the phone. You should detach the battery pack (if possible) and leave it in the uncooked rice for at least 6 hours. This should be done as soon as possible for maximum effect.

8. Turn a DVD Lens into a Cameraphone Lens

Maybe your cellphone's camera lens is broken or scratched, or maybe you just want to take higher quality closeup photos. If you have an old or broken DVD player lying around, you can actually salvage the small lens it uses and use it as a camera lens on your phone. If you're replacing your current lens, you'll have to open your phone up and do some surgery, but if all you want is a few macro pictures, you can set it on top of your current lens to get the same effect.

Turn a DVD Lens into a Cellphone Macro Lens

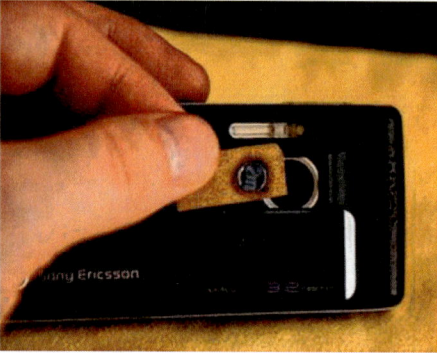

You've always got your cellphone handy, but it's not really ready to take a close-up shot. With parts recycled from an old DVD player or drive, you can craft a makeshift macro lens for your tiny camera.

It turns out that the little lens inside DVD players is just about the perfect size and magnification to turn the tiny lenses of cellphone cameras into a macro tool. All you need is a drive to hack apart, a piece of stiff posterboard or plastic to mount the lens in, and a little bit of poster tack or painter's tape to hold the lens mount in place over your cellphone's camera lens.

The result? Your cameraphone now has a significantly more intense gaze.

Check out the photo to the below for an example of what the dvd-macro-lens is capable of

7. Cool Down an Overheating Phone

This can be both a software and a hardware problem, but we've all been there: your cellphone is burning a hole in your pocket it's so hot. Well, often this is because of the battery so turning off battery- and CPU-draining apps can help a lot. However, you should also try and let it breathe a little bit. If possible, don't stifle it in your pocket, and take off that non-breathable case and see if that helps. The cooler you can keep your phone, the longer it will last and the better battery life you'll get throughout the day.

6. Repair Stuck and Unresponsive Buttons

Got a button that only works half the time, or a button that won't seem to press all the way down? Sometimes, you can fix it just by giving it a small dose of rubbing alcohol with a cotton swap wipe it on, press the button a few times, and hope for the best. If not, it's more likely you need to replace the button entirely. You can often find them as spare parts online for cheap, then use your tool kit to open up your phone and replace the button. If that sounds a little scary, you can always make up for the broken button with software solutions, too.

5. Replace a Dying or Dead Battery

Batteries don't last forever. After a few years, it's likely your battery won't hold the same charge it used to, so it's time to get a replacement. That's easy for Android users, but iPhone users have to do a bit more work. You can usually buy replacement batteries online and replace them yourself without too much hassle. We've shown you how to do it on an iPod, and it isn't that much different on an iPhone grab your toolkit, open up your phone, and carefully replace the battery with the one you bought online. You'll be surprised how much longer your new battery will last.

4. Revive a Seemingly Bricked Phone

If you like to jailbreak or root your phone, you're probably well aware with the possibility of bricking your phone that is, breaking your phone so horribly that it no longer turns on and has become, for all intents and purposes, as useful as a brick. Luckily, it's very hard to brick a phone, and what may *seem* like a brick could be a perfectly fixable issue.

How to Jailbreak Your iPhone: The Always Up-to-Date Guide [iOS 6.1.2]

Jailbreaking is a process that changes little by little with each iOS upgrade. Rather than always publishing new guides.

Everything You Need to Know About Rooting Your Android Phone

We love Android, but rooting your phone can give you the opportunity to do so much more than your phone can do out of the box

How Do I Fix My Bricked iPhone, iPad, or iPod touch?

How Do I Fix My Bricked Android Phone?

Save a Bricked Phone Using Paper Clips and Pencil Graphite

If you've managed to brick your phone while attempting to root it or flash a custom kernel, you can force it to boot back up using paper clips

3. Smooth Out Stubborn Scratches

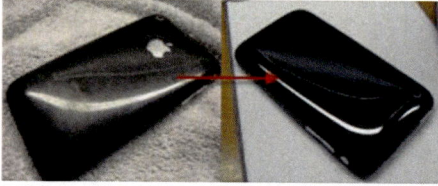

It's unavoidable: phones get scratched up. It isn't your keys or the coins in your pocket, either, it's the sand and dirt. If you want to keep your phone scratch-free, you can brush the bezel or sandpaper the back to get it shiny and smooth again. Your screen is another matter screen protectors will keep it from getting scratched (and you can make your own for about a nickel, but if your phone's already scratched up, refer to #1 before to see how to replace the screen.

Your Keys Aren't Scratching Your Smartphone; It's the Sand in Your Pocket Most modern smartphones use scratch-resistant glass on their screens, but every once in a while you'll see that your phone still gets some fine
Brush Your iPhone's Bezel to Hide Scuffs and Scratches
If the shiny metal bezel around your iPhone has seen better days, and that nags at your perfectionist instincts, a quick protective taping and smooth
Restore a Scratched-Up iPhone with Sandpaper
iPhones are scratch-resistant, but life throws some tough stuff at our phones. One MacRumors user, owning a phone that looks pretty beat
Are Screen Protectors Necessary Anymore?
Make Your Own Vinyl Screen Protector for Less Than a Nickel
Whether you have a screen protector because your device scratches easily or you just hate seeing your greasy fingerprints, the cost always seems

2. Resurrect a Soaked Phone with Rice

Many of you have probably heard of this trick before, and it really does work. If your phone takes an unexpected swim, you can save it by removing the battery (if possible), getting it to a bag of rice as quickly as you can, and leaving it there for a day or two (the longer, the better). If your screen's having problems due to moisture, you can often massage stuck pixels away with your fingers, too.

Testimonial: Rice Resurrects Even the Most Soaked of Gadgets Nobody wants to lose their favorite new electronic gadget to a dunk in the drink. Resurrect your phone in 30 minutes or less Save Your Cell Phone Screen by Massaging Dead Stuck Pixels Away Your cell phone's screen has some dead stuck pixels. You're not too excited about the prospect of shelling out for a new phone do this now...

1. Replace a Scratched or Shattered Screen

All it takes is one fateful drop to render your phone's screen useless, and it may seem like the only course of action is to upgrade. However, replacing your phone's screen is actually pretty easy, not to mention cheap. Don't believe us? All you need are some tools and a little bravery, and you'll have your phone looking good as new in no time.

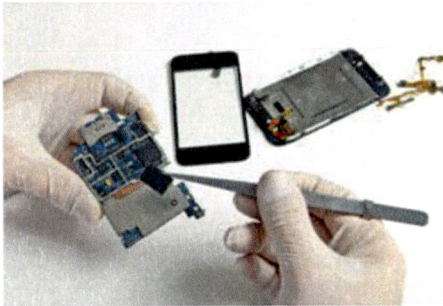

PART 09

Basic Hardware Handling Procedures

Proper Disassembling and Assembling Methods
How to Test Mobile phone Speaker, Buzzer or Ringer
How to Test Mobile phone Microphone or Mouthpiece
How to test Mobile Phone Charger Voltage
How to Test Mobile Phone Vibra Motor
How to check Mobile Phone Battery Voltage
How to test Power ON OFF Switch

How to Properly Dismantle Mobile Phones Handsets

Before Proceeding to dismantle any mobile Phone Handset make sure to ask your costumer about the warranty period of the said handset. Attempting to open it, may lose service warranty, just unless you are working in any authorized service center which is you are the one who decides.

Dismantling mobile handset needs extra care to avoid further damaged.

Scratches and breakage also takes place if unhanding carefully. On the internet you can easily find disassembly guide just type the following keywords example

"brand + model number + Disassembly guides" you may also find it in Youtube for video guides.

Even Professionals needs extra care how to dismantle mobile handset. Various brands have different types of packaging types. Opening Tools also varies according what they suggest including torx screw number and other opening kits.

keep your time and don't rush in, always keep in mind that you are handling fragile object.

Wearing white cotton hand gloves is a good advice for beginners and even Pros, to avoid risk of Electro Static Discharge

(ESD) There are components like CPU and Memory Chips which is can be easily damaged by Human Interference, a ground strap is also required as advice.

Make your working table free of dust and dirt's and other objects which is not part of disassembling tools, to keep a place where all part have to put when opening operation is done.

Here's an example dis-assembling of Nokia handset looks like.

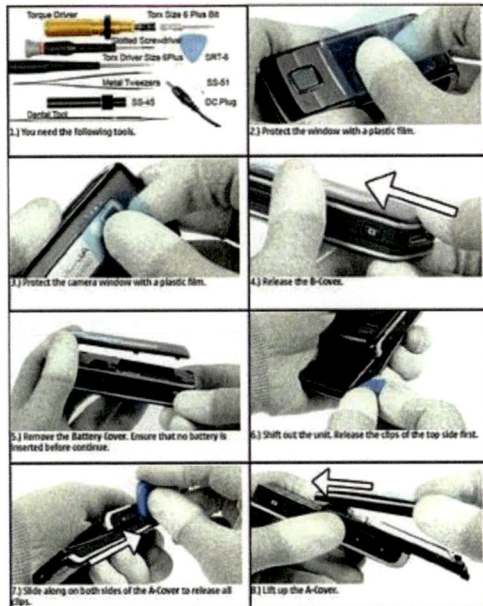

Latest released of mobile Phone products doesn't have guides available like shown above. Pros and masters defends only their instincts to tear it down, with out any guides available.

Here is set example of a teardown with iphone 3G courtesy of **iFixit**

iphone 3G

Tools Used in this Guide

*Dental Pick
*Metal Spudger
*Paper Clip
*Phillips #00 Screwdriver
*Spudger

Step 1 — Battery

*Remove the two Phillips #00 screws from the dock-connector end of the iPhone.

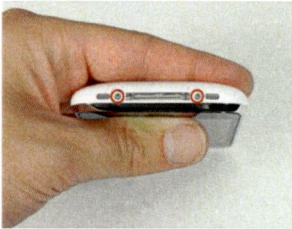

Step 2

*There is a rubber gasket between the silver front bezel and black display assembly. A bit of force is required in this step to separate the iPhone's display assembly.
*Use a small suction cup near the Home button to gently pull up the bottom portion of the iPhone's display assembly.

Step 3

*The display assembly is still connected to the iPhone by several cables, so don't try to remove it entirely just yet.
*Rotate the display assembly up until it is at an angle of approximately 45 degrees.

Step 4

*Continue to hold the display assembly with one hand, and use your other hand and a spudger to disconnect the black ribbon cable labeled "1."

Step 5

*Rotate the display assembly up until it is roughly vertical. This will allow easier access for disconnecting the remaining cables.
*Use a spudger to disconnect the black ribbon cable labeled "2."

Step 6

*Use a spudger to flip up the white plastic tab holding the remaining ribbon cable in place. The white tab will rotate up 90 degrees, releasing the ribbon cable.
* Slide the black ribbon cable out of its connector, and remove the display assembly from the iPhone.

Step 7

*Insert your SIM eject tool or a paper clip into the hole next to the headphone jack.
*Press down on the tool until the SIM card tray pops out.
*Grasp the SIM card tray and slide it out of the iPhone.

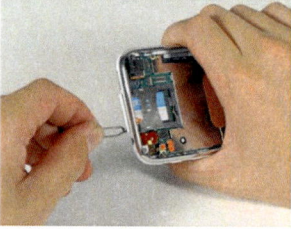

Step 8

*Use a spudger to disconnect the ribbon cable labeled "4."

Step 9

*Use a spudger to disconnect the ribbon cable labeled "5."

Step 10

*Use a spudger to disconnect the ribbon cable labeled "6."

Step 11

*Carefully peel up the small sticker labeled "Do not remove."

Step 12

*Remove the following 8 screws:
oFive 2.3 mm Phillips #00 screws with partial threads securing the logic board to the rear panel.
oTwo 2.3 mm Phillips #00 screws with full threads securing the logic board and camera.
oOne 2.9 mm Phillips #00 screw from beneath the "Do not remove" sticker.

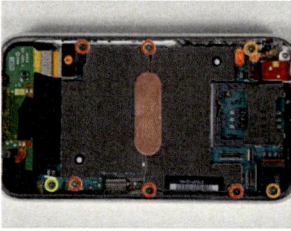

Step 13

*Use a spudger to gently pry the camera up and out of its housing in the rear panel. The camera cannot be removed entirely yet because it's connected to the bottom of the logic board.

Step 14

*Use a spudger to gently pry up the end of the logic board closest to the dock connector.
*If the board won't lift up, double check to make sure all the screws securing the logic board have been removed.

Step 15

*Slide the logic board towards the dock connector and out of the iPhone.

Step 16

*Use a spudger to pry the battery up from the rear panel. The battery is attached with an adhesive strip around the perimeter of the battery. To prevent the battery from bending during the removal process, we recommend against using just the plastic pull-tab .

Step 17 — Headphone Jack

*Remove the two Phillips #00 screws securing the on/off switch to the front bezel.

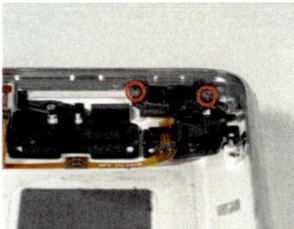

Step 18

*Carefully peel up the orange ribbon cable from the rear panel.

Step 19

*Remove the following 4 screws:
oThree 1.8 mm Phillips #00 screws securing the headphone jack and GPS antenna to the rear panel.
oOne 3.8 mm Phillips #00 screw in the plastic loop near the headphone jack.

Step 20

*Remove the four Phillips #00 screws securing the volume and vibrate buttons.

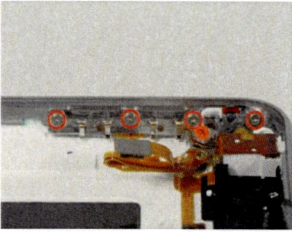

Step 21

*Lift the volume button circuitry away from the side of the iPhone, and carefully peel up the orange ribbon cable from the rear panel

244

Step 22

*Carefully lift the headphone jack assembly out of the iPhone.

Step 23 — GPS Antenna

*Remove the single Phillips #00 screw securing the black plastic spacer.

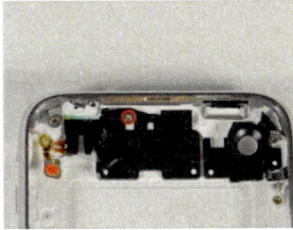

Step 24

*Use a spudger to pry up the black plastic antenna housing from the rear panel.
*Lift the black plastic antenna housing out of the iPhone.

Step 25 — Rear Panel

*Remove the on/off switch button from the iPhone.

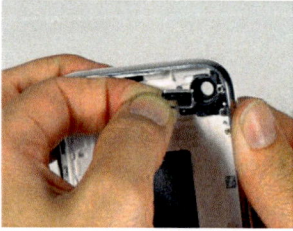

Step 26

*Remove the vibrate button from the iPhone.

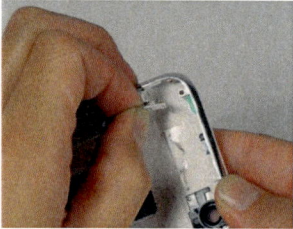

Step 27

*Remove the two Phillips #00 screws securing the vibrator to the rear panel.
*Lift the vibrator up and out of the iPhone.

Step 28

*Remove the following 3 screws:
oTwo 1.5 mm Phillips #00 screws, one on either side of the dock connector.
o One 2.4 mm Phillips #00 screw near the ribbon cable labeled "4."

Step 29

*Lift the dock connector assembly up and out of the iPhone.

Step 30

*The rear panel and attached front bezel remain.

iPhone 3GS Teardown

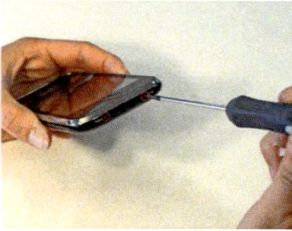

Step 2

*A small suction cup is your friend. A large suction cup may also be a fun toy.
*There are seven numbered connectors on the 3GS, up from six on the 3G. Connector number seven is in the lower right corner, just above the dock connector.

Step 3

*There are three cables holding the LCD and digitizer to the rest of the logic board. Disconnecting them is as easy as 1-2-3.

1: LCD panel

2: Digitizer

3: Ear speaker

Step 4

*Here's the two halves.

*All the chips on the logic board are hidden beneath two large EMI shields. We'll have those removed in just a bit.

Step 5

*Just like the iPhone 3G, the LCD is pretty easy to replace. After removing 7 screws, the LCD simply lifts out.
*On the iPhone 3G, we see a lot more cracked digitizers than cracked LCDs. Replacing the digitizer is a little more work, and requires breaking out a heat gun or hair dryer.

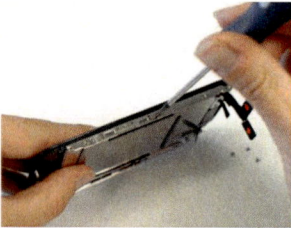

Step 6

*Here's the fabled "Do not remove" sticker. It didn't stop us last year, and it's certainly not going to stop us this year.

Step 7

*Removing the logic board. Like the 3G, there is a single large PCB with all components.

Step 8

*The main logic board. There's a lot packed in here. Here's a high-res image of this shot.
*The Apple-logo chip is the primary Samsung ARM processor.
*The 16 GB of Toshiba flash are now on the front of the board, just below the Samsung ARM.

Step 9

*The other side of the logic board. You can see the battery contact pads in the lower right corner. Apple was again kind enough to not solder the battery to the logic board.
*Here's a high-res image of this shot.

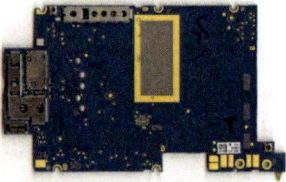

Step 10

*Apple promises improved battery life with the 3GS. The battery is listed as 3.7V and 4.51 Whr. This comes out to 1219 mAh, compared to 1150 mAh on the 3G. That's only a 6% increase.

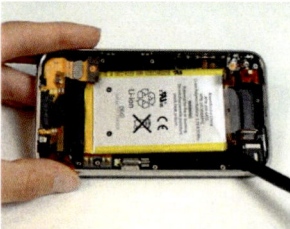

Step 11

*Video recording is a long-overdue feature of the iPhone 3GS. The 3GS records video at 640x480 resolution and 30 fps.
*The video recording quality appears acceptable, although not exceptional. You can see a video (taken using another iPhone 3GS) of us opening the phone.

Step 12

*The 3GS offers Voice Control. We're not sure yet why this feature couldn't be added via software to earlier iPhones. Perhaps the voice recognition requires a better microphone than in earlier iPhones or a lot of processing power, or maybe Apple just wanted to differentiate the 3GS.

*According to Richard Lai, the "Chinese (Cantonese) voice control works, but took a while to work out the magic words as there is no guide released yet (not out in Hong Kong until early July)." He also tested the "Chinese (Mandarin) and Chinese (Taiwanese), although the latter didn't work as well since [he doesn't] do the accent well."

Step 13

*Here's all the parts. We'll continue to perform further analysis.

How to Test Mobile phone Speaker,Buzzer or Ringer

Speakers also known as earpiece is the device that allows the handset user to hear the other user during call conversations.

While the **Buzzer** or a **Ringer** is the one that sends out the ringtone to be heard by the handset user.

Both Earpiece, buzzer or ringer are same speaker. it only varies the loudness of it sounds being produce.

Ringer buzzer generates more loudness than the earpiece speaker.

A speaker is a device that converts electrical signal into sounds.

It is made by a magnetic wire winded into a coil and a metal piece of magnet.

below is an example oh how to test of a good and working speakers .

Test procedure on Speaker,Buzzer or Ringer

Simply set the analog or digital multi-tester to X1 resistance value, and attach one probe to one the speakers terminal while tick tacking the other one unto it.
A working speaker produce a crackling sounds and the multi-tester pointer moves, while the a busted one will not and have no reading.

How to Test Mobile phone Microphone or Mouthpiece

Mobile phone microphone also known as mouthpiece is the one that intercepts the voice to transmit to other mobile phone users. Without it or a defective one will result that the other user on a phone cannot hear the one with a defective microphone on its mobile phone handsets.
 A technical term of a microphone is a device used to convert sounds into electrical signal.
A microphone is made of an electrical magnetic wire shaped into a round coil with a magnet metal surrounds it, the mechanical vibration generated by it will then produce an electrical voltage signal.

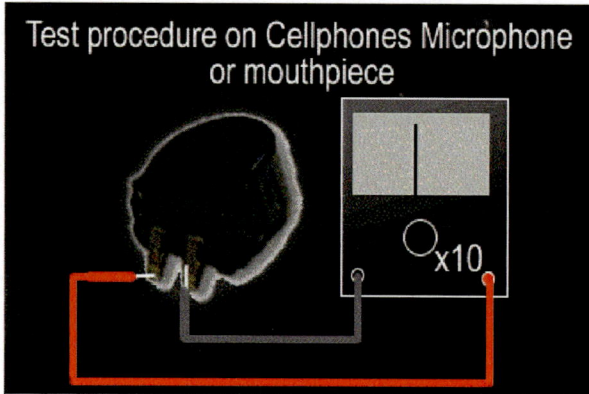

Test procedure on Cellphones Microphone or mouthpiece

Checking the microphone is also been so easy, Just set the analog or digital multi-tester to x1 resistance value then attach both test probe to its terminal. A good sign of a working microphone tends to have a reading while the busted one will have no reading. In some other cases types of microphones may only have a reading to the range of x10 for some high resistance value.

How to test Mobile Phone Charger Voltage

Learning to check mobile phone charger voltage is also a big help when it comes to troubleshooting charging problem.
Various mobile phones have different varieties of charger packaging and designed but almost all of them have one the same operational concepts.

A picture below is an example of a charger used in **Nokia Mobile Phones**.
The concepts is that the positive voltage is in the inner side of the connector pin while the negative voltage is in outer side of the pin. Charger voltage range from 4.5 to 6 volts and an average rating of 800 milliAmpere current.
Checking it output voltage will be on its connector pin tips. Just set the analog or digital multi-meter to 10DCV or higher range. and connect both test probe to its corresponding polarities. A good and working charger will get the approximately correct reading while the busted one will get no reading.

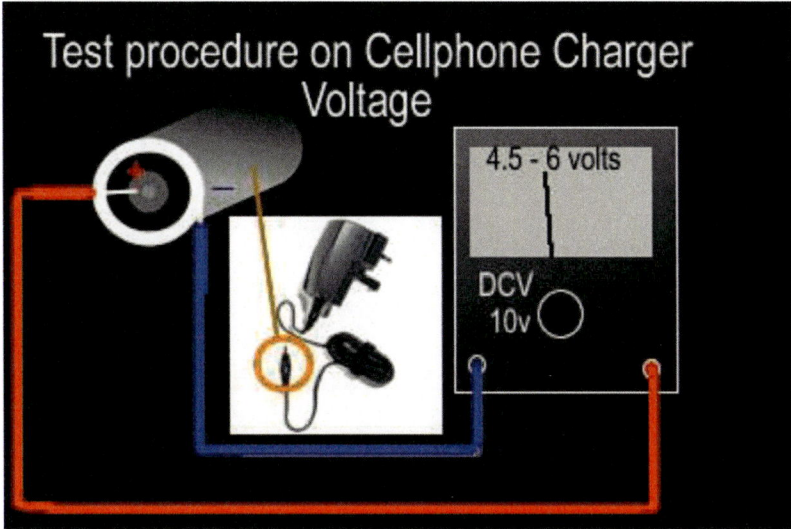

Test procedure on Cellphone Charger Voltage

4.5 - 6 volts

DCV
10v

Many experts know how to fix mobile phone charger for they know the whole designed of its circuitry inside it, but I'd rather not encourage to the newbies to teach about it because it is so complicated and might result risk of electric shock or any possible accident. It is because that circuit involves AC (alternating current) on it, *NOTE: Alternating Current is a dangerous voltage and can kill if not have much knowledge about it.*

How to Test Mobile Phone Vibration Motor

A mobile phone vibration is created by a small motor called **Vibra motor**. when applied by a voltage or current it rotates and the vibration is generated by a small tiny piece of metal attach to its tip.

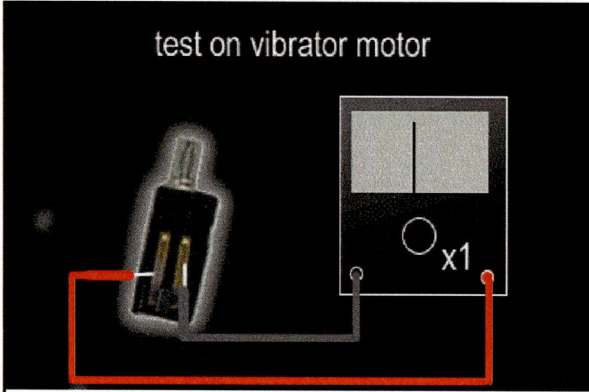
test on vibrator motor

Checking this small piece of motor was so very easy just set the analog multi-tester range to X1 in resistance
settings then connect the both probes to each terminals, polarity doesn't matter here for the motor will rotate clockwise if its in the right polarity. and rotates counter clockwise when not in each corresponding polarity.
A good and working vibration motor will then rotate and a bad or busted one will not.

How to check Mobile Phone Battery Voltage

A good and working battery voltage is approximately 3.7 volts DC(direct current), below that maximum voltage range the phone will not be able to power on.
Checking the battery voltage by an analog multi-meter is so easy, just set it to a DC range 10volts then attach the both test probes to each corresponding polarity, positive probe to positive terminal, then negative probe to negative battery terminal. Check the maximum battery voltage reading 3.7 volts.
A battery voltage lower than 3.7 volts can power on the handsets but it shows Battery Low on a screen.
A battery voltage lower than 2 to zero volts will hardly charge the phone and won't power up the phone.

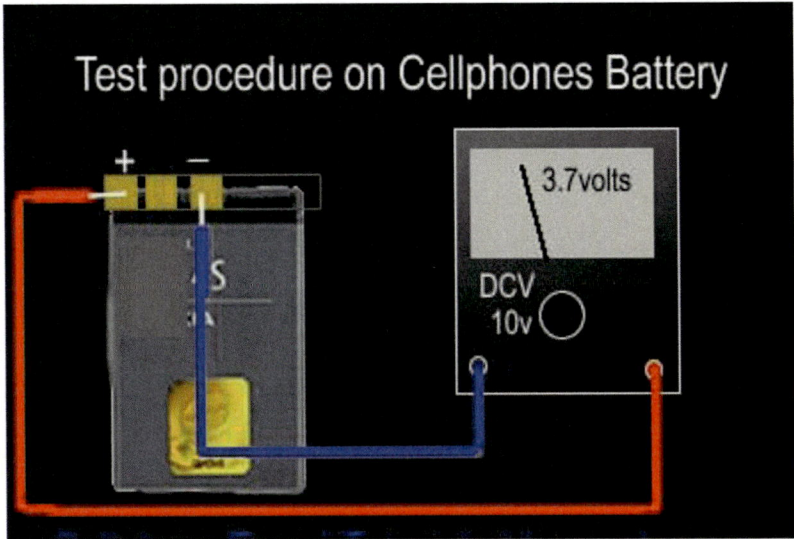

Test procedure on Cellphones Battery

A drain battery voltage approximately down to zero volts will not be able to accept charge when a charger is being plug-in. A drain battery will be **shock** by a a higher voltage range from 6 to 12 volts for a quick charging point as possible to avoid damaging the battery, a **DC regulated power supply**. is the equipment used to shock a drained battery. just connect both probe to each corresponding polarity for a quicker period of time, prolonging it will damage the battery itself. You may ask an experience technician in your neighborhood about this method for assistance and safety guidelines.

Power ON OFF Switch on Mobile Phone - Test and Check Up Procedures

ON/OFF Switch on cell phones comes different varieties and forms or designs but the fundamentals on how does it work or where to use it is the same. On Off switch can be determine by the number of its legs or terminals.

This cell phone repair tutorial for beginners covers on how to check the power on off switch on mobile phones and also work on volume key switches.

Here's a brief information on every ON and OFF switch which covers how the components being

259

assembled and by this information you can easily test and check up the said switch if it is good or in working condition.

By checking on off switch is been so simply by just only checking its terminals conducting continuity. A broken power on off switch can be easily determine when its visual assembly is busted out, so this procedure below covers only when the said switch visual assembly seems to be good.

This also the first step to repair the mobile phone if unable to power up, its like happens when the phone can accept and show charging if at charging state but unable to power up while pressing the power ON OFF button switch.

The two Legs On OFF switch assembly:

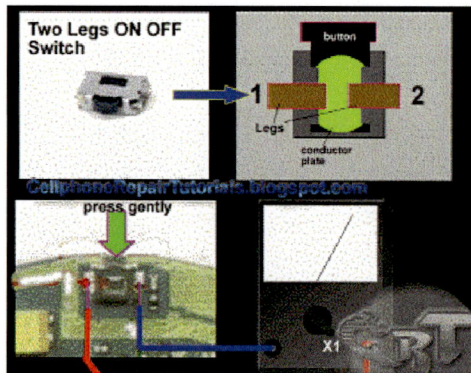

This check up procedure can work even if the ON OFF switch is mounted on the printed circuit board or isolated.

Two check this two legged kind of ON OFF switch is by simply set the multimeter to X1, then connect the two test probes of the multimeter to both legs of the switch, we are just simply trying to check here if the on off switch continuity. Then hold it so that it won't move then simply press it gently. You can easily determine it here when the said switch is working or not by the multimeter response, If the pointer moves approximately 0ohms the switch is good and working, but while if it is not moving at all it means the switch is faulty.

The four legs ON OFF switch assembly:

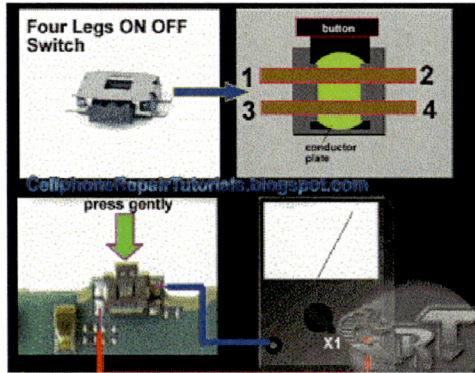

This check up procedure can work even if the ON OFF switch is mounted on the printed circuit board or isolated.

Four legged On off switch has its both opposite two terminal connected which other, so by checking this said switch is similar to the two legged on off switch. Again. just set the multimeter to X1 and connect the both probes to both opposite terminal of the said switch then simply hold and gently press it to get readings.

If the the multimeter's pointer moves it means it is working while if not the switch is faulty.

Read below for understanding how ON OFF switch works for advance power ON OFF switch problem repair troubleshooting techniques.

Cell Phone Power ON/OFF switch line paths, Basic test procedure

If you ever wonder how to determine if the power on off switch line paths is working or not or being cut or open, when proceeding to repair a dead cell phone handset?
This one will help you to a more specific troubleshooting steps,
before looking for or applying a power ON OFF ways solution or modified jumper on it.

This tricks can be applied before or after doing the following steps in repair procedures,

1. the flash firmware is okay

2. the power switch is okay

3. the phone can charge up or accept and show charging indication on LCD display but won't power up

Here's a simple Tricks on how to determine faulty power ON/OFF switch line path on mobile phone's circuit.

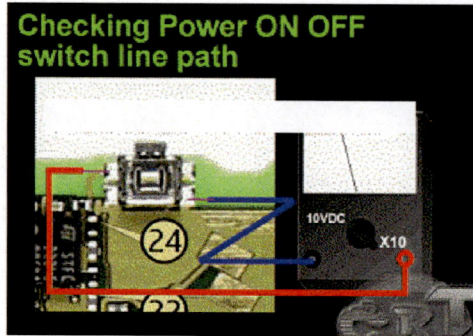

Checking Power ON OFF switch line path

By a way of Checking Resistance: This one can be applied if the power on/off line is directly connected to the Power Management IC terminal itself and no other components or open tests spot on the PCB's layout.

Set your multimeter tester to X10 or X 100 and connect the one probes to the power line path terminal of the power on off switch and the other one to the ground. Do this twice by reversing both probes position. If there is an indication of reading it means that line paths is okay, but without any response from the multimeter tester this means that the power on off switch line path is being cut or open. This technique is not just considering that every components needs a connection to the ground to work but definitely it won't work exactly without the ground connection.

By a way of checking voltage: This method can be applied by using a temporary voltage from DC Power Supply Regulator or even a battery itself, if the said handset is manageable to attach the battery without the pcb casing on it. Some mobile phones can be attachable when the battery pin connector is mounted and soldered on the PCB and unlike those have not.

Okay by checking voltage, just set the multimeter tester to 10volts DC, connect the negative probe to the PCB's groundings, then the other other one which is positive to the power on off line path. The voltage reading can reach up to 1 to 4 volts DC depending on which particular mobile phones models. The most important part on this, is that you should get readings to determine if the line paths is okay. Without any reading, the line path is seemingly open or cut.

PART 10

Troubleshooting

Fixing hardware problems is not been easy and takes a lot of time to consume rather than software problems, it is because when it comes to software handling you don't really need to open or dismantle a mobile phone handset, because only few of them really need to. In most cases like this, many among mobile phones technician focus on software handling like especially **unlocking**, for it less time consuming and more flexible to do with. This is been true that mobile phone technicians were separated into two specialties, like Hardware expert and Software expert, that is what the term they called it; It because mobile phones is a combination of software and hardware mechanism.

But there are also many mobile phones masters that can manage and do both hardware and software specialty and skills. They gained this knowledge by years of experience, and not only that they also earned much more income rather than to those staying at one particular specialty.

Now, here is the basic step by step repair procedure on hardware troubleshooting on mobile phones. Various mobile phones have different circuits and components or parts layouts and designs. First thing you must learn and be familiar with is, how each circuit components or parts is being mounted, connected, assembled or designed.

First step in handling troubleshooting procedure.

1. **Visualization Checkup**- Before proceeding to anything always consider the fact that a mobile phones handset is fragile object. Check and have take a look around every inch of the handsets package and layout, In this manner you can identify if the handset is in repairable condition, something like checking the whole printed circuit board components and parts, if it is free from dust, corrosion, bended, breakage etc.

2. **Know the Phones Status** - Ask the the user or the costumer about the phones history before the problem occurs. Letting know the phones history like accidentally soaked into a liquids or water, dropped, throwned and etc.

In this manner you can get an idea where to start or begin with.

3. **Do Software Check up** - Use a certain **flashing device** for that particular handset product to be able to read **logs**, logs is a reading of mobile phones firmware programmed and installed unto it. This is a big help for most advance mobile technician this days, A logs reading can help you where the faulty line or parts occurs. If you are not familiar about how to read logs you can ask to that certain flashing device product supporters and creator.

You can do flash, reformat at first hand if found something wrong with the mobile phones firmware. If all methods of software already done and nothing happens, proceed to hardware troubleshooting.

4. **Analyze The Circuit** - After dismantling and do visualization check up,be patient and take your time to

analyze the whole circuits layout, and **think of a step by step plan procedure** in your mind where or how to begin with. A **Special Operation Procedure** is good way and a reliable source of idea within yourself, not only by enhancing your skills but you are also practicing a self discipline method.

Now lets take one example of basic hardware troubleshooting methods in one particular mobile phone handsets. In this simple way you can then manage how to troubleshoot or been able on finding faulty parts or components within a mobile phone circuitry.

An example here is Nokia 6300, now assuming that this handset having a faulty microphone or mouthpiece.

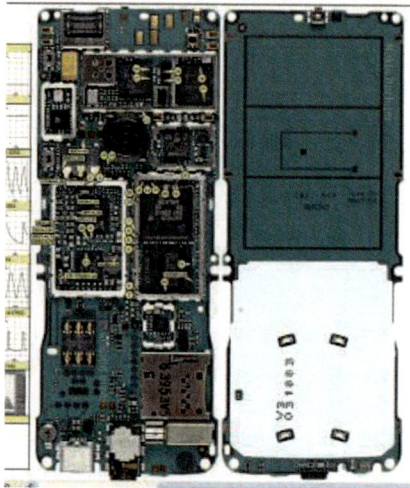

Do the basic procedures mentioned above, assuming that you are familiar with the Mouthpiece or microphone circuit, and already know how to check a microphone or mouthpiece component. you can now do this step below;

1. Find any available schematic diagram and locate the microphone circuit layout on it. Remember where each parts and components location and do a mapping like this.

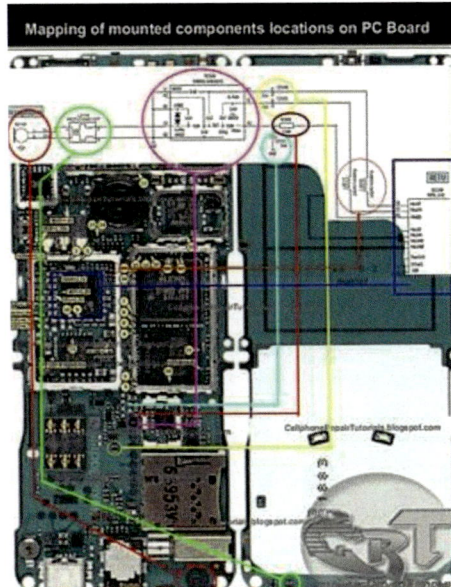

Mapping of mounted components locations on PC Board

2. Use a multi-tester and check the pads for a short circuit, this is not always happen but it is also unpredictable to a mobile phones short circuit might occurs, you are not checking the outer mounted components but the internal lines with it. Just set the tester to x1 resistance value, I preferred analog multitester in this lesson for it is cheaper to purchase rather than the digital. Now connect both test probe to the inner and outer layer of the mouthpiece terminal pads, then do it again in opposite manner, a short circuit have both readings closer to zero ohms.

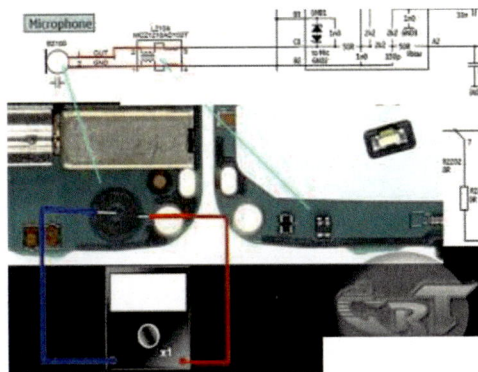

3. Trace the line paths between the first or the closest component connected to each terminal pads. The circuit diagram shows that there are coil filter in both lines, connect the tester across each coil terminal leds, your not just checking the lines here but also checking the coil as well.

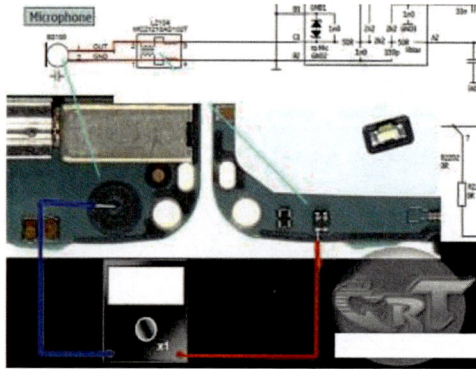

4. Now the next step is to leave behind the line paths between the coil to the EMI-Filter for it is uncheck able beyond that paths for the EMI- filter is an IC. you need to remove it first before you can check on that lines , which will be done later at the last steps of procedures. Now next to move on to the opening lines and component where the test probe can connect with, the two filter capacitors and both coils which are an open path where you can connect the test probe on it. now connect or attach both probes at the end of each line indicated in red.

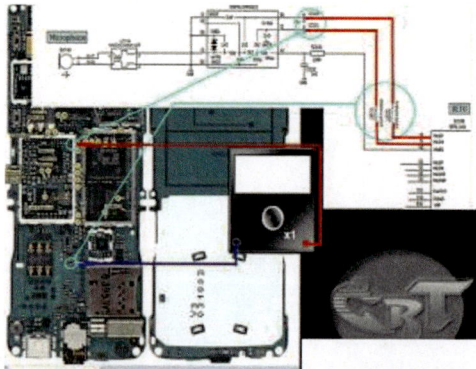

5. Now check the remaining open path which is the Resistor, you can't check the line paths on those area for it ends up connected to Retu IC. So just then proceed to check its resistance value instead.

266

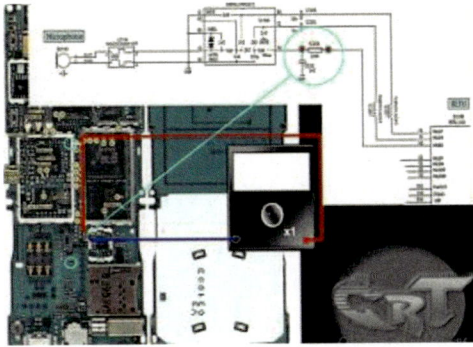

6. If all those mentioned lines above is all in good condition you may now proceed to suspect the EMI-Filter is having a problem or faulty. You then now remove it from the Printed circuit board then do a line check up from the mouthpiece terminal to that EMI-filter terminal bumps where it is being connected.

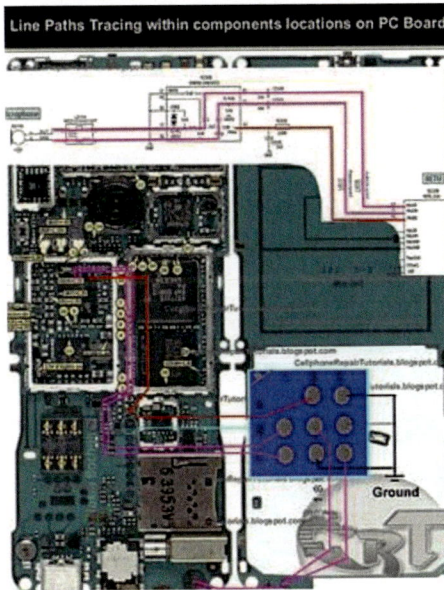

You can refer to the schematic diagram for each terminal specification. You may now can check the IC itself by analyzing the internal circuitry inside it. I advice just replace a good and working one if not so sure about.

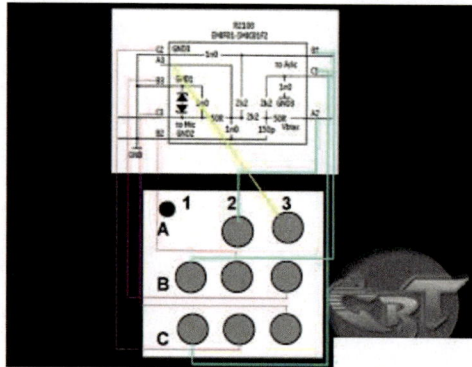

8. It this step is most complicated job to do with, specially for beginners. This is one of advance troubleshooters skills. If found all of those line paths and components above were in good conditions. The last part is to work a power management IC itself for the audio codec circuit is also within that chips. Now, if the last and final suspected parts is the chips, you must need to rework it, Reheating it the first will do and might as well also work. But if the problem still remain, Reworking it is the best advice that suites out.

but also do not forget to check the line paths between the mouthpiece circuit area, while the chips is being remove and out on the PCB layout, it is a proper time to check the ball bumps terminal where that certain microphone is being connected. an example of tracing the ball bumps terminals below.

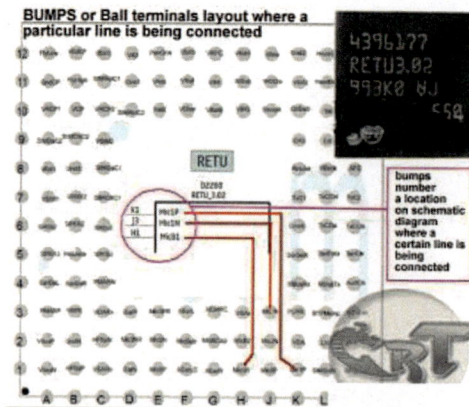

okay, that's it for a while, for there are lots of techniques we are going to tackle sooner, hope you do understand a little bit with this method.

PART 11

Troubleshooting and Repairs

How does Charging Circuit Works from a Battery Charger to charge a Mobile phone Battery

This lesson is also important for charging problem troubleshooting for knowing which parts or components has being used to make a charging circuit. Many mobile phone technicians had been asking me, **how does mobile phone charging circuit works? How does a battery charger can charge a mobile phone battery?**

To tell the truth many of them has never heard of this even they already fix thousands of mobile phones in their years of cellphone repair careers." and I am one of them.

I don't know but I know how fix it, its so easy" that's what we've often said.

Well, we all know that all mobile phones are all battery operated handsets that needs to charge the battery so that it will continue working, failure to charge it will result to unable to power up the mobile phone handsets.

Here's a brief explanation of how charging circuit works,

I prepare this simple idea and diminished some electronics technical terms so that everyone without adequate knowledge on electronics technical terms might can catch up with this.

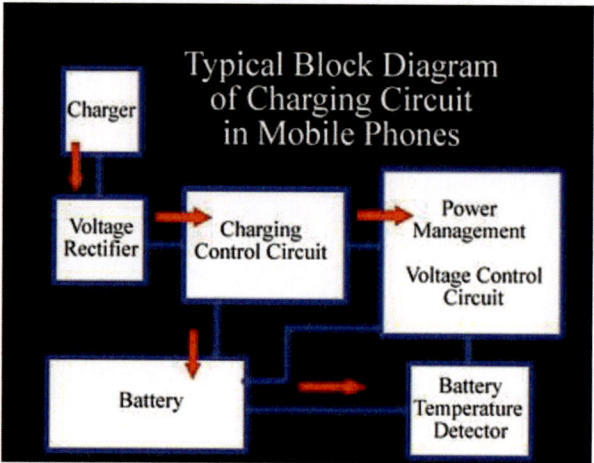

Typical Block Diagram of Charging Circuit in Mobile Phones

A charging circuit is composed of the following stages or sections.

1. **Battery Charger Circuits** - Although this is not found on mobile phones PC board circuit and have separate circuit but definitely this is also part of charging circuit; without this, the charging circuit is not complete and will not work completely.

This circuit is all parts and components that being mounted on any mobile phone charger, this is the one that converts **AC** (Alternating Current)voltage to **DC** (Direct Current)voltage.

What is AC Voltage? This voltage is a power source that we used in our household appliances to work and operate, this voltage can cause risk of electric shock and very dangerous to humans when being touch. This kind of voltage has **an alternate polarity.**

What is DC voltage? This voltage is a low level voltage which typically found on any kind of batteries. This kind of voltage have two polarities, the negative and the positive.

Here's how the battery charger works, the 110 or 220 AC volts coming from the electrical outlet at home or etc. will be converted to a desired DC voltage like 4.5 to 6 volt DC because the phone only accepts and can be operated into small amount of DC voltage.

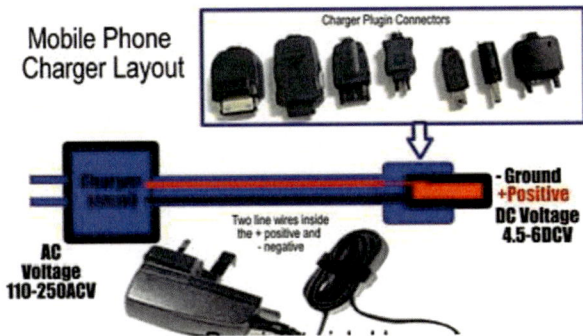

Mobile Phone Charger Layout

Charger Plugin Connectors

- Ground
+Positive
DC Voltage
4.5-6DCV

Two line wires inside
the + positive and
- negative

AC
Voltage
110-250ACV

A DC voltage output of a charger is only an artificial DC voltage, why is that? because only a battery cell can produce a 100% pure DC voltage.

2. **Protection Circuit**- this circuit is composed of a Fuse, Inductor coil Diode and Capacitors, before the DC voltage reach to the charging voltage control circuits the protection circuit is the one that control and check if that voltage is in exact amount. Let say the desired amount of DC voltage is only 5.6 volts above that point the fuse will be blown out to stop the voltage to flow so that it prevents damaging to another corresponding circuits.

In a protection circuit below of Nokia BB5 mobile phones a diode is the one that measure the amount of voltage from the battery charger, this diode has a reaching point of desired voltage to measure of how much amount of voltage will be allowed to flow within that line, when exceed to that desired point of voltage the diode will then cut it off.

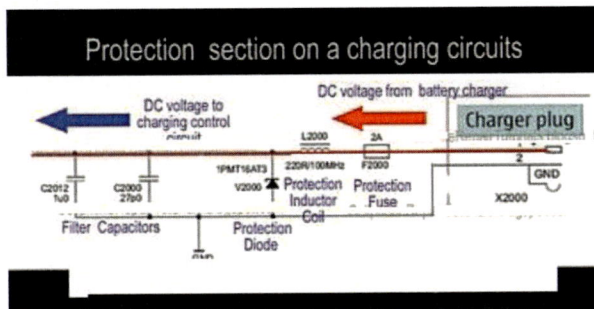

Protection section on a charging circuits

DC voltage from battery charger

DC voltage to
charging control
circuit

Charger plug

L2000   3A

1PMT16AT3   220R/100MHz   F2000
V2000   Protection   Protection
Inductor   .Fuse
Coil

GND

X2000

C2012   C2000
1u0   27n0

Filter Capacitors   Protection
Diode

like for example if that **diode** is being designed that only allows only 7 volts from the battery charger to flow on that line. Now, above that desired voltage let say that the voltage becomes 8 or higher the diode will then be reacts and destruct itself, this is what then so-called shorted component; so that the current will flow directly to ground and will not reach to the following or corresponding circuit. If the diode will cut off or shorted the **fuse** will tends to blow and totally cut the voltage line. The inductor coil's role is to filter unwanted voltage saturation, it rejects abnormal voltage modulation caused by electrostatic interference.

3. **Charger Voltage Control Circuit** - This is the stage where the charger voltage and current is being stabilized, amplified, rectified, regulated and other voltage purification process is being held in this area before it feeds to the battery. This kind of circuit commonly being pack in a chips together with another circuits.

A failure of this certain area will result on charging problem status. This area mostly called by most technician as a **Charging IC** it is because this circuit is inside in a particular IC chips, but eventually this circuit also accompanied by many other circuit types and not exclusive to a certain charging area.

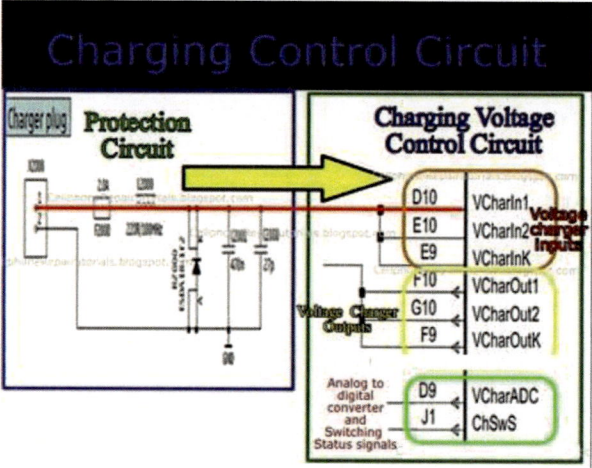

This pictures shows is the next corresponding circuit from the protection circuit area. The voltage from charger is now then feeds into three terminal inputs of the charger voltage control circuits.

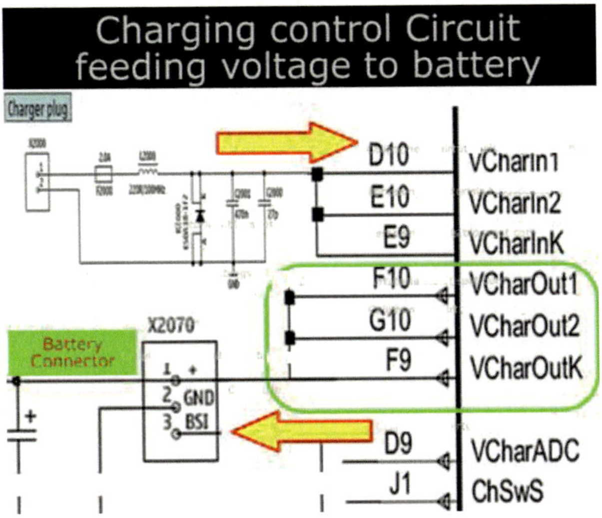

Charging control Circuit feeding voltage to battery

D10	VCharIn1
E10	VCharIn2
E9	VCharInK
F10	VCharOut1
G10	VCharOut2
F9	VCharOutK
D9	VCharADC
J1	ChSwS

in this figure shows after the voltage stabilization and purification process the voltage is now then feeds to the battery terminal.

4. **Charging Control Circuit** - this is the area where the charging process is being monitored, this is the one that sends information to the application processor to start or stop the charging process. This area is part of **Power management circuit,** so-called **POWER IC** by many technicians**.**

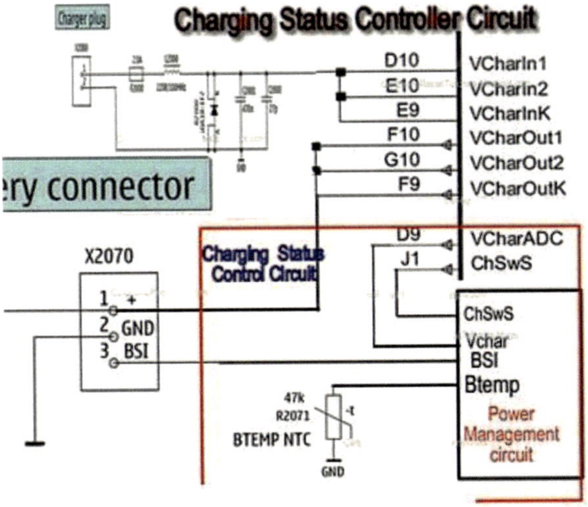

Charging Status Controller Circuit

In this picture that there are two terminal signal from the voltage control that sends data to the Charging control circuit, this two data signals will inform to the charging control circuit that a charger voltage is being entered or plug-in. After this charging control circuits receives the data it will then analyze and convert that data into digital signal then sends it to the Application processor.

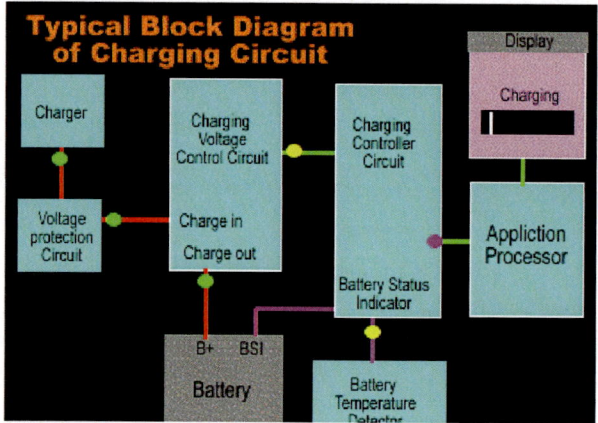

Typical Block Diagram of Charging Circuit

The application processor which is the brain of all the circuits now then decide if all the data's are in correct or in right information to begin the process,
It always relies on the data that sends by the charging control circuit, then decide all data and completely process it.

Okay now lets take an example and apply this particular method on a mobile phone circuitry component layout, I have here a Nokia N95 board, which is a good way to start with, while we still working on advance training. Now, try to analyze and compare all of those previous picture above and combined them into each corresponding stages or section, in this manner you can build an step by step tracing procedure on how to deal charging problem issues.

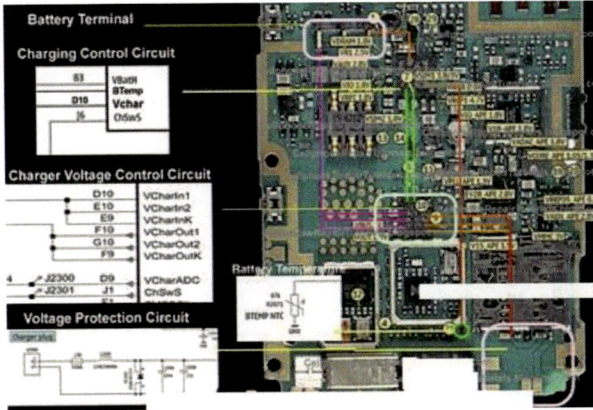

In the picture above shows, how and where the voltage flow from a charger voltage source through the entire PC board circuit. This is the method where you can start and manage how to locate and trace each and every component to find possible problems regarding charging problem issues.

How to Repair Cellphone Not Charging, No Response, Charger Not Supported Problem Issues

There are few types of charging problem issues like Not Charging, No Charging Response and Charger Not Supported.

A problem issues with "Not Charging" shows on a display when a charger is being plug-in, this problem occurs when a required current or voltage is not enough to boost up and charge the mobile phones battery.

One reason of this problem is a faulty BSI Line, a BSI line is a Battery Size Indicator that tell the charging control circuit how's the batteries working status.

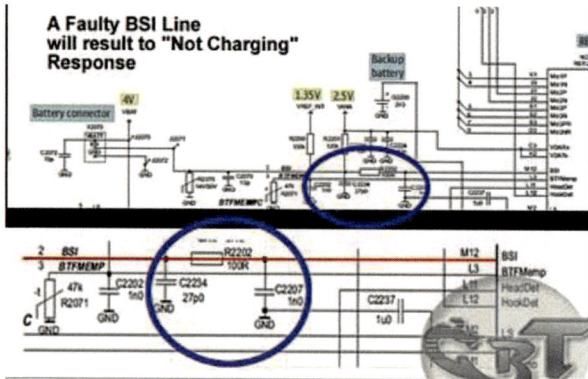

A Faulty BSI Line will result to "Not Charging" Response

The battery has a BSI output indicator terminal that connected to its negatives terminal with desired value of resistor on it.

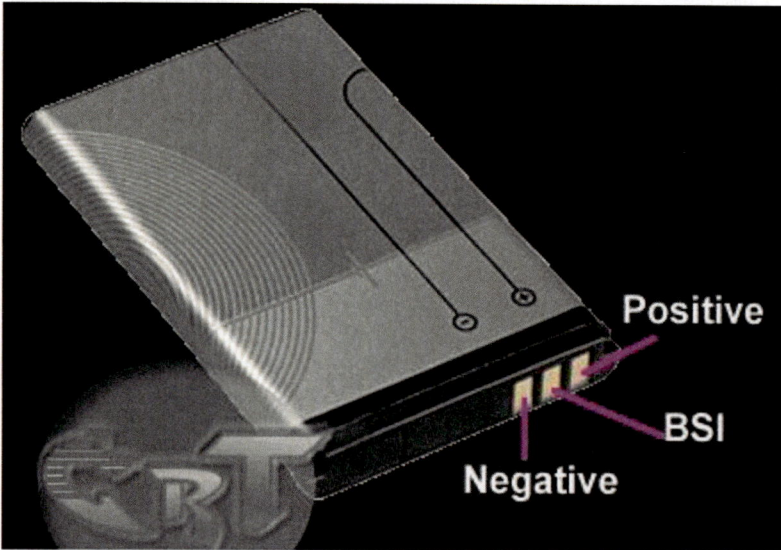

Positive

BSI

Negative

One other charging problem issues is the No charging response when a battery charger is being plug-in, it stays no response or nothing happens.

One reason of this is a faulty protection circuit section. this happens when there is no voltage reach to charging circuit indicators and controls. If the protection circuit breakdown this will result to "charging no response" situation. You need to check each components for short and open circuits. You may start from the fuse then to the coil and the diode.

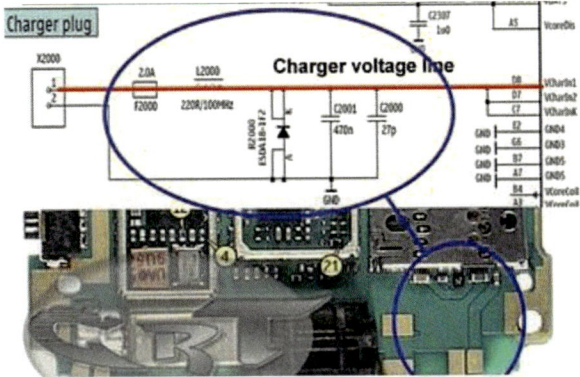

Charger Not Supported problem is cause by a faulty BTEMP thermistor component, BTEMP stands for Battery Temperature, This is the one that monitors the battery temperature status during at charging status, if this one having a problem , it wont allow any charger to proceed to charging stage.

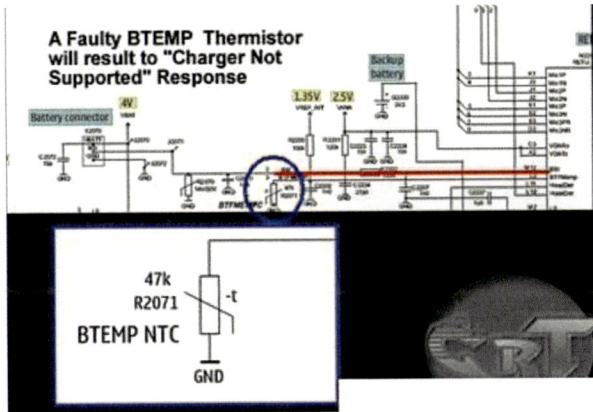

A Faulty BTEMP Thermistor will result to "Charger Not Supported" Response

47k
R2071
BTEMP NTC
GND

This all, is only a brief explanation of how charging problem issues occurs, while charging the mobile phones .

There are lots of ways on how to troubleshoot each and every kind of handsets. Hope at least, this one let help you understand how charging problem issues occurs, and by this you can gain ideas to move into a stage where you can practice how to troubleshoot this kind of issues.

How Do SIM Card Works on Mobile Phones Circuit

A **SIM Card** also known as **Subscriber Identity Module**, A SIM is a **Smart Card** that can store data from a cellular phone. Those data like identity, location and phone number, network authorization data, personal security keys, contact lists and stored text messages. Security features include authentication and encryption to protect data and prevent eavesdropping.

But how does this SIM card works within the mobile phones circuit? How does mobile phones reads and write data unto it?

In those particular questions above, If we learn answers unto it, we can solve problem issues regarding SIM related problems, like **Insert Sim Card** and etc.

Now here's a brief explanation on how does SIM Circuit Works on a mobile phones circuit.

A Sim Card have six pads that also corresponds to the six SIM connectors pins, but only five has totally have connection on the entire layout.

SIM DATA - this is a digital data that being stored on a SIM memory

SIM Clock - this is a clock frequency signal that being synchronize to the digital data to create data signal in order transfer or sends and receive data information.

SIM Reset - this is also a frequency signal that triggers or reset all synchronization process.

VSIM B+ Supply Voltage- This a power supply voltage used to activated the SIM circuit.

SIM Ground - a ground line voltage

The other one is not connected

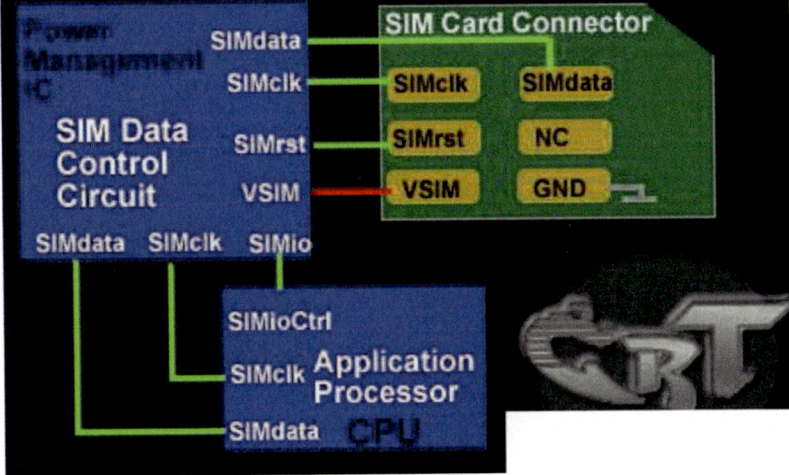

Typical Block Diagram of SIM Circuit

A Typical block Diagram above shows on how SIM Circuit Works on a Cellular phones circuits.

In the layout the **Sim Interface Connector** connected directly to SIM Control Circuit. The SIM Control Circuit is the one the generates Clock frequency that triggers the SIM data storage, once the SIM is now being triggered, it is then now sends data information to the application processor to begin the process with. The application processor is the one that gathered all data information from the SIM memory, initiate and activate it, if all information is in desired status.

Those three particular lines of signal flows associated in the circuit shows how the synchronization is being applied. If one of those lines being cut off the sending and receiving process will breakdown, and will result to SIM problem issues. The Power Supply Voltage through the SIM is also remain stable otherwise a lack of voltage will not activate the SIM to work.

SIM Circuit on Schematic Diagram

Power Management IC

CPU

SIMClk1
SIMDctrl1
SIMODa1

Application Processor

1.8/3V

SIM connector

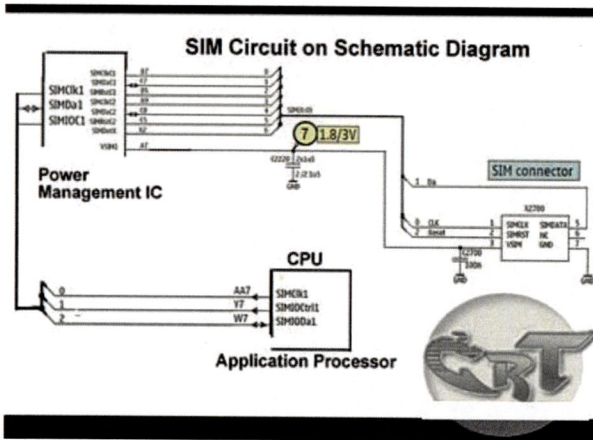

In a picture below an EMI-ESD Filter has been added to protect the circuit to an Electro-static Discharge and Electro-magnetic Interference disorders. This type of SIM connection circuit is an advantage to mobile phone technician for troubleshooting SIM related problem issues. Thus, type of particular EMI filter is very vulnerable and mostly create breakdown to the entire SIM connection.

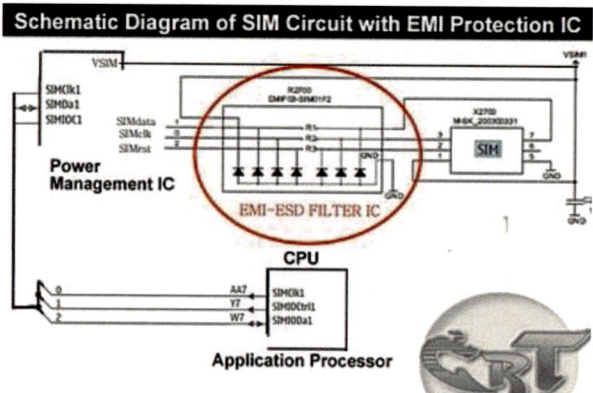

Schematic Diagram of SIM Circuit with EMI Protection IC

Power Management IC

SIMClk1
SIMDa1
SIMIOC1

SIMdata
SIMclk
SIMrst

EMI-ESD FILTER IC

SIM

CPU

SIMClk1
SIMDctrl1
SIMODa1

Application Processor

The picture below is an equivalent layout of an EMI filter and its internal circuitry, only both frequency and data lines is being filtered.

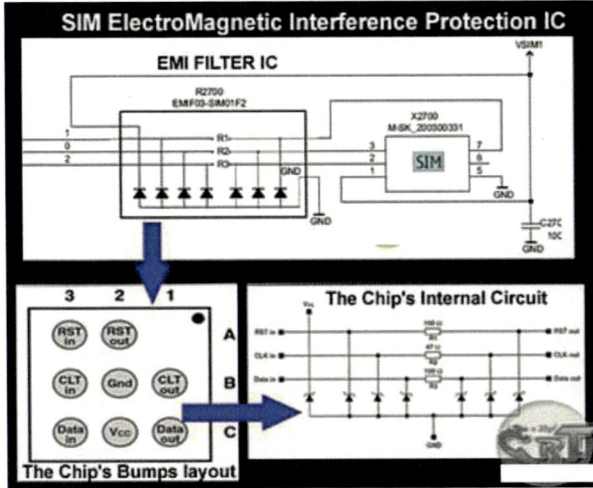

SIM ElectroMagnetic Interference Protection IC

EMI FILTER IC

The Chip's Internal Circuit

The Chip's Bumps layout

The EMI Filter is a tiny chips designed to protect SIM DATA, SIM Clock and SIM Reset data signals that flow across trough the SIM connector.

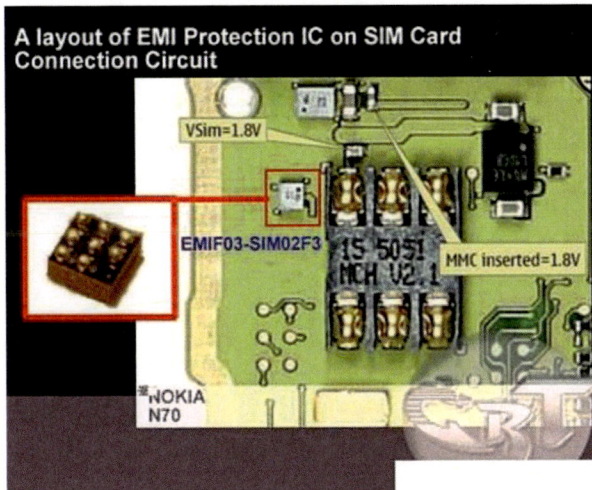

A layout of EMI Protection IC on SIM Card Connection Circuit

The EMI-ESD Filter is a highly integrated device designed to suppress EMI(Electromagnetic Interference) and RFI(Radio frequency Interference in a circuit. This filter includes ESD protection circuitry which prevents damaging the mobile phone application when subject to ESD (ElectroStatic Discharge) surges up to 15 kV.

Here's an example of how the the SIM data signal flow across the printed circuit board.
Note: this is only shows where the signal flows from component to component connections.

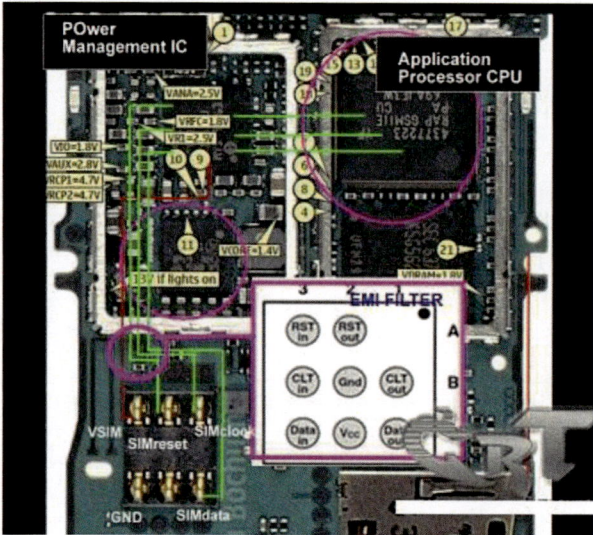

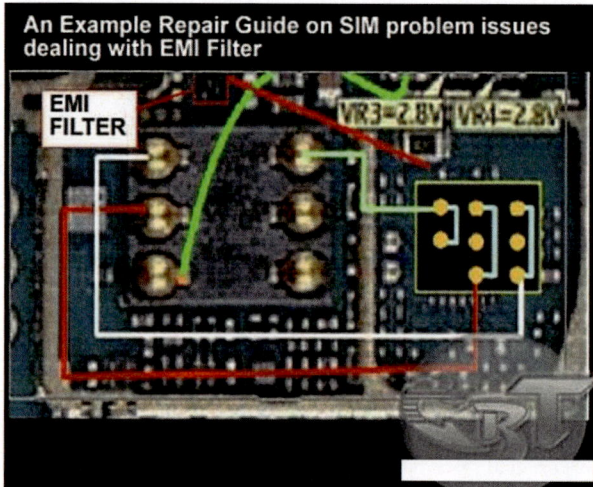

 A picture above is an alternative way by many mobile phone technicians dealing with SIM problem issues on most Nokia Mobile Phones.

Understanding Keypads Circuit, a way to Learn How to Repair Keypad Problem

Understanding the Keypad circuit may help and boost your knowledge on fixing keypad problem issues on mobile phones. Keypads is a part of user interface being used to navigate or enter numbers, letters and characters, browse application, sends information and etc.

An schematic diagram below will help us understand how keypad circuits works and which components or parts did this circuit is being connected.

In this diagram the each and every key switching pads is being divided and grouped into **rows and columns**. Each rows and columns were group into 2 -5 keypads switch. This rows and columns have each corresponding lines according to each and every group of switching pads.

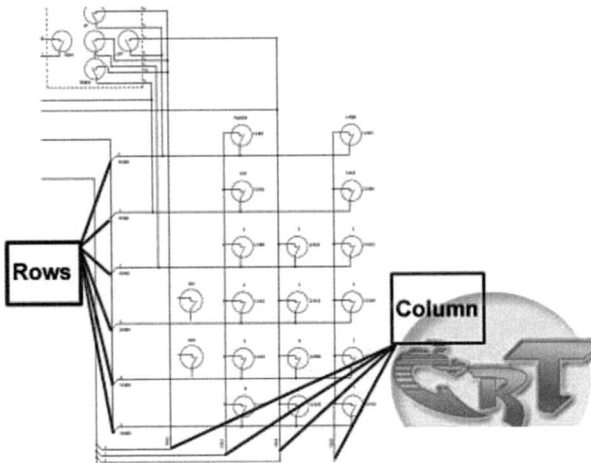

This lines of rows and columns is being filtered for EMI and ESD protection the EMI filter is made of tiny chip that used to protect such EMI and ESD interference.

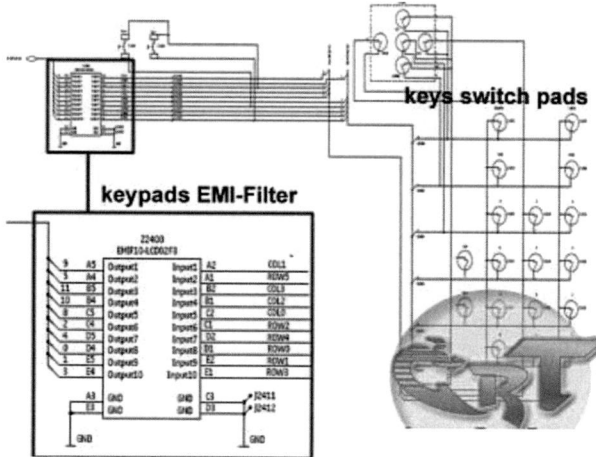

keys switch pads

keypads EMI-Filter

This rows and columns lines are digital switching signals generated by the application processor to trigger or activate every corresponding **digital data** that is being stored and programmed within the mobile phone **system memory**. This diagram below is an **Application Processor** that generates and feeds then receives digital data switching signals.

Keypads Rows and Column Lines on EMI Filter

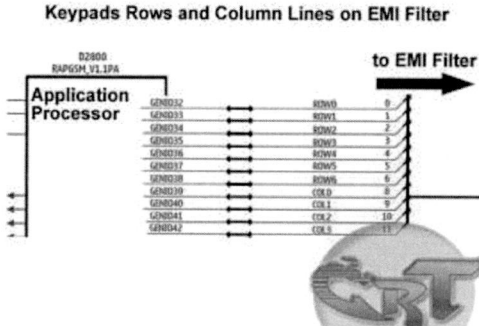

to EMI Filter

This digital data frequency signals corresponds and interpreted to each key characters that are marked on each keypads. Like for example a combination of row 2 and column 3 will triggered the number 3 when hitting on it.

this block diagram below shows how the switching signal is being triggered to process a command data.

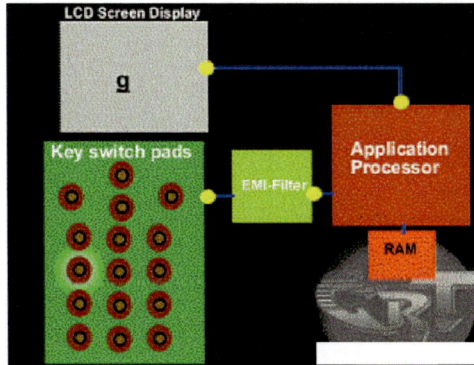

Various mobile phones have different keypads layouts and specification. A joystick and a volume switch is also parts of keypads switching circuits. Some keypads module designs are made into a flexible wire like those **Slide Type package** of mobile phones. Some flexible wires are very vulnerable and common cause of keypad malfunction.

How to Trace and Map Keypads Layout on Mobile Phone Printed Circuit Board (PCB)

There are few methods in tracing and mapping the keypad layout on a mobile phones keypads on printed circuit board. One of this quick and very easy method is by using an schematic diagram, if that certain mobile phones have available unto it. Schematic diagram is very useful guide in every aspects of hardware troubleshooting.

Now assuming that you already have knowledge how to use and read it, follow this simple steps below. Browse to bottom of the pages where you can locate and find like the picture below., it is the keypad circuit section. In that schematic layout you will notice that each corresponding key characters is being group into lines. This group of keypad switch lines is being marked with **rows and columns.**

285

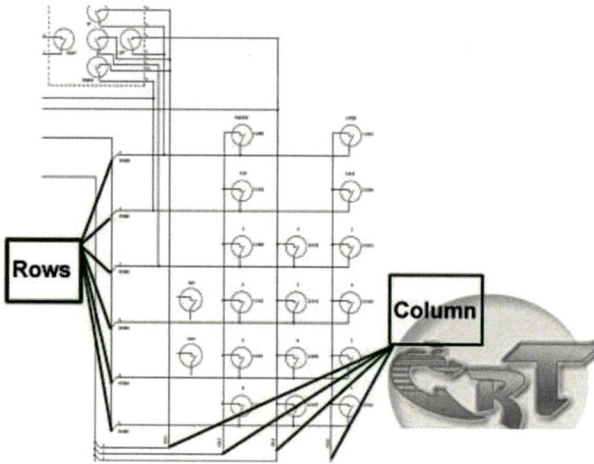

Rows

Column

trace each and every lines where those keypads switch symbols is being connected, once you been manage to trace it. configure and trace it on the printed circuit board by using an analog or digital multimeter, just set it the resistance value X1 and attach both probes to corresponding keypads groups in every rows and column

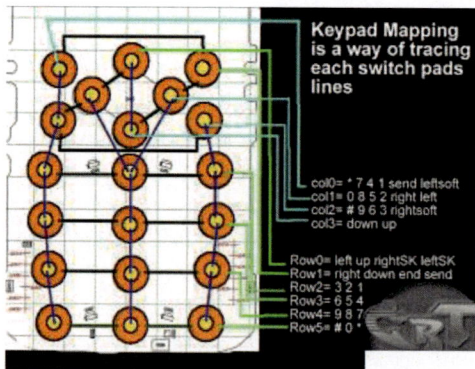

Keypad Mapping is a way of tracing each switch pads lines

col0= * 7 4 1 send leftsoft
col1= 0 8 5 2 right left
col2= # 9 6 3 rightsoft
col3= down up

Row0= left up rightSK leftSK
Row1= right down end send
Row2= 3 2 1
Row3= 6 5 4
Row4= 9 8 7
Row5= # 0 *

Practice this kind of method with an aide of schematic diagram, in this way if you're skills grows further, you can then trace any other mobile phones without any schematic diagram available at first hand.

How Do LED light bulbs works on Mobile Phone Circuit

An **LED** - light emitting diode is used to illuminate keypads keys and LCD screen displays on all mobile phones handsets. It is being controlled by a voltage or current draws on its terminal leds.

a picture below is an Schematic Diagram that tells us how does the LED circuit works on cellular phone whole circuitry.

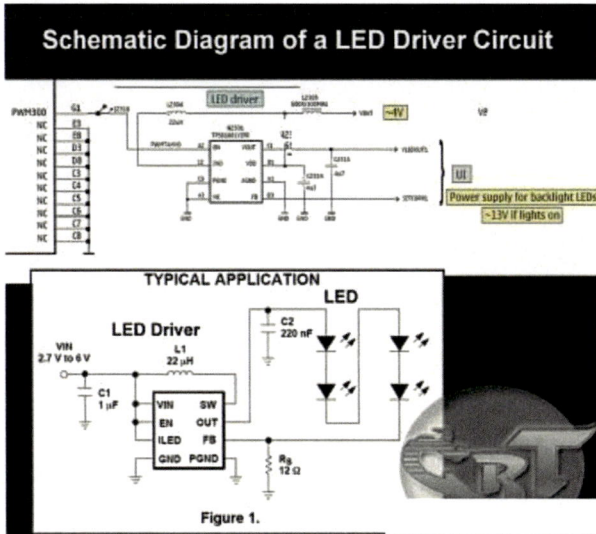

On schematic diagram we notice that the LEDs is driven by an **LED driver** chip's, and an **Switching Control** circuit that also being packed in a chip. The LED driver is being used to stabilized the voltage and current and do take control on engaging ON and OFF status of an LEDs to light up or not.

It also drives the amount of brightness or dimming status of the LEDs by applying Pulse Width Modulation signal from the Switching control circuit.

The block diagram below interpreted a component and section or parts of an LED circuit to work during application process.

The Switching control circuit feeds and release a **Pulse Width Modulation** Signal (**PWM**) to switch and light up the LEDs light bulbs. A pulse width modulation signal is a type of digital frequency signal range up to 1khz to enable and implement to take control of LED brightness.

Once that certain signal is being received by the LED driver, the LED driver now will engage and release the voltage or current that being feeds up from the mobile phones battery supply voltage;

The output voltage release by the LED driver is the one that draws the LED light bulbs to light up.

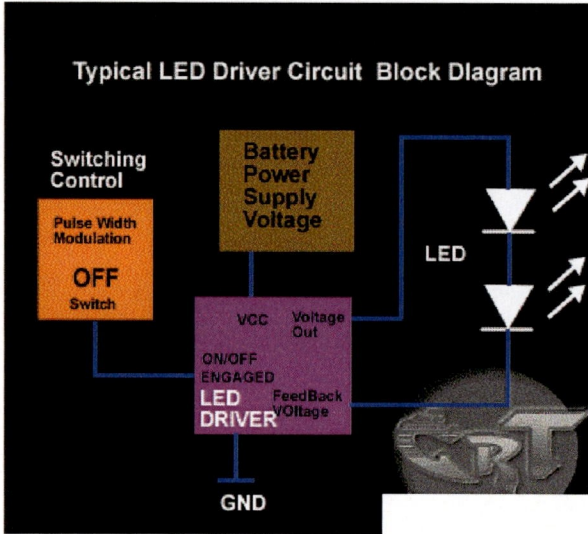

Typical LED Driver Circuit Block Diagram

Switching Control
Pulse Width Modulation
OFF
Switch

Battery Power Supply Voltage

VCC Voltage Out
ON/OFF ENGAGED
LED FeedBack VOltage
DRIVER
GND

LED

LED drivers is a high frequency, synchronous boost converter with constant current output to drive up to 5 white LEDs. This device circuit is designed for maximum safety, it integrates overvoltage and short circuit protection when the output is being shorted to the ground. Meaning this chips circuitry will not easily breakdown for it is designed to protect when short circuit happens.
like for example, the two LED light bulbs commits short circuit to its terminal
In mobile phones application methods; the switching control circuit that release pulse switching signal is also being synchronized programmed by the application processor (CPU) to engaged a full control on how and which proper situation that the LED will be switch to light up or not.
like for example the LED will only switch and light up, if the handset is being in used and remain off if the handset is not in used.

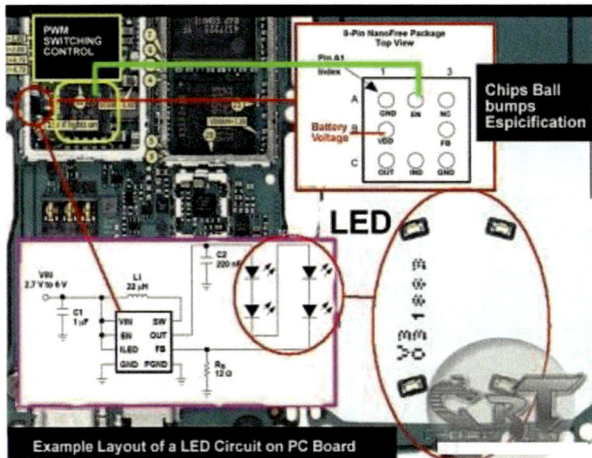

Example Layout of a LED Circuit on PC Board

The above image is an example of the LED circuit, how those particular stages and components being mounted on a phones circuits. Note that the LED driver and switching control circuits is being packed into an Integrated Circuit or ICs.

To all beginners: A bunch of simplified STEP By STEP Procedures On Troubleshooting LED Problem issues on various mobile phones product will be Posted Here Later.. Just keep on visiting this blog more often.

How Audio Codec do on Mouthpiece, Earpiece, IHF speaker or Buzzer and Vibrator on mobile phone circuits

The Audio Codec is a circuit that controls sound signals in a cellphone circuits. It acts like an **audio amplifier** or an **audio mixer** or a sound booster.

Audio codec is the main area in a mobile phone where all audio properties is being process, during transmission and reception. It converts the sound signal into radio frequency signal, and also converts radio frequency signal into a sound signals.

Like for example a microphone's sound signal is being amplified then converts and feeds to radio frequency before it send to the network airwaves. Opposite to that process is the conversion of radio frequency into an audible or understandable sound, and that sound is that what we hear on the earpiece speaker.

A typical block diagram below show how audio interfaces being connected to an **audio codec circuit**.

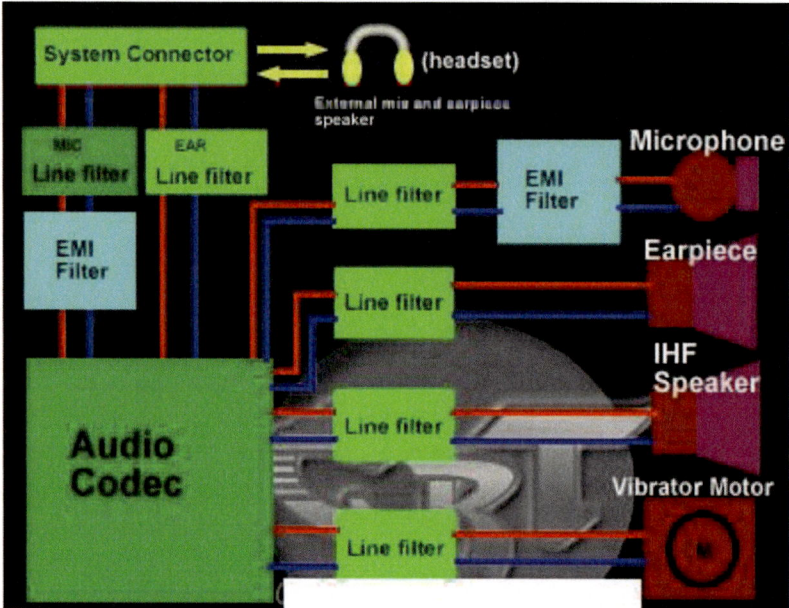

The Audio codec is the main part which control all audio properties from all audio interfaces like the microphone, earpiece, IHF (integrated hands free) speaker or a buzzer, ringer, head set and vibrator motor. A typical audio circuit is being filtered from any sound interference signal to avoid sound interruptions.

Understanding Mouthpiece or Microphone, Earpiece and IHF or Buzzer Speakers Circuit on mobile phones

A mobile phones microphone or mouthpiece is a component used to convert sound signal into an electrical signal. The earpiece speaker is the one that converts electrical signal into a sound signal, likewise also the IHF , buzzer or ringer speaker do.
These certain parts works as a user interfaces components on a mobile phone.

And controlled by an **Audio Codec Circuit** which is the part that relatively controls and converts all audio frequency signal.

see picture below

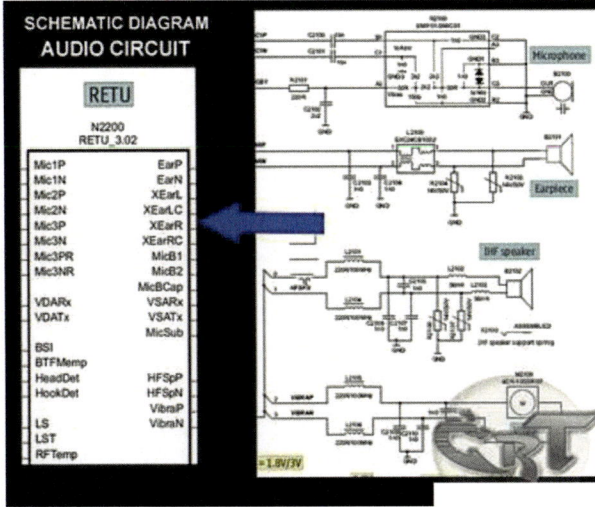

A picture below is an schematic diagram microphone or mouthpiece circuit,
A typical and modern designed of mouthpiece circuit is being protected by an EMI- Filter to prevent sound interruption, before it then feeds the audio signal to the audio codec circuit. Some microphone circuit other mobile phones have no EMI Filter like the one showed below. The microphone line signal is being presented into positive and negative polarity, and those two polarity lines is being filtered again by two capacitor after being pass by from an EMI-Filter, in order to remove the DC (direct current) coming from the EMI-filter.

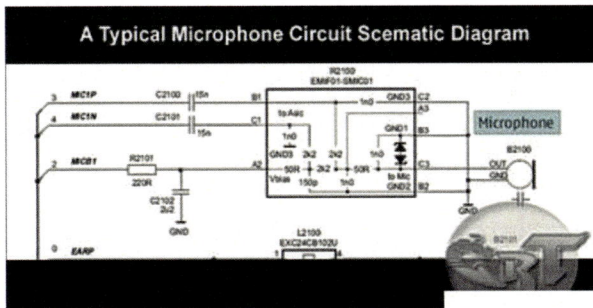

The earpiece circuit is also filtered by inductor coil to reduce sound saturation cause by any radio frequency interruption.

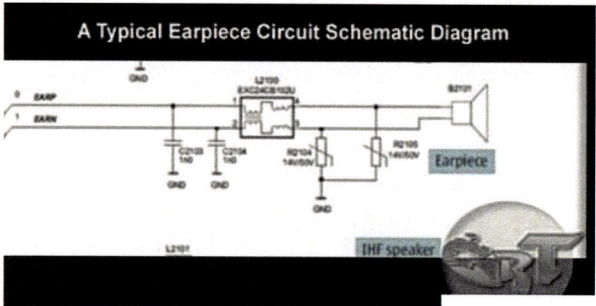

A Typical Earpiece Circuit Schematic Diagram

And same also in an IHF speaker circuit. The IHF speaker also have two lines which is positive and negative line.

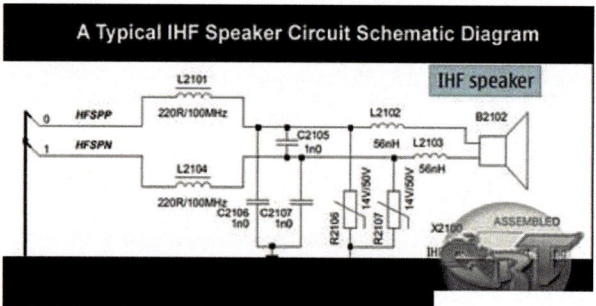

A Typical IHF Speaker Circuit Schematic Diagram

A vibrator motor although this is not a sound converting device but it generates a vibration which generates sounds, this one is also included in audio circuitry.

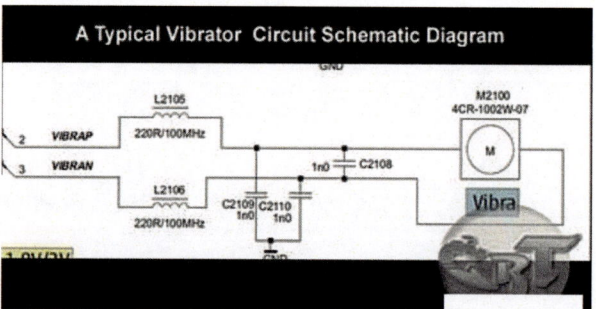

A Typical Vibrator Circuit Schematic Diagram

Here's an example mapping layout of a Microphone, Earpiece, IHF speakers and Vibrator motor connections on a mobile phones printed circuit board. Each connection were both separated and apart from each other but all of each line is being pointed towards in audio codec circuit.

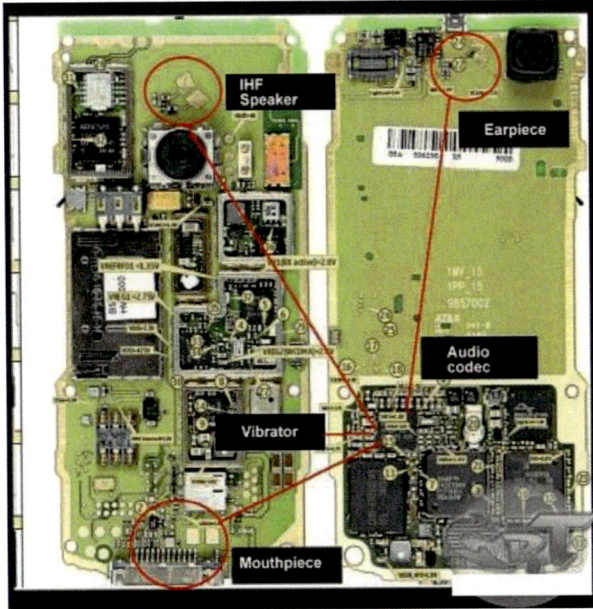

The above picture is only an interpretation of how audio circuit is being connected or mounted in a mobile phones printed circuit board.

How LCD Display Interface Circuit works

An **LCD -liquid crystal display** is an electronically-modulated optical device made up of any number of pixels filled with liquid crystals and arrayed in front of a light source (backlight) or reflector to produce images in color or monochrome.
They can be optimized for static text, detailed still images, or dynamic, fast-changing, video content.
Old type of LCD are monochrome types which only display one certain color while the modern types are colored ones that can display rich text and images.

LCD's resolution of display depends on the amount of pixels into it, the highest amount designed looks and displays best.

Now, LCd wont work without a **light source** and a **reflector** to drive it pixels to form an image information.
This typical block diagram below will help us a brief explanation oh how the LCD can produce an text and images on mobile phones handsets.
The block diagram shows the LCD gets a data source from the application processor, so therefore LCD is being controlled by the application processor to produce a detail images,
LED is a light emitting diode that can produce light, this light source of an LED is the one that reflect at the back of an LCD, without this **LED light reflection** on the back of an LCD it will result a black or dark screen displays.
LCD also needs a power supply voltage to activate its liquid crystal arrays inside of it, so that is why a voltage supply is also very important for that matter.

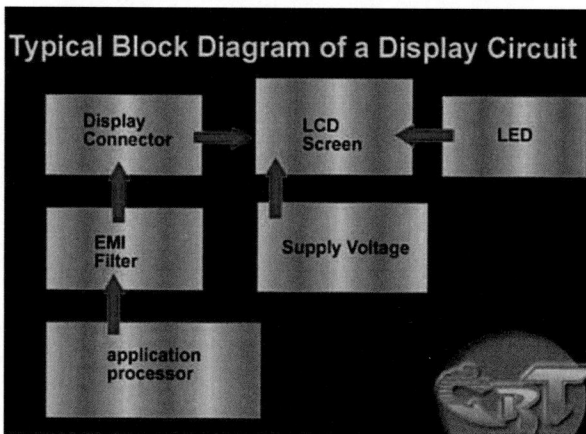

Typical Block Diagram of a Display Circuit

An LCD Display Circuit Schematic diagram of a mobile phones below interprets how the whole circuitry of an LCD being connected and designed. A circuit start from an application processor that controls and sends data to LCD connector which where the LCD is being connected. Before the data reach to the LCd connector it is being filtered for Electromagnet Interference protection. The LED light circuit and a power supply voltage is also provided for it is also work an important part on LCD circuit.

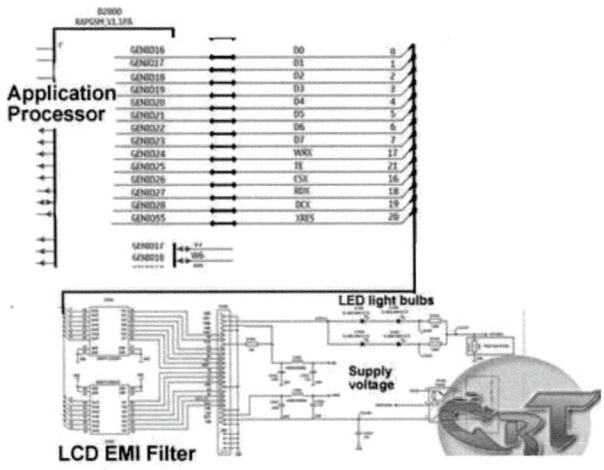

The picture below interprets the schematic diagram above on how each components layout are being mounted on a particular mobile phones printed circuit board.

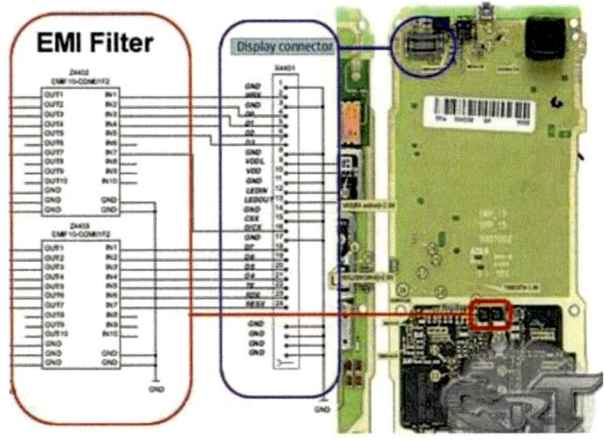

Always keep in mind that LCD needs the following sources to make it work completely,

1. Data control signal from the application processor
2. LED light that reflects on it back so that display will reveal completely.
3. A power supply voltage to turn the LCD activated.

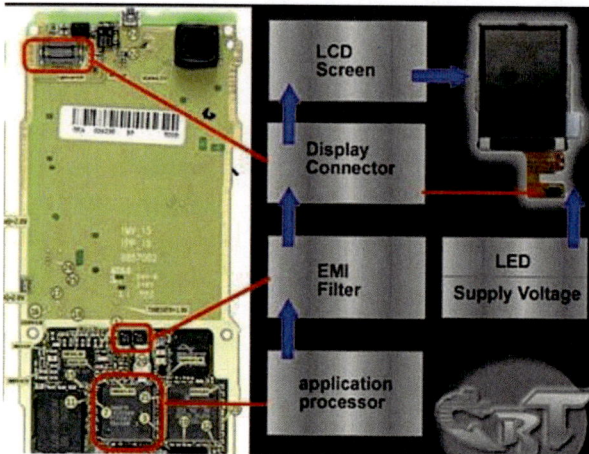

A failure of these three sources will result on display problem issues.

Understanding how RF circuit Works on Cell Phones

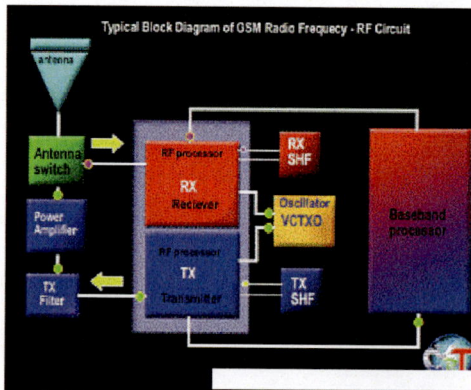

In cell phone repair it is very helpful to understand how the RF circuits works , for this is a big help when troubleshooting No signal problem issues.

RF stands for radio frequency , this frequency is used to transmit and receive the data signals from a mobile phone.

Here's a brief explanation on how does RF circuit works on mobile phones.
This is for GSM RF circuit only, although the WCDMA circuit and WI-FI circuit have similarity on this but I will try to explain both of it hereafter.

See the block diagram below. Observe how the frequency data signal feeds from a certain parts of an RF circuit design.
A breakdown or failure of each certain part will result to signal loss and the capability to generate, amplify, control , process, send and receive the desired radio frequency during transmission process.

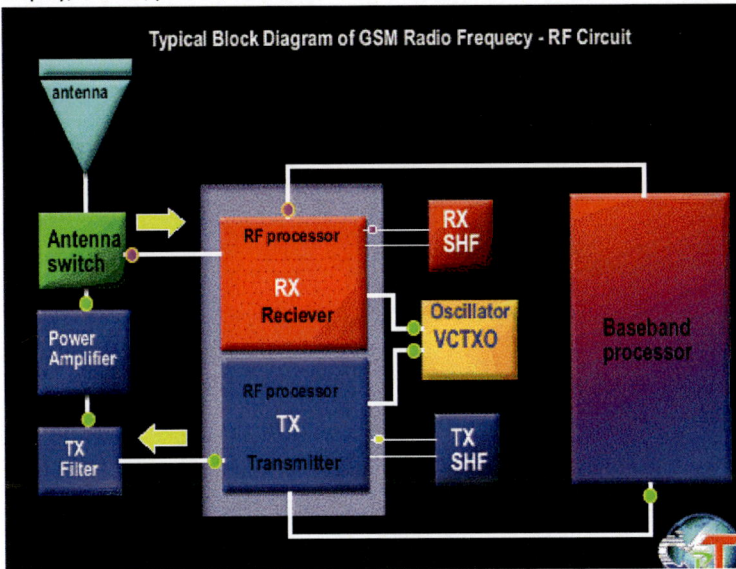

Typical Block Diagram of GSM Radio Frequecy - RF Circuit

antenna

Antenna switch

RF processor

RX SHF

RX Reciever

Oscillator VCTXO

Baseband processor

Power Amplifier

RF processor TX

TX Transmitter

TX SHF

TX Filter

In mobile phones transmission there are two types of operation took place, the receiving operation and the transmitting operation.
In normal mode, RX part is always active in receiving operation the antenna switch is always open its gateway through to the RX circuit, It is always ready to receive and intercepts the radio waves and wait for the desired frequency signal to catch up.
During transmission like making a call or sending a text message the antenna switch will close the gateway of the RX and open the gateway of the TX in order not to interfere the data signal during transmission.
All data that has been receive and before to transmit or send, all this data signals are feeds to the baseband processor.

An explanation of an RF Circuit Parts and what possible problems if a certain part is damaged.

RF Receiver - (RX radio receiver)

The rf receiver are called RX, this circuit is design to receives, and process the data signals from the airwaves during transmission process. A failure of this circuit will result to unable to receive data signal during transmission.

RF Transmitter - (TX radio transmitter)

the rf transmitter are called TX which is the one that process, amplify the data signals from a mobile phone .

Once failed to initiate a failure to transmit radio frequency signal, this will result to unable to send data signal during transmission. .

Power amplifier - RF amplifier

The power amplifier is used to amplify, boost up the radio frequency signal before it feeds to the antenna before it thrown over the air waves during transmission. If damaged will result to signal loss, a dropping signal indication on the display.

The Antenna is used to intercepts and thrown the radio frequency in the air during transmission
When electricity is "thrown" into the metal of an antenna, the metal reacts to the electricity at an atomic level in the form of a wave.
if damaged or due to a corroded terminal pads, will indicate and show a poor signal or low level frequency signal.

Antenna switch

The antenna switch is used as a gateway that controls and manage the frequency to pass through, it switch the RX frequency signal and TX frequency signal during transmission process. literally the antenna is the signal catcher and likewise the signal thrower. If damaged the gateway to the antenna will be closed and result to network signal indication.

Crystal oscillator

Generates a desired frequency that feeds to the RX and TX circuits. In mobile phones a Voltage controlled Oscillator (VCO) and Voltage Controlled Temperature Compensated Crystal Oscillator (VCTXO) is used in rf circuit.
If damaged the RX and TX will not work and the RF circuit is at full failure.

SAW filter

Surface Acoustic Wave filter used as an rf synthesizer to purify a desired level of frequency. If damaged result also to no network signal indication.

An example of the RF circuit components layout on a PCB board.

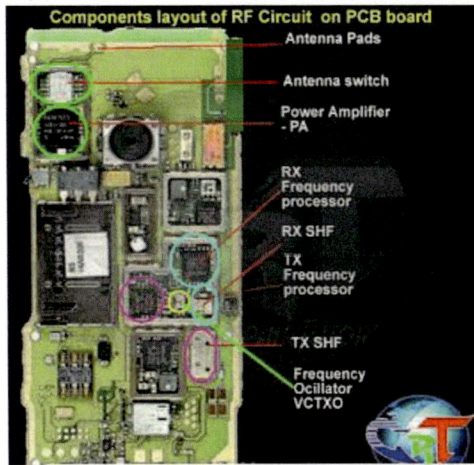

Components layout of RF Circuit on PCB board
- Antenna Pads
- Antenna switch
- Power Amplifier - PA
- RX Frequency processor
- RX SHF
- TX Frequency processor
- TX SHF
- Frequency Ocillator VCTXO

The rf circuit components are often covered with shielding metal case unlike the baseband processor parts which is oftentimes not. This is because frequency is very vulnerable with unwanted radio waves interference and destroys data signals. Using the shielding metal will minimize the radio waves interference.

PART 12

What is Flashing

What is Unlocking

What is Flashing on Mobile Phones

Flashing is installing a new firmware to a cellphone flash memory. When the cellphones firmware is being damaged or interrupted, this one particularly result on not powering the phone, hang up, or keep on re-starting and a lot more software problem issues.

This firmwares were comes with different versions.

Each mobile phones product has unique firmware versions. And have also specific software that to be use for it.

If you have a basic computer knowledge is more advantage, but even if none you can still do and learn easily.

What things do we need in flashing cellphones?

In flashing phones we need ob-course

1.)A desktop or laptop computer to run the software program, with a USB (universal serial bus) port.

2.) Flashing Device- It is programmed circuit that can synchronize the mobile phone and the computer.

3. Flashing Software - this software is provided by the flashing device seller or even you can download it on the internet.

4. A USB cable and a flashing Cable wire- this the wire that used to connect the mobile phones to the flashing device that also connect to the computer.

This one is also provided by the flashing devices seller or you can purchased a pre designed one.

Every mobile phone products have different kinds of flashing devices used, and also have different methods and procedures.

5. Flashfiles and Firmware collection- this are the programmed data used in the phones. See here of exmples of flashfiles in Nokia Mobile Phones.

Below are the list of Flashing devices which is being used to flash a certain and particular mobile phone products.

Advance-Box

Axe Box

Cruiser Team Products

CPF-box Products

Cyclonebox

Easy-Unlocker

ET-BoX

FuriouS TeaM Products

Genie Universal

GM-Box

GsmMagicBox G

SMServer Products

Infinity-Box

J.A.F - Just Another Flasher

Kulankendi Box / Dongle

Martech products

Mastertools

McnPro Box

Micro-Box.com Team Products

Multi-Box TEAM Products

MXKEY (by Alim Hape)

NEROkey

NSPRO

POLAR Team Products

Rocker Team products

T-BOX Products

SAGEM JTAG UNLOCKER

Saras Boxes

SMTi Support Sections

SpiderMan

SPT BOX

Super Doctor Box (MTK-BOX)

TEST-BOX 2

TGT Products

Ultimate-Sam

Universalbox

UST Pro II

Ve Box

Vodafone Star

VygisToolbox

Z3X-Team Products

What is Phone Unlocking and How to Unlock a Mobile Phones

There are many mobile phones are "locked" into one particular service provider once purchased it. A user cannot use the handset to switch into another service provider by replacing available SIM card module into it.

So the best reason is to unlock the phone so it will be used into another network which is very useful when traveling from country to country.

Unlocking is completely legal and not illegal, because every phone user own the phone after all!
the only reasons that the networks do it is to try to make sure that the phone users don't move to another network, but all it really does is stop them using the phone as they would like to!

But how to Unlock a Phone

There are two methods in unlocking mobile phones, It varies a certain products of mobile phones some can be easily unlock and some are not.

1. Unlocking by entering an unlock code. Many Nokia, Samsung, Siemens, Sony, Panasonic and some other brands of mobile phone will unlock if you enter a specific code based on your phone's IMEI (serial) number. This is the most easy method of unlocking - all you have to do is get hold of the code!
There are some that offers free unlock codes and some you need to purchased it via online.

2. If a model of phone does not support unlocking by code, you need to get the phone unlocked using a unlocking device and a unlocking software tool.

Glossary

Definition of Abbreviations on Mobile Phones Circuit

0

2G 2nd Generation

3G 3rd Generation

3Gs 3rd Generation speed

4G 4th Generation

A

A/D-converter Analog-to-digital converter

ACI Accessory Control Interface

ADC Analog-to-digital converter

ADSP Application DPS (expected to run high level tasks)

AGC Automatic gain control (maintains volume)

ALS Ambient light sensor

AMSL After Market Service Leader

ARM Advanced RISC Machines

ARPU Average revenue per user (per month or per year)

ASIC Application Specific Integrated Circuit

ASIP Application Specific Interface Protector

B

B2B Board to board, connector between PWB and UI board

BB Baseband

BC02 Bluetooth module made by CSR

BIQUAD Bi-quadratic ,type of filter function)

BSI Battery Size Indicator

BT Bluetooth

C

CBus MCU controlled serial bus connected to UPP_WD2,UEME and Zocus

CCP Compact Camera Port

CDSP Cellular DSP (expected to run at low levels)

CLDC Connected limited device configuration

CMOS Complimentary metal-oxide semiconductor circuit (low power consumption)

COF Chip on Foil

COG Chip on Glass

CPU Central Processing Unit

CSR Cambridge silicon radio

CSTN Color Super Twisted Nematic

CTSI Clock Timing Sleep and interrupt block of Tiku

CW   Continuous wave

D

D/A-converter   Digital-to-analouge converter

DAC Digital-to-analogue converter

DBI Digital Battery Interface

DBus DSP controlled serial bus connected between UPP_WD2 and Helgo

DCT-4 Digital Core Technology

DMA Direct memory access

DP   Data Package

DPLL Digital Phase Locked Loop

DSP Digital Signal Processor

DtoS Differential to Single ended

E

EDGE Enhanced data rates for global/GSM evaluation

EGSM Extended GSM

EM Energy management

EMC Electromagnetic compatibility

EMI Electromagnetic interference

ESD Electrostatic discharge

F

FCI Functional cover interface

FPS Flash Programming Tool

FR Full rate

FSTN Film compensated super twisted nematic

G

GND Ground, conductive mass

GPIB General-purpose interface bus

GPRS General Packet Radio Service

GSM Group Special Mobile/Global System for Mobile communication

H

HF Hands free

HFCM Handsfree Common

HS Handset

HSCSD High speed circuit switched data (data transmission connection faster than GSM)

HW Hardware

I

I/O Input/Output

IBAT Battery current

IC Integrated circuit

ICHAR Charger current

IF Interface

IHF Integrated hands free

IMEI International Mobile Equipment Identity

IR Infrared

IrDA Infrared Data Association

ISA Intelligent software architecture

J

JPEG/JPG Joint Photographic Experts Group

L

LCD Liquid Crystal Display

LDO Low Drop Out

LED Light-emitting diode

LPRF Low Power Radio Frequency

M

MCU Micro Controller Unit (microprocessor)

MCU Multiport control unit

MIC, mic Microphone

MIDP Mobile Information Device Profile

MIN Mobile identification number

MIPS Million instructions per second

MMC Multimedia card

MMS Multimedia messaging service

N

NTC Negative temperature coefficient, temperature sensitive resistor used as a temperature sensor

O

OMA Object management architecture

OMAP Operations, maintenance, and administration part

Opamp Operational Amplifier

P

PA Power amplifier

PDA Pocket Data Application

PDA Personal digital assistant

PDRAM Program/Data RAM (on chip in Tiku)

Phoenix Software tool of DCT4.x

PIM Personal Information Management

PLL Phase locked loop

PM (Phone) Permanent memory

PUP General Purpose IO (PIO), USARTS and Pulse Width Modulators

PURX Power-up reset

PWB Printed Wiring Board

PWM Pulse width modulation

R

RC-filter Resistance-Capacitance filter

RF Radio Frequency

RF PopPort TM Reduced function PopPortTM interface

RFBUS Serial control Bus For RF

RSK Right Soft Key

RS-MMC Reduced size Multi Media Card

RSSI Receiving signal strength Indicator

RST Reset Switch

RTC Real Time Clock (provides date and time)

RX Radio Receiver

S

SARAM Single Access RAM

SAW filter Surface Acoustic Wave filter

SDRAM Synchronous Dynamic Random Access Memory

SID Security ID

SIM Subscriber Identity Module

SMPS Switched Mode Power Supply

SNR Signal-to-noice ratio

SPR Standard Product requirements

SRAM Static random access memory

STI Serial Trace Interface

SW Software

SWIM Subscriber/Wallet Identification Module

T

TCXO Temperature controlled Oscillator

Tiku Finnish for Chip, Successor of the UPP, Official Tiku3G

TX Radio Transmitter

U

UART Universal asynchronous receiver/transmitter

UEME Universal Energy Management chip (Enhanced version)

UEMEK See UEME

UI User Interface

UPP Universal Phone Processor

UPP_WD2 Communicator version of DCT4 system ASIC

USB Universal Serial Bus

V

VBAT Battery voltage

VCHAR Charger voltage

VCO Voltage controlled oscillator

VCTCXO Voltage Controlled Temperature Compensated Crystal Oscillator

VCXO Voltage Controlled Crystal Oscillator

Vp-p Peak-to-peak voltage

VSIM SIM voltage

W

WAP Wireless application protocol

WD Watchdog

X

XHTML Extensible hypertext markup language

Z

Zocus Current sensor, (used to monitor the current flow to and from the battery)

Highly Recommended

www.laptoprepairtrainingcollege.com

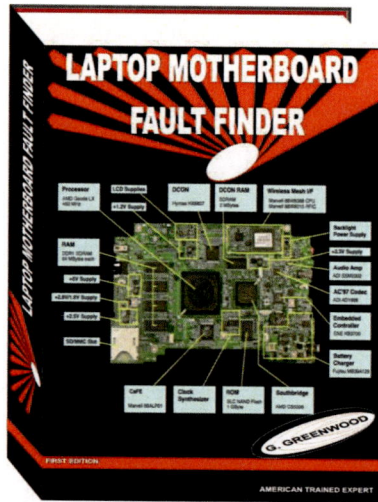

Made in the USA
San Bernardino, CA
20 March 2015